Lessons on Leadership by Terror

NEW HORIZONS IN LEADERSHIP STUDIES

Series Editor: Joanne B. Ciulla
Professor and Coston Family Chair in Leadership and Ethics,
Jepson School of Leadership Studies, University of Richmond, USA
and UNESCO Chair in Leadership Studies,
United Nations International Leadership Academy

This important series is designed to make a significant contribution to the development of leadership studies. This field has expanded dramatically in recent years and the series provides an invaluable forum for the publication of high quality works of scholarship and shows the diversity of leadership issues and practices around the world.

The main emphasis of the series is on the development and application of new and original ideas in leadership studies. It pays particular attention to leadership in business, economics and public policy and incorporates the wide range of disciplines which are now part of the field. Global in its approach, it includes some of the best theoretical and empirical work with contributions to fundamental principles, rigorous evaluations of existing concepts and competing theories, historical surveys and future visions.

Titles in the series include:

Moral Leadership in Action
Building and Sustaining Moral Competence in European Organizations
Edited by Heidi von Weltzien Hoivik

Beyond Rules in Society and Business
Verner C. Petersen

The Moral Capital of Leaders
Why Virtue Matters
Alejo José G. Sison

The Leadership Dilemma in Modern Democracy
Kenneth P. Ruscio

The New Russian Business Leaders
*Manfred F.R. Kets de Vries, Stanislav Shekshnia, Konstantin Korotov
and Elizabeth Florent-Treacy*

Lessons on Leadership by Terror
Finding Shaka Zulu in the Attic
Manfred F.R. Kets de Vries

Lessons on Leadership by Terror

Finding Shaka Zulu in the Attic

Manfred F.R. Kets de Vries

*The Raoul de Vitry d'Avaucourt Chair of
Leadership Development and Director, INSEAD
Global Leadership Center, France and Singapore*

NEW HORIZONS IN LEADERSHIP STUDIES

Edward Elgar

Cheltenham, UK • Northampton, MA, USA

Published by
Edward Elgar Publishing Limited
Glensanda House
Montpellier Parade
Cheltenham
Glos GL50 1UA
UK

Edward Elgar Publishing, Inc.
136 West Street
Suite 202
Northampton
Massachusetts 01060
USA

A catalogue record for this book
is available from the British Library

ISBN 1 84376 933 6 (cased)

Printed and bound in Great Britain by MPG Books Ltd, Bodmin, Cornwall

Contents

Preface   vii
About the author   xiii
A note about source material   xvi

Introduction   1

PART I   THE HISTORICAL CONTEXT

1   A school for tyranny: learning from hardship, betrayal and
    humiliation   15

2   The making of a military state: honing the *assegai*   31

3   Ruling by fear: bringing enemies and allies alike to submission   39

PART II   THE QUESTION OF CHARACTER

4   The inner theatre of the king: acting out personal concerns on
    a public stage   57

5   Monte Cristo in Africa: seeking revenge for past wrongs   75

6   The nature of relationships: being unable to establish real
    intimacy   83

7   Paranoia – the disease of kings: exercising caution beyond the
    bounds of danger   93

8   The terrorist mind: protecting the self by victimizing others   103

PART III   LEADERSHIP BY TERROR

9   Following the leader: colluding in cruelty   117

10   Lessons in leadership: teaching by example and omission   139

PART IV   DECONSTRUCTING TOTALITARIANISM

11   A throne of blood: deploying the tools of tyranny   161
12   Dancing with vampires: preventing tyranny through effective
       governance   175

Bibliography   186
Index   193

Preface

Wake, Amakó, wake!
And muster for the war:
The wizard wolves from Keisi's brake,
The vultures from afar,
Are gathering at Uhlanga's call
And following fast our westward way,
For well they know, ere evening fall,
They shall have glorious prey!
      (George F. Angas, *The Kafirs Illustrated*)

Vain the ambition of kings
Who seek by trophies and dead things
To leave a living name behind,
And weave but nets to catch the wind.
      (John Webster, *Vanitas Vanitatum*)

... [S]o shall you hear
Of carnal, bloody, and unnatural acts,
Of accidental judgments, casual slaughters,
Of deaths put on by cunning and forc'd cause,
And, in this upshot, purposes mistook
Fall'n on the inventors' heads.
      (William Shakespeare, *Hamlet*)

I make war on the living, not on the dead.
      (Charles V, comment made after the death of Martin Luther)

I shall be an autocrat: that's my trade. And the good Lord will forgive me: that's his.
      (Catherine the Great, attributed)

Power is the ultimate aphrodisiac.
      (Henry Kissinger, quoted in the *New York Times*)

Dionysius, a Greek tyrant of Syracuse in the fourth century BC, once invited a courtier named Damocles to dinner. Damocles had earlier flattered him about the might of his army, the magnificence of his treasures, the beauty of his palaces and the immense resources at his disposition. He had exclaimed, 'With those riches, no one could ever be happier.' To which Dionysius had responded, 'Since you think that my life is so pleasant, would you like to have a taste of it yourself?' Predictably, Damocles had answered in the affirmative, saying that he would be delighted. The dinner invitation had followed.

On the night of the dinner Dionysius laid out a magnificent banquet for his guest. When Damocles arrived, he was ushered to a couch of gold, covered with beautiful tapestries, and offered perfumes, garlands, the best food in the land, and beautiful men and women eager to be of service. But Dionysius had included one small extra item in his opulent setting. He had ordered a sharp-edged sword to be suspended from the ceiling by very slender horsehair, just over the seat his guest would be offered. When, after taking his seat, Damocles saw what was suspended over his head, he had neither the courage to rise and remove himself, nor the ability – given the threat – to enjoy his meal. In spite of the splendid meal and the magnificence of the surroundings, Damocles was in a complete state of terror, expecting the string to break at any moment. Dionysius took note of his fear and remarked, 'Now you know what this glorious life I live is all about! There will never be any happiness for me, because I am threatened continually by danger. I can never feel safe.'

This anecdote illustrates the dilemma faced by tyrants such as Dionysius. In spite of all their possessions, in spite of all their power, such people have to be perpetually on their guard. Haunted by anxiety and the constant fear of assassination, they trust nobody. The resulting strain makes them unpleasant to be with and influences the way they deal with others. The absolute rulers of today – men such as Robert Mugabe, Fidel Castro, and Kim Jong-Il – must all live with this kind of pressure.

For years I have been curious about what makes despotic leaders tick. As a lifelong student of leadership, I have often wondered what motivates political leaders who resort to destructive activities unimaginable to the normal mind. What can be said about the personality structure of such despots? What makes them behave the way they do? How did they become so cruel? On a lesser (and far more common) scale, what can be said about people who engage in ruthlessly abrasive behavior in the workplace? What is wrong with business leaders who seem to have lost their sense of humanity? Why and how do they create a culture of terror in their companies?

The behavior of such people raises questions about power. What happens to human beings when they acquire power? Is the abuse of power inevitable? Apparently Thomas Jefferson thought so: he once wrote in a letter, 'Whenever a man casts a longing eye on offices, a rottenness begins in his conduct.' Power can be like pestilence, contaminating those who touch it; it can be like a narcotic, turning the power-hungry into addicts. Many people who seem quite sane to all outside appearances have suddenly engaged in pathological behavior when given power. In fact, we all seem to possess a darker side – one that shows itself only in certain situations, such as the acquisition of power. The violent potential deep within has surprised many a person.

Although each tyrant is unique in what he or she tries to accomplish, this book focuses on a single ruler, in order to illustrate the characteristics of despotism and gain insight into its psychodynamics. For this purpose, one of the most controversial African leaders of all time has been selected: the Zulu king Shaka kaSenzangakhona – or Shaka Zulu. During his short reign, this unusual leader established one of the most successful regimes based on terror that has ever existed. Although some people idolize this great warrior-king and excuse his excesses, to many inhabitants of southern Africa his name still inspires fear. His life story – rich in adventures and battles and decisions that had an enormous impact on the geography of southern Africa – is the stuff of which legends are made. A close look at that life story will allow us to better understand the psychology of terror. Shaka Zulu serves, in the pages of this volume, as a proxy for all despots in all times. Using his short, dramatic life as a case study, we will discover what drives despots and what makes for totalitarian societies. We will also examine human nature more generally. We may learn that all of us have a Shaka Zulu in the attic.

A ROAD MAP

The primary objective of this book is to give the reader a greater understanding of what despotic leaders are all about, what leadership lessons can be learned from them, what makes for totalitarian states, and what can be done to prevent despotic leaders from coming to the fore. To provide a modicum of structure to this vast topic, I have divided the book into four parts.

I begin with an introduction to set the stage, explaining the kind of magnifying glass used to examine the actions of this despot. Then, in the three chapters of Part I, I offer a historical description of the life of Shaka in the context of the Zulu culture. In these opening chapters I give an account of the dramatic career of this warrior-king. In Part II, consisting of five chapters, I scrutinize the question of character, attempting to get inside the despotic mind. Integrating developmental, interpersonal, cognitive, psychodynamic and biological configurations, I explore the personality make-up of the despot, paying close attention to the psychopathological aspects of his character. Although Shaka is still the focus in Part II, this psychological exploration extends far beyond the character of Shaka. Many of the insights provided are applicable to any despot in any time.

In Part III, consisting of two chapters, I explore the nature of the interface between the leader and the led, studying the complex group dynamics that enable despots to manipulate their subjects. I offer a pragmatic discussion of what makes for exemplary leadership as a way to highlight its converse, suggesting a number of lessons on leadership that can be learned from Shaka's behavior – both from what he did well and from his failures. In the two chapters of Part IV, I deconstruct the self-destructive cycle of totalitarianism, scrutinizing the levers of power used by totalitarian leaders and inspecting the building blocks of totalitarianism. I conclude by offering suggestions on how to prevent totalitarian leaders from gaining power.

This book on the psychology of leadership by terror is not meant to be a linear study. I discovered when I first approached this subject matter that it does not lend itself to straightforward investigation. Thus I have indulged in considerable divergent thinking, shifting as the topic demanded within a constant interplay of intrapersonal, interpersonal, group and societal perspectives. My purpose is to demonstrate to the reader how, and to what extent, the 'inner theatre' of leaders – the demons that populate their internal stage, and the script from which those demons read – influences the architecture of the societies they create. I want the reader to recognize how powerfully each leader's dreams, aspirations, fears and anxieties affect his or her external world.

Because understanding is the first step toward prevention, it is my hope that the reader will become more sensitized by these pages to the psychology of terror and totalitarianism, recognize the societal abyss created by despots, and take a stand when the situation warrants it – in other words, that the reader will resist when the sirens of demagoguery are singing. Too many despots have created too much misery throughout the ages. They continue today, in many cases unchallenged, leaving their devastating mark in the form of genocide, war crimes and other forms of cruelty. *Caveat emptor*!

ACKNOWLEDGMENTS

Fortunately, only extremely rarely, during a personal consultation or at one of the two leadership seminars I run at INSEAD, have I come across someone whose personality make-up bears close resemblance to Shaka's. However, participants in my top-management seminar, The Challenge of Leadership: Creating Reflective Leaders – all of whom wield considerable power in their organization – offer important insights into the despotic mind, albeit it on a modest scale. Aspects of the behavior of some of these participants mirror the behavior of what we know of despots – an insight that surprises (and even alarms) these executives.

One important task during the above-named seminar is to make the senior executives who participate aware of how their behavior and actions affect others – in other words, what influence their behavior has on their organization's culture and patterns of decision-making. During the course of the program some of the participants come to realize that one or more of their behavior patterns are destructive to self, others and/or the organization. Although my interactions with these participants can be difficult, they generally result in a great learning experience, not only for them but also for me. I have learned a lot about my own foibles and frailties during my interactions with these men and women. As I respond to these executives during the seminar, my reactions, along with the comments of their peers, help them to better understand their actions. Such insight is a precondition to change – and in fact changes in destructive behavior patterns often result from the seminar.

I would like to thank all of the seminar participants who have struggled with me to create healthier organizations. More than any other source of information and insight, these executives have helped me make sense of the vicissitudes of leadership – and indeed to recognize, on rare occasions, psychopathology. Their contributions, and those of my other faculty members of INSEAD's Global Leadership Center – Elisabet Engellau, Sudhir Kakar, Roger Lehman, Erik van der Loo and Martine van den Poel – are very much appreciated.

I realized as I began this project that to understand the inner world of a Zulu king, I would need to understand the Zulu culture. My starting point for this aspect of the project was certainly not highbrow: I watched period movies such as *Zulu* and *Zulu Dawn*. Watching the controversial television mini-series *Shaka Zulu* at a later date augmented my preliminary visual indoctrination. The next step – reading about the battles of Isandlwana and Rorke's Drift – led to deeper insights about Zulu culture than the big screen can convey. Nothing, however, is better than actual interaction. Once, many years ago, I spent some time at the World Economic Forum in Davos with Chief Butelezi, the leader of the Inkatha Freedom Party, as he advocated his view of a post-apartheid Africa. Subsequently, during occasional visits to KwaZulu Natal, I have met a number of people who informed me about some of the intricacies of the Zulu culture. That personal contact is in part what led me to delve deeper into the subject. The observations and aspirations of the people I spoke with helped me better understand cultural behavior patterns. I am no expert, however, and as a novice I hope that in my portrayal of the Zulu culture of old I have not engaged in too many faulty representations.

I am grateful to INSEAD for providing me with the time and space to engage in what surely is an unusual research topic for a business school. Members of the research department and committee – particularly Landis Gabel, Anil Gaba and Alison James – have been extremely helpful, supporting me in my activities. For helping to create writing space in what can be an intrusive environment, I am very much indebted to my personal assistant and administrator at the Center, Sheila Loxham. Her talent at what now is called 'positive organizational behavior' – that is, the constructive reframing of situations that are potentially difficult – has always been encouraging. My research project manager, Elizabeth Florent, has created a working environment for our leadership research group, enabling me to devote a considerable amount of my time to writing. I would also like to thank my irrepressible editor, Kathy Reigstad, who has taught me a great deal about the English language – often more than I care to know! In the end, all errors and omissions in this research project are mine.

Paris

About the author

This study of Shaka Zulu and leadership by terror takes Manfred F.R. Kets de Vries out of his usual territory. In most of his writings, he brings a different view to the much-studied subjects of leadership and the dynamics of individual and organizational change. Relying on his knowledge and experience of economics (Econ. Drs., University of Amsterdam), management (ITP, MBA and DBA, Harvard Business School), and psychoanalysis (Canadian Psychoanalytic Society and the International Psychoanalytic Association), Kets de Vries typically scrutinizes the interface between international management, psychoanalysis, psychotherapy and dynamic psychiatry. His specific areas of interest are leadership, career dynamics, executive stress, entrepreneurship, family business, succession planning, cross-cultural management, team-building, coaching and the dynamics of corporate transformation and change.

A clinical professor of leadership, Kets de Vries holds the Raoul de Vitry d'Avaucourt Chair of Leadership Development at INSEAD, Fontainebleau, France. He is the Director of INSEAD's Global Leadership Center. He is program director of INSEAD's top-management seminar The Challenge of Leadership: Creating Reflective Leaders, and its seminar Coaching and Consulting for Change (and has five times received INSEAD's distinguished teacher award). He has also held professorships at McGill University, the Ecole des Hautes Etudes Commerciales (Montreal) and the Harvard Business School, and has lectured at management institutions around the world. He is a founding member of the International Society for the Psychoanalytic Study of Organizations. The *Financial Times*, *Le Capital*, *Wirtschaftswoche* and *The Economist* have named Manfred Kets de Vries one of the world's leading management thinkers.

Kets de Vries is the author, co-author or editor of 20 books, including *Power and the Corporate Mind* (1975, new edn 1985, with Abraham Zaleznik), *Organizational Paradoxes: Clinical Approaches to Management* (1980, new edn 1994), *The Irrational Executive: Psychoanalytic Explorations in Management* (1984, editor), *The Neurotic Organization: Diagnosing and Changing Counter-Productive Styles of Management* (1984, new edn 1990, with Danny Miller), *Unstable at the Top* (1988, with Danny Miller), *Prisoners of Leadership* (1989), *Handbook of Character Studies* (1991, with Sidney Perzow), *Organizations on the Couch* (1991), *Leaders, Fools and Impostors*

(1993, new edn 2003), the prize-winning *Life and Death in the Executive Fast Lane: Essays on Organizations and Leadership* (1995) (the Critics' Choice Award 1995–96), *Family Business: Human Dilemmas in the Family Firm* (1996), *The New Global Leaders: Percy Barnevik, Richard Branson, and David Simon* (1999, with Elizabeth Florent), *Struggling with the Demon: Perspectives on Individual and Organizational Irrationality* (2001), *The Leadership Mystique* (2001), and *The Happiness Equation* (2002), *The New Russian Business Leaders* (2004) and *Are Leaders Born or Are They Made: The Case of Alexander the Great* (2004, with Elisabet Engellau). He has also developed two 360-degree instruments: *The Global Executive Leadership Inventory* (2004) and *The Personality Audit* (2004). These instruments are used in leadership development programs around the world.

In addition Kets de Vries has published over 200 scientific papers as chapters in books and as articles in such journals as *Behavioral Science, Journal of Management Studies, Human Relations, Administration and Society, Organizational Dynamics, Strategic Management Journal, Academy of Management Journal, Academy of Management Review, Journal of Forecasting, California Management Review, Harvard Business Review, Sloan Management Review, Academy of Management Executive, Psychoanalytic Review, Bulletin of the Menninger Clinic, Journal of Applied Behavioral Science, European Management Journal, International Journal of Cross-Cultural Management, International Journal of Human Resource Management, Harper's* and *Psychology Today*. He has also written numerous case studies, including seven that received the Best Case of the Year award from the European Case Clearing House. He is a regular writer for a number of magazines, and his work has been featured in such publications as the *New York Times*, the *Wall Street Journal*, the *Los Angeles Times*, the *International Herald Tribune, Fortune, Business Week*, the *Economist*, the *Financial Times* and the *International Herald Tribune*. His books and articles have been translated into 18 languages. He is a member of 17 editorial boards. He has been elected a Fellow of the Academy of Management.

Kets de Vries is a consultant on organizational design and transformation and strategic human resource management to leading US, Canadian, European, African and Asian companies. As a global consultant in executive development, he has worked with an array of clients including ABB, Aegon, Air Liquide, Alcan, Alcatel, Accenture, Bain Consulting, Bang & Olufsen, Bonnier, BP, L.M. Ericsson, GE Capital, Goldman Sachs, Heineken, HypoVereinsbank, Investec, KPMG, Lego, Lufthansa, Novartis, Nokia, NovoNordisk, Rank Xerox, Shell, SHV, Standard Bank of South Africa, South African Breweries, Unilever and Volvo Car Corporation. As an educator and consultant he has worked in more than 30 countries.

The Dutch government has made him an officer in the Order of Oranje

Nassau. He was the first fly fisherman in Outer Mongolia and is a member of New York's Explorers Club. In his spare time he can be found in the rainforests or savannas of Central Africa, in the Siberian taiga, in the Pamir mountains or within the Arctic circle.

A note about source material

The search for authenticity concerning Shaka Zulu poses a challenge, because it is based on (1) the imagery of Shaka available within African society, a blending of oral and written tradition, and (2) perceptions of traders and colonial officials. Over time Shaka's image has become mythopoetic, its details contested between white and black historians. Many writers have demonized him, creating a figure of inhuman qualities, a symbol of violence and terror. European writers with this perspective have been accused of reinventing Shaka as a monster as justification for stealing African land. (It should be noted, however, that many of the most horrendous stories drew on tales already in existence before the arrival of whites.)

Shaka's early life is remembered through oral tradition, which was the way traditional Zulu society kept records. Separating first-hand accounts from hearsay leads to problems of intepretation. In contrast, many facts of his later life are based on the written accounts of the first white adventurers, who established a settlement at Port Natal – modern-day Durban – in 1824. Predominantly British, they thrived under Shaka's protection, hunting for ivory and trading with the Zulu kingdom.

The main source of written information, not only for me but for researchers generally, is the detailed eyewitness accounts of Nathaniel Isaacs (1836) and Henry Francis Fynn (1833/1950), both of whom had personal contact with Shaka. These two traders wrote accounts of their interactions with the African king that smack of sensationalism, probably in order to capture the attention of their audience.

Analysis of the texts of Isaacs and Fynn reveals that both accounts are highly problematic, containing internal contradictions. Nathaniel Isaacs's portrait of Shaka was, in his own words, 'somewhat incredible, if not highly exaggerated'. When Isaacs heard that Fynn was writing a book on Shaka, he advised him to depict the African leader as being as bloodthirsty as possible (though neither writer had had significant problems dealing with him), to get the attention of the readers. Fortunately, Fynn does not seem to have taken Isaacs's advice to heart. Thus his diary, from the point of view of perspective, is a more reliable source. However, the diary had to be reconstructed later from fragmentary notes, because the original was lost. (According to one romantic version it was buried by mistake – wrapped in an elephant's ear – in the grave of the writer's brother.)

Other information comes from colonial administrators. One colonial official in particular – James Stuart – engaged in systematic research of the reign of Shaka. Between 1897 and 1924 he collected the stories of nearly 200 informants concerning the history of the Zulu and neighboring people. His collection of oral history is the main source for historical research of that period, and I have relied on it heavily.

In addition, the first book ever written in Zulu by a Zulu author, Magema Fuze, contains a rich store of oral knowledge that the author gathered through his wide network of contacts. This book, *Abantu Abamnyama* (*The Black People*), was privately published in 1921, when the author was approximately 82 years old.

One very popular book on Shaka by Edward Ritter needs to be called into question. Notwithstanding its listing of many original sources, it plagiarizes extensively (particularly from Alfred Bryant's book *Olden Times in Zululand and Natal*), embellishing and fantasizing the original texts. Other works verge into historical invention because their authors were determined to fit the facts to a specific worldview.

Three kinds of Shaka sources are used in these pages:

1. Narratives of people who knew (or at least met) Shaka personally.
2. Accounts from people who knew people who knew Shaka (including contributions from Europeans and researchers who collected oral history).
3. Zulu praise songs, known as *izibongo* – portrayals of Shaka that have evolved over the years

All these accounts need to be treated with care, given problems of translation of accounts from the Zulu language, and problems of interpretation resulting from the subjectivity and the biases of the authors. Because the early traders and colonists gave a Eurocentric interpretation of the behavior of the Zulus, perceptual confusion was compounded.

Because of the emotional symbolism attached to the person of Shaka, it is particularly difficult to separate fact from fiction in accounts of his life. Indicators for the existence of a twilight zone surrounding the man include the many versions circulating about his birth and early life, the nature of his personal relationships, and his much-recounted cruelty. Given the great confusion concerning certain episodes and events in his life, I have tried to be parsimonious and have aimed at triangulation. I have focused on episodes in Shaka's life where many different authors have reached some form of consensual agreement, and on themes implied in the mythopoeic presentation of Shaka.

To Alicia,
Eva,
Fredrik
and Oriane
who helped me
retain my sense of
imagination, curiosity
and wonder.

Introduction

Hail! Hail! This land is yours, child of my compatriot,
You shall rule over nations and their kings
You shall rule over peoples of diverse traditions
You shall even rule over the winds and the sea storms
And the pool of large rivers that run deep;
And all things shall obey you with unquestioning obedience,
And shall kneel at your feet!
O yes, oi! oi! Yet you must go by the right path.
   (Thomas Mofolo, *Chaka*)

The strongest drink or smoke of all, however, is power. Be careful, then, to mix it well with mercy, and the reasoning of your counselors and friends, lest it overwhelm you and you become like a mad bull, who, having killed all his opponents, starts goring his defenseless cows and calves and finally charges against the walls of his own kraal and senselessly breaks his neck instead of walking through the open gate of reason.
   (E.A. Ritter, *Shaka Zulu*)

The people always have some champion whom they set over them and nurse into greatness. ... This and no other is the root from which tyranny springs.
   (Plato, *The Republic*)

Awe is composed of reverence and dread. I often think that people today have nothing left but the dread.
   (Christa Wolf, *Cassandra*)

The goal of this book is to better understand a special type of leadership: leadership by terror. Whether we talk about autocrats, tyrants, despots, totalitarian regimes or violent rule, the subject of terror is a contemporary problem, though this generation did not invent it. Indeed throughout the ages autocratic governments have been more the rule than the exception; democratic forms of government have been relatively rare. In the recent past, despots such as Joseph Stalin, Adolf Hitler, Mao Zedong, Pol Pot, Idi Amin, Nicolae Ceausescu, Joseph Désiré Mobutu, Kim Il-Sung, and Slobodan Milosevic, replaced Caligula, Nero, Tamerlane, Vlad the Impaler and Ivan the Terrible; and these leaders have themselves been followed by the likes of Saddam Hussein, Fidel Castro, Kim Jong Il, Muammar Qaddafi and Robert Mugabe. Although some of these leaders have been lionized as nation-builders in spite of their atrocities, they stand out as examples of the kinds of horror humans can bring to other humans, many having murdered millions. They stand as horrendous examples of how to inflict human misery and suffering. Hitler, Stalin, Mao Zedong and Pol Pot in the previous century were grandmasters of bloodshed, leaving tens of millions of dead in their wake.

What makes the existence of such violent leaders particularly disturbing is that it seems so inevitable: the history of absolute, totalitarian regimes is a long one, with no apparent beginning and no end in sight. We like to think that the world is growing more civilized, and yet the crop of potential new despotic leaders is burgeoning. The explanation is disturbing: studies of human behavior indicate that the disposition to violence exists in all of us; *everyone has a Shaka Zulu in the attic.* Lord Acton's dictum, 'All power tends to corrupt, and absolute power corrupts absolutely', is truer now than ever. Humankind appears to be the only member of the animal kingdom that has the potential for mass murder, and we realize that potential with disturbing frequency. Given the psychological make-up of the human animal, we must assume that there are untold numbers of tyrants in the making among us, who will be revealed if and when the opportunity for power arises. The human tendency to lionize leaders and excuse their excesses encourages an endless line-up of new candidates for fame and glory.

In engaging in a study of this human tendency toward tyranny, I took an elaborate journey that not only included such fields of study as psychoanalysis, developmental psychology, psychopathology and the psychology of groups, but also spanned philosophy, history, sociology, anthropology, ethology, political science and management. Working at the boundaries of these various disciplines proved to be fruitful in obtaining insight into the complex human phenomenon of terror.

Because prevention requires knowledge, and change requires insight, an understanding of the psychology of terror can be seen as a modest step toward preventing despotic leaders and totalitarian regimes from coming to the fore. Such an understanding will help us find our way through what remains a largely unexplored domain. It will for example give us insight into the unusual relationship between leaders and followers in totalitarian regimes, help us deal more effectively with potential and existing tyrants, and give us tools of prevention. As an additional benefit, making sense of the tyrant's inner theatre will contribute to a better comprehension of leadership generally, helping us to grasp what both effective leadership and ineffective leadership are all about.

TERROR AND ITS VICISSITUDES

My definition of 'leadership by terror' is leadership that achieves its ends and gains compliance through the deliberate use of violence and fear. It is the use of arbitrary power beyond the scope permitted by law, custom and tradition. The lust for power pushes true despots beyond the boundaries of their mandate to rule, causing them to abandon respect for human rights and individual freedom and to behave in ways that prevent others from living their lives with dignity and self-respect. In a nutshell, tyrannical leadership is the arbitrary rule by a single person who, by inducing a psychological state of extreme fear in a population, monopolizes power to his or her own advantage (unchecked by law or other restraining influences), exercizing that power without restraint and in most cases contrary to the general good. Despots hamper justice, fair process, excellence and the development of the human potential of a population (Arendt, 1973; Boesche, 1996; Chirot, 1994; Glass, 1995; Herschman and Lieb, 1994; Reich, 1990; Robins and Post, 1997; Walter, 1969).

Clarifying Confusing Terminology

In contrast to many other writers, I use the terms 'dictatorship', 'despotism', 'tyranny' and 'totalitarianism' somewhat interchangeably. The polemics of the various nuances of these terms is not the objective of this study; classification is a topic unto itself. I will simply mention briefly that some writers have made an effort to classify nondemocratic forms of government, putting at one extreme traditional, relatively benevolent authoritarian regimes and at the other extreme totalitarian governments of the Nazi and Soviet variety.

Totalitarianism
At the most dangerous extreme of the control spectrum, the term 'totalitarianism' is used by these writers to refer to regimes under which a population is completely subjugated to a political system that aspires to total domination of the collective over the individual. Totalitarian regimes strive to invade and to control their citizenry's social, economic, political and personal life. Such forms of government are typically permeated by a secular or theocratic ideology that professes a set of supreme, absolute values that are propagated by the leadership. Repression of individual rights and loyalty to that ideology are their salient characteristics. The overriding importance of ideology means that every aspect of every individual's life is subordinate to the state. Because totalitarian governments want to transform human nature, they exercise thought-control and control moral education. In other words, repression is carried out not only against people's actions but also against their thoughts.

Such regimes retain control only so long as the terror of totalitarianism does not ease up. Thus any objection to governmental control is viewed as a danger to the regime, a threat to its delicate equilibrium. As a result, such regimes are more likely than others to 'eat their own' – that is, to do away with (by exile, imprisonment or death) government supporters tainted by the merest suspicion of rebellion. These regimes need the sacrifice of an endless stream of new enemies to retain their focus (Arendt, 1969, 1973; Boesche, 1996; Friedrich, 1954; Friedrich and Brezezinsky, 1965). This is the category into which I would place Shaka Zulu and his reign of terror.

Authoritarianism

Authoritarian regimes, on the other hand, are perceived by those who make this distinction as being less intrusive. Although repression of the populace takes place, there is no intrusive ideology. Such regimes do not profess the benefits of a future utopian state; they do not want to transform human nature. The goal of authoritarian leadership is much more mundane: retaining power. Authoritarian rulers want to keep the riches and privilege that come with holding on to power, and they exert whatever level of repression that takes.

Although both types of regime can be extremely brutal to political opponents, in an authoritarian state the government's efforts are directed primarily at those who are considered political adversaries. The government lacks the desire (and often the means) to control every aspect of each individual's life, and thus intervention in the day-to-day life of the citizenry is limited. Grounded in greed rather than ideology, authoritarian leadership does not claim to represent a specific historical destiny or possess the absolute truth; it is not in the business of creating a new type of social life or a new kind of human being.

Under the guise of promising social reform, authoritarian leaders seize power only to enrich themselves and their friends, ruling with brutal terror and arbitrary force for enrichment only. The amassing of wealth, the betrayal of social reforms, the development of a military power base, and rampant paranoia are characteristics associated with authoritarianism.

Riding the Waves with Despots

Whenever people gather in groups, there is the potential for the abuse of power. Would-be despots are everywhere, although they thrive best in the fertile ground of tribal or nation formation. The turbulence of the formative period makes people anxious, and anxiety prompts them to search for strong leadership. The prevalence of human anxiety explains why totalitarianism and leadership by terror have been with us since the dawn of time. The early civilizations that grew up along great rivers such as the Nile, the Tigris, the Euphrates, the Yangtze, the Yellow and the Ganges clamored for leaders to give their public waterworks a modicum of centralized direction. As we will observe in the course of this book, however, centralized leadership can easily become perverted. Looking back into history, we can see how ancient Egypt, Mesopotamia, China, India, and the pre-Columbian Central and South American cultures positioned an absolute ruler at the center of the ruling bureaucracy. We can also follow the rise and inevitable fall of such regimes.

Much has been said and written about absolute rulers. Philosophers in particular have tackled this subject. Plato, for example, was one of the earliest recorded observers of tyranny. Tyranny evoked for him associations of disharmony and disease, and he viewed tyrants as individuals governed by out-of-control desires. According to Plato, 'drunkenness, lust, and madness' differentiate the tyrant from other people. A tyrant 'becomes in reality what he was once only occasionally in his dreams, and there's nothing, no taboo, no murder, however terrible, from which he will shirk. His passion tyrannizes over him, a despot will be without restraint or law' (Plato, 1955, p. 348). In other words, tyrants act out in the light of day what most of us only dare to dream about at night. Plato concluded that to act on such dreams – to satisfy one's darkest desires – leads the tyrant into an unending, spiraling cycle of desire, gratification and more desire.

Most students of totalitarian regimes acknowledge that leadership by terror involves the application of violence. As Niccolò Machiavelli (1966) advised cynically half a millennium ago, 'Men must either be caressed or else annihilated.' Machiavelli, who was one of the first statesmen to build a political science based on the study of humankind, saw no alternative to love and violence as motivators. But tyranny goes beyond the 'simple' violence of, say, execution; it evokes images of madness and sadistic desires run amok. Tyrants would do well to remember the Chinese proverb 'He who rides a tiger cannot dismount', because they create behavior that gives a wild and uncontrollable ride. They hurtle roughshod over anything that dares to cross their path. And yet their violence is likely to be their own undoing in the end: as the saying goes, 'He who lives by the sword will die by the sword.'

The terror and violence that characterize tyranny take two forms: outwardly directed and inwardly directed. Both forms often lead to mass murder and genocide. Outwardly directed terror is used to intimidate or even exterminate enemies outside one's borders. Typically, enemies are viewed by despots as forces of darkness that need to be destroyed by a force of light. They are described with derogatory remarks and depicted by tyrannical leadership as less than human. This dehumanization makes the administration of violence more palatable to members of the enforcement arm of the government. After all, it is only the enemy – no more than a subspecies – upon whom violence is inflicted.

Leadership by terror is particularly devastating when it is directed – as it often is – not only outward but also inward. Inwardly directed terror heightens considerably the fear and anxiety of living with totalitarianism. Characterized by violent acts against the despot's own population, inwardly directed terror results in subjugation of the citizenry, classification as a subspecies of one part (or multiple parts) of the population, loss of various freedoms, and ultimately the suffocation of the mind. A reign of terror is superimposed on the conventional systems of power and authority.

The ability to enact terror – whether against an external enemy or against one's own people – is viewed by many tyrannical leaders as a sign of privilege, a special prerogative. To despots, boundaries of acceptable behavior apply only to others. Living in a narcissistic 'soup,' having little concern for the needs of others, despots perceive few restraints on their actions. They believe that 'divine providence' (however they construe divinity) has given them power over life and death. In other words they believe that they have the right to act as they do. This sense of entitlement is especially frightening when it spreads: the specific psychology or psychopathology of a leader can become institutionalized (as with Hitler, Stalin, Pol Pot and Bin Laden), loosing demons on the population at large, so that the common people come to support the distorted and dangerous ideology articulated by the leadership.

Leadership by terror succeeds only in the hands of a despot skilled at the fine art of boundary management. If terror is taken to its extreme and executed too forcefully, there is soon nothing left to terrorize; the 'objects' of terror are destroyed. If, on the other hand, terror is applied too lightly, it does not result in the desired compliance. Maintaining the devilish bond between the terrorized and the tyrant requires a delicate balancing act: traditional mechanisms in society need to be modified but cannot be destroyed.

My journey into the rocky terrain of leadership by terror has raised many questions for me. For example, what kind of psychological processes make a society (or portion of society) more susceptible than others to political terror? What can be said about the peculiarities of regimes that engage in tyrannical practices, and what processes and levers do such regimes use to maintain terror? What is the role of leadership in creating tyrannical regimes? What can be said about the personality make-up of the despotic leader? How do early developmental experiences contribute to the tyrannical mind-set? What is the nature of the psychological dynamic between the healthy leader and the democratically led? And between the pathological leader and the terrorized led? What can be said about the psychology of a group willing to participate in violent, destructive behavior?

In referring to the tyrannical mind-set, this is not to say that traumatic childhood experiences inevitably result in psychopathology. Human development is a complex interface of genetic predisposition, birth order, family status, the history of a child's successes and failures, serendipity – and, for the unfortunate few, trauma. Development follows an innate timetable that determines successive maturational sequences depending on the above-mentioned factors.

Given the devastating consequences of leadership by terror, all these questions warrant careful investigation. I approach that investigation here through the tale of Shaka Zulu. His story will help us decipher the psychodynamics of terror.

HERO FIGURES AS MYTHIC REPRESENTATIONS

Although Shaka Zulu will be our vehicle into the terrain of terror, and as such is representative of tyrants everywhere, he is not just another name in the world's list of disreputable leaders. Although he has been portrayed as an example of barbaric despotism and as the creator of a semi-celibate people-slaying juggernaut, he has also been glorified (to some extent rightly so) as a true nation-builder. Leading from the front, he gathered many dispersed and warring tribes and built them into a single cohesive entity – the Zulu nation. Within a period of 12 years, this warrior-king (called by some 'the Black Napoleon' and by others 'the African Attila') conquered a territory larger than present-day Western Europe, unifying the tribes of southern Africa. Due to his efforts, the Zulu influence eventually extended from the Drakensberg Mountains in the west, to the Indian Ocean in the east, to the Transkeian territories in the south, to the southern regions of what is now Swaziland and Mozambique in the north. Shaka's attempt at nation-building had a tragic ending, however: the nation he built was eventually torn apart, he and his successors were humiliated, and most of their land was taken over by European settlers (a state of affairs that is only now gradually being redressed).

Because Shaka Zulu was not a one-dimensional leader, but a blend of good and evil in which evil eventually won out, he can as well stand in our stead as in that of tyrants everywhere. Our study of him will give us a better grasp not only of tyrants, but of the major motivational needs of humankind generally – of the rational and irrational forces that drive each of us. In Shaka we can see a reflection of many of these needs: strivings for love, solidarity, power and autonomy alongside of needs to dominate, to control, to envy, to hurt and to destroy. It is those complex needs, projected on the vast stage of Africa, that both enabled him to be a nation-builder and brought him to his knees.

Reviewing Shaka's history will help us enter the mind of the absolute ruler, investigate the nature and causes of violence and destructiveness in human society, and explore the making of a totalitarian state. As a leader, Shaka can be viewed as the quintessential *tyrannos* – a Lydian word used to describe a cruel and oppressive ruler in ancient Greece. In him we will see the megalomania, the paranoia, the underlying insecurity, the tactics of terror and the flawed reality-testing that characterize most despots. His case will demonstrate that tyrannical leaders are driven to do what they do by the psychological forces that dominate their inner theatre.

The Romantic Imagination

Shaka's life story touches humankind's romantic imagination. It is a tale of ordeal, exile, exposure, destitution and humiliation – all common elements of romantic fantasy. The existence of these themes makes it hard to distinguish between what is myth and what is reality. Compounding the difficulty of distinguishing between fact and fantasy is the fact that stories told about Shaka's birth, childhood and early career have their origin in the oral tradition, with all its embellishments (Stuart, 1976, 1979, 1982, 1986, 2001; MacLean, 1992). As the oral tradition took written form, many of those poetic embellishments, along with the ideological influences of the day, made their way into history. This problematic interface between oral and written traditions keeps Shaka enigmatic today (Bird, 1888/1965; Cope, 1968; Delegorgue, 1847; Fuze, 1921/1998; Fynn, 1950; Gibson, 1911; Golan, 1990; Haggard, 1882; Hamilton, 1998; Isaacs, 1836; Knight, 1995; Kunene, 1979; Laband, 1997; Mofolo, 1981; Ritter, 1978; Rycroft and Ngcobo, 1988; Stuart, 1927; Thompson, 1967; Webb and Wright, 1978; Worger, 1979; Wylie, 1993). Because of all the mythology that surrounds his persona, he remains the most talked about and the least understood of all African kings.

Myths and legends are an essential part of every culture. These stories are first passed down orally from one person to the next; only later (in a culture that knows the written word) are they committed to writing. While myths tend to be sacred stories, legends generally center on real people, places and events. The tale of Shaka, with its larger-than-life hero symbolism, contains both elements: it portrays Shaka as savior and soldier. Shaka's life story is metaphor as well. Shaka is a bearer of meanings: he symbolizes the aspirations of a people; he represents the birth of a nation; he stands for power and independence. He also served during his lifetime as a means of defending against anxiety, fear and despair. Through his life story – the reality and the fantastic embellishments alike – we can retrace the trials and tribulations of life in general. We can engage in a mythic journey like the one Shaka himself took, because many of his life themes – alien as they may seem to us at first – resonate deep inside all of us.

The psychoanalyst Otto Rank pointed out the power of such resonance, noting that some individuals elevated by culture to heroic status touch the deep recesses of our minds. He also noted that the hero's journey often follows a predictable outline:

The hero is the child of most distinguished parents, usually the son of a king. His origin is preceded by difficulties, such as ... secret intercourse of the parents due to external prohibition or obstacles. During or before the pregnancy, there is a prophecy, in the form of a dream or oracle, cautioning against his birth, and usually threatening danger to the father. ... As a rule, he is surrendered to the water, in a box. He is then saved ... by lowly people. ... After he has grown up ... he takes his revenge on his father, on the one hand, and is acknowledged, on the other. Finally he achieves rank and honors. (Rank, 1932, p. 65)

Imagination or Reality?

Given their universal structure, myths and legends (particularly in primitive society) are not just stories; they are a reality lived. With their symbolism and metaphor, they are products of imagination in response to stressful situations. Because they are successful at relieving stress, they are relived throughout the ages. As they are repeated through the generations, they help in sense-making – that is, in trying to interpret what otherwise would be a bewildering world (Levi-Strauss, 1955, 1969; Malinovsky, 1926). Some myths and legends are pre-scientific attempts to interpret what happens in the physical world around us. They help us understand the metaphysical dimension, explain the origins and nature of the cosmos, validate social issues and, on the psychological plane, address themselves to the innermost depths of the psyche (Campbell, 1949).

The universality of the events described in myths and legends – the repetitiveness of their structure (as in Rank's 'formula' for the hero, above) – makes these stories the expressed products of our unconscious. These tales are like dreams expressed in the public domain – dreams that, like private dreams, emerge from the unconscious mind (Freud, 1900). As shared, institutionalized dreams, they become moral tales to a society. This power of myth in the figure of Shaka Zulu was picked up both by the Zulu Inkatha movement and by Afrikaner right-wingers.

THE PROJECTION OF FANTASIES

Myths and legends are important for cultural identity formation, but they have a downside as well: the mythopoetic imagination taints whatever real story the life of a particular hero represents. That has certainly been the case with Shaka Zulu's story. People interested in Shaka have tended to project their own fantasies onto him, in order to enhance the desired identification (Wylie, 1992). In the case of Shaka the poetic imagination has taken over, and he has become different things to different people.

Some writers – most of them white – have portrayed Shaka Zulu as a person possessed by animalistic drives, madness and violence, a savage and bloodthirsty despot who kept his people under control through sheer terror.

Others have presented Shaka as symbolizing the forces of order over barbarism. To these latter writers, he is a symbol of inviolate law, an individual in total self-control. They argue that the gruesome reputation that has been cultivated by other writers is totally unwarranted, that Shaka has been the victim of deliberate acts of character assassination by whites for political purposes.

For many black writers, Shaka has become a symbol used to explain the origin and destiny of a people. They argue that Shaka needs to be viewed in the context of his time and culture. Given the harshness of the time he lived in, his aggression and ruthlessness were essential to his victories over rivals and enemies. He would not have been able to build a nation, in that time and place, had he not used extremes of force. People who put forward this perspective point out that, in light of his accomplishments, he should be seen as a successful nation-builder, a visionary leader who created order and social security where chaos once reigned.

As these contrasting views attest, Shaka's image is infinitely manipulable. Many people interested in Shaka seem to be less concerned with revealing his actual past than with creating a coherent account that fits their particular objectives. In other words, they project their own meanings on the material available. As a result the real Shaka has been all but lost. With so many people endlessly reworking him as a symbol or myth, projecting their fantasies onto him, he has become a profoundly ambiguous, mysterious figure. It is difficult now to distinguish between propaganda and reality, to separate psychological truth from historical truth. Probably we never will. In the context of this book, however, the question of what he was really like is less important than what he stands for as representative of a whole line-up of despots.

To some extent, of course, the contrasting views of Shaka Zulu do reflect the real person. As was noted earlier, he was a man of daunting complexity, a person not easily labeled – a cruel despot, but also at times a brave and generous leader. That complexity leads us to wonder whether he destroyed for destruction's sake or whether he destroyed in order to construct. In any case, as he attempted to deal with the complexity within – to shape his own identity, as it were – he touched and changed the lives of countless Africans. Those changed lives became elements of the cultural myth surrounding the ruthless leader. Thus Shaka, in creating his own personal identity, created a political and national identity for the Zulu.

Problems of Countertransference

The contradictions as presented in the 'texts' that exist about Shaka – texts that include not only purportedly historical accounts, but also myths, legends and symbols – place a special burden on any author hoping to add to the

Shaka literature. Because this is a book dealing with the relationship between personality, leadership practices and despotism, I will focus not on verifying or disproving specific events but on revealing patterns of outlook and behavior as recounted by many different sources. I will highlight those events that provide the most insight into Shaka's personality and leadership style.

As a psychoanalyst using all the therapeutic and scholarly tools available to me, I will try to listen to what Shaka has to say, to observe his behavior and to understand why he did what he did. The danger in trying to 'diagnose' his behavior is that psychological diagnosis inevitably results in reductionism – that is, oversimplification of the enormous complexity of human behavior. Furthermore, as we all discover in the course of daily life, the better we know a person, the more difficult it is to put a label on him or her. Consequently I will ground my modest attempt at diagnosis, at understanding Shaka's intrapsychic and interpersonal processes, in the larger context of societal forces. In other words I will study the environmental context within which behavior occurs.

In identifying themes that provide us with insight into Shaka's inner theatre – themes such as narcissism or paranoia – I cannot hope to arrive at the objective truth about him; I can only identify what feels true. And yet that perceived truth may be truer than any fact. Because a theme by definition implies repetition (just as a motif in music returns again and again), it tells us more than a discrete action does. Each theme that comes to the fore in Shaka's life serves as a window into his personality and helps to explain his public actions. Taken together, these themes tie together what would otherwise be an enigmatic character engaged in enigmatic activities. We choose our life-themes – though rarely consciously, of course – as a way of making sense of our own existence and gaining mastery over our unpredictable environment.

It is impossible for any researcher (or reader) to interpret a historical person – to listen, observe, feel with, and attempt to understand that person – without projecting his or her own meanings on the material available. This phenomenon, known in the context of psychotherapy as 'countertransference', is inevitable in historical studies of this kind (Devereux, 1978; Loewenberg, 1982). Consciously or unconsciously, researchers are influenced by the people they decide to study. I will combat that influence by engaging in a process of 'objective subjectivity'; that is, I will make an effort to detach my attachment to the material presented. In addition I will attempt to remain open to the multiple meanings any material has, rather than trying to make the material fit predetermined conclusions.

The Clinical Perspective

The psychoanalyst Erik Erikson, in his psycho-historical writings, described quite well the hurdles that a clinically oriented student of historical leaders is up against:

> [T]he clinician turned historian must adapt himself to and utilize a new array of 'resistances' before he can be sure to be encountering those he is accustomed to. There is, first of all, the often incredible or implausible loss or absence of data in the post-mortem of a charismatic figure which can be variably attributed to simple carelessness or lack of awareness or of candor on the part of the witnesses. ... The myth-affirming and myth-destroying propensities of a post-charismatic period must be seen as the very stuff of which history is made. Where myth-making predominates, every item of the great man's life becomes or is reported like a parable. (Erikson, 1971, p. 198)

Shaka Zulu is a clinical historian's dream. His life story is a good illustration of the psychodynamics of leadership, revealing as it does the extent to which a person's inner theatre affects the behavior and action that are externalized on a public stage (Erikson, 1975; George, 1969; Kets de Vries, 1993; Lasswell, 1960; Zaleznik and Kets de Vries, 1975). It also elucidates how early life-events can determine a person's character and influence behavior. Finally, it gives us at least a glimpse into the dynamics of terror – a subject that is tragically topical.

In analyzing Shaka Zulu's personality and behavior, I will use a clinical perspective (Kets de Vries, 2000). What does this mean? I will try to understand the role that conscious and unconscious conflict played in the making of his personality. I will look at his strengths and weaknesses and seek to understand how those affected him. I will apply concepts of developmental psychology, family systems theory, cognitive theory, dynamic psychiatry, psychotherapy and psychoanalysis (particularly object relations and self-psychology) in an effort to untangle the relationship between child and man, between personal peculiarities and public acts.

Discussing Shaka Zulu without putting him into the context of time and place would limit our comprehension of psychological issues. Therefore when appropriate I will offer information about cultural themes. To prevent oversimplification I will pay attention both to the sociopolitical situation of Zulu society at a certain historical period, and to the group, interpersonal and intrapsychic forces affecting Shaka. Tying Shaka's behavior patterns to psychological theories and to recorded history will help us gain a better understanding of historical, cultural and psychological change; and it will help us deconstruct the psychological forces that make for despotic regimes. By his example (both positive and negative) Shaka will teach us several crucial lessons on leadership. He will remain elusive to the end, however, an enigma protected by myth and the passing of time.

PART I

The Historical Context

1. A school for tyranny: learning from hardship, betrayal and humiliation

Of all the animals, the boy is the most unmanageable.
(Plato, *Laws*)

For where no hope is left, is left no fear.
(John Milton, *Paradise Regained*)

Man, who wert once a despot and a slave;
A dupe and a deceiver; a decay;
A traveler from the cradle to the grave
From the dim light of this immortal day.
(Percy Bysshe Shelley, *Prometheus Unbound*)

And it came to pass, when the evil spirit from God was upon Saul, that David took a harp, and played with his hand: so Saul was refreshed, and was well, and the evil spirit departed from him.
(*The Holy Bible*, Book of Samuel)

The infliction of cruelty with a good conscience is a delight to moralists. That is why they invented Hell.
(Bertrand Russell, *On the Value of Skepticism*)

What canst thou know of happiness,
If in the vale of misery thou hast not walked?
What canst thou know of freedom,
If against bondage thou hast not cried aloud?
(Jiddu Krishnamurti, *The Song of Life*)

The early life of Shaka sounds like many a mythical tale of triumph over misfortune and adversity. According to the 'formula' for such tales, the hero faces severe hardships and obstacles, overcoming each in turn before coming into his own (Campbell, 1949; Rank, 1932). These obstacles prepare the persevering struggler for his future role as leader. The tale of Shaka closely follows that formula: Shaka endured significant adversities, including expulsion and exile, performed heroic deeds that saved his people from disaster, and was eventually recognized triumphantly as their leader, setting the stage for a life of glory.

The tales told about Shaka Zulu – particularly those that were in circulation before the existence of written accounts – have a dreamlike quality to them.

Like all tales that are told generation after generation, they contain not just a
kernel of history but layer upon layer of make-believe. Speaking to the
collective unconscious, they touch on basic themes of humanity: love, hate,
pride and revenge. Though these tales make it clear that Shaka was destined
from an early age for great achievements, the student of history finds it hard
to distinguish myth from reality, fact from fantasy, as the tumultuous life of
Shaka Zulu unfolds (Mofolo, 1981; Worger, 1979; Wylie, 1992).

THE BIRTH OF A LEGEND

To the best of our knowledge, Shaka was born about 1787 in what is now
known as KwaZulu Natal. This area was populated by many clans belonging
to the Nguni cultural and linguistic group – clans that included the Zulus, who
traced their descent from an ancestor named uZulu ka Malandela (Zulu, son of
Malandela), a man thought to have settled beside the White Mfolozi River
during the seventeenth century (Knight, 1989). (The word *izulu* means 'the
heavens'; thus the title *amaZulu*, by which the Zulu clan is known, means 'the
People of the Heavens'.)

At the time of Shaka's birth his father, Senzangakhona kaJama (a name that
means 'He who Acts with Good Reasons'), was the chieftain of the small, then
unknown Zulu clan. The smallest of the more than 800 Eastern Nguni-Bantu
clans, probably numbering not more than 1500 people at the time, the Zulus
still occupied an area along the White Mfolozi River in the Mkhumbane
Valley, as had the ancestor after whom they were named. Shaka's mother
Nandi was a child of a deceased chieftain of the neighboring eLangeni
clan.

Both oral and written accounts include many versions of what happened
between Senzangakhona and Nandi. One account tells that Shaka's father,
when traveling, saw Nandi bathing in a stream. The two young people were
immediately attracted to each other and engaged in an activity called *ukusoma*
('thigh sex'). This form of sexual play without penetration (and thus without
conception) was a socially acceptable way for young unmarried individuals to
release sexual tension. Senzangakhona and Nandi lost their heads in the
process, however, and broke the rules concerning acceptable sexual relations,
an outcome that, because pregnancy resulted, concluded in serious disgrace
for all parties involved.

The oral accounts about Shaka not only differ regarding the details of
conception; they also reflect enormous controversy about his legitimacy.
Some declare that an *ilobolo*, or 'bride's price,' was paid for Nandi (meaning
that a marriage was at least planned if not already transacted); others make no
mention of a dowry. Some say that Senzangakhona had been circumcised

(meaning that he had the right to marry); others stipulate that he had not (Stuart, 1976, 1979, 1982, 1986, 2001).

When it was first reported to the neighboring clan that Nandi was pregnant – so says one account – Zulu elders indignantly dismissed the claim, suggesting instead that she was suffering from an intestinal parasite, a stomach beetle or bug called *ishaka* that was alleged to suppress menstruation and enlarge the belly. The elders of the tribe could not believe that their chief would have disgraced himself with a woman of the eLangeni clan. The selection of a wife for a chieftain was a serious matter of tribal politics, not a fleeting matter of sexual desire. When the baby was born, Nandi named him Shaka, after the stomach beetle the Zulus had invoked by way of explanation for her symptoms of pregnancy. Another account of the birth suggests that when asked what was wrong with her, Nandi replied that she had *ishati*, a bad body disease (Fuze, 1921/1998). A similar word, *chaka*, which means a poor fellow, a servant, is employed in still other accounts.

The illegitimate birth was not the only taboo that was broken, however. In creating a child, Senzangakhona and Nandi transgressed cultural rules concerning proper social behavior. Nguni kinship rules disallowed marriage or sexual relations between kindred, which meant that no sexual play of any kind was permitted among members of the closely linked eLangeni and the Zulu clans. This social convention carried such weight that both clans were publicly humiliated by the baby's birth. The stigma of this double dishonor – illegitimacy coupled with violation of exogamy rules – would not only have been a heavy burden on the mother but would also have extended to the child.

The accounts of what happened after Shaka's birth vary greatly as well. One version reads that Nandi was sent to Senzangakhona and quietly installed as his third wife (Stuart, 1986). Another reads that she never became the wife of Senzangakhona but brought Shaka up on her own (Fuze, 1921/1998). Still another (mirroring the many mythological narratives of fathers killing their sons) reads that Senzangakhona's guardians sent out warriors to Nandi's home to kill the child, because Senzangakhona was not yet allowed to marry (Stuart, 1986, pp. 222–3); but Senzangakhona's mother, wanting to spare her grandchild, hid the boy until he could be turned over to Nandi's people.

A more common version of the tale suggests that the couple lived together after Shaka's birth but the relationship soon turned sour. Although another child, a girl named Nomcoba, was born to the pair, Senzangakhona's love for Nandi cooled and the young chieftain came to neglect Shaka and his mother. Some sources claim that Nandi refused to conform to the proper behavior expected of a Zulu wife (a fondness for impropriety foreshadowed by her willingness to engage in forbidden sexual play with Senzangakhona). Although her name means 'the Sweet One', Nandi appears to have been anything but. Many oral sources describe her as a woman with a difficult, fierce temperament. According to these sources, she was a strong-willed and sharp-tongued woman who made life miserable for those around her (Stuart, 1986).

An event that occurred when Shaka was six years old brought matters to a head, according to some sources. Because of inattention, the youngster allowed a dog to kill one of his father's pet animals (a sheep or a goat, depending on the account). Nandi took Shaka's side, and a serious fight ensued between the parents. Because of this fight, the Zulu clan cast out Nandi and her children. Another version of the marital break-up says that Nandi struck one of her husband's leading advisors over the head with a knobkerrie (a wooden club used in warfare), prompting a fight between Senzangakhona and Nandi and resulting in her expulsion from the clan.

Nandi felt disgraced, having to return to her own people. She and her son and daughter were even less welcome among the eLangeni than with the clan of her husband. This negative reception was due in part, say some accounts, to the fact that her family had to give back to her husband the *ilobolo* of cattle paid for her – a serious loss of face. Moreover a returned woman was considered disgraced and had no real stature in the social structure of the clan. With Nandi's father no longer alive, the small family had very little political support. Only Shaka's maternal grandmother offered some comfort.

Shaka hated living with his mother's family. Growing up fatherless and despised among people of his mother's clan, he was treated like an outcast. According to legend he had to endure many humiliations, including the cruel bullying of the other children, who referred to him as 'the fatherless one' and treated him like a dog. They smeared him with excrement, tortured him by giving him burning food to eat, trampled on his belongings, made him the butt of jokes, and taunted him with being the son of a chief who had deserted him.

In particular he was ridiculed about his body. He was supposedly quite scrawny as a youngster – a fact that would have been obvious, since Zulu boys walked around naked. A number of sources mention that Shaka was frequently teased about his supposedly undersized sexual organ. His tormentors would say, 'On no account will we speak to a little Ntungwa [those people who come from the North] with a little penis that sticks up' (Stuart, 1982, p. 216). A sense of physical inadequacy may have added to the shame, hostility, and bewilderment that the clan's ostracism had ignited (Bryant, 1929; Ritter, 1978; Roberts, 1974). All these factors worked together to turn Shaka into a lonely, bitter and angry young man. His only companion was his mother, whom he worshipped. Her life too was made miserable by the villagers. The negative treatment they received was etched in his mind, becoming a red thread that would color his outlook on life. Harboring great hatred for his tormentors, he grew increasingly revenge-focused, vowing never to forget what had been done to him.

But the tragic tale of mother and children is not yet finished. In 1802 the eLangeni clan expelled Nandi and her children. A persistent drought threatened the clan's survival, and there was no longer enough food for the unwelcome. Possessing no wealth and having no one to stand up for them, Nandi and her children were outcasts again, sent away to fend for themselves. (This is one among many reasons given in various accounts for their departure. One source says that Shaka caused the chief's son great distress by breaking his toy bull while playing. Another says that Shaka, in an act of rage after being cheated while playing a game with one of his cousins, stabbed a beast belonging to his cousin's family – a terrible crime for a herdboy.)

Popular legend agrees that whatever the reason for their departure, the three were forced to move hungrily from clan to clan until they obtained a degree of acceptance with a subclan of the neighboring Mthethwa tribe. Nandi found here a new husband – a commoner, Gendeyana – with whom she had one more son, Ngwadi. For the first time there seemed to be a certain amount of stability in the life of mother and children. During these years the chief of the Mthethwa, Jobe (and after his death his son, Dingiswayo), took Shaka under his wing, eventually becoming his mentor.

Shaka grew to young manhood herding sheep and cattle. Oral history tells that by the time he was 21 he was 6 foot 3, with a very well-proportioned body and a truly royal bearing. According to certain written sources, however, he was not a handsome young man, his looks marred by a large nose; and he may have suffered from a speech impediment (Fynn, 1950; Lyndon Dodds, 1998; Stuart, 1927). Already as a teenager Shaka showed exceptional fighting ability – an ability he had had to hone to defend himself against his early tormentors. In addition, over the years he had worked hard at learning to use his spear effectively. One story claims that Shaka, at the age of 19, showed extraordinary bravery by using two throwing spears and a club to singlehandedly kill a leopard that was attacking the livestock. Another tale relates how as a warrior for Dingiswayo he slew an invincible 'madman' who had robbed the tribe of many cattle (Stuart, 1982, p. 198).

Because of Shaka's growing physical prowess, both his father's and his mother's clans began to show an interest in him (though neither clan was much interested in having Nandi back). Good warriors were always welcome to strengthen the group. Returning to his father's clan was an unattractive proposition, because his father had recognized another of his sons as his heir. (Shaka may also have worried that, if he were with his father's clan, other family members would take the opportunity to put him out of the way, perceiving him as a threat.) Returning to his mother's clan was likewise unthinkable to the proud young man, given their earlier treatment of him and his mother and sister. Thus when the time came to leave home and join one of the national regiments – the *amabutho* – Shaka offered his services to Dingiswayo and the Mthethwa clan rather than to his father or to his mother's people.

THE ZULU WAY OF LIFE

The Zulu society into which Shaka was born was collectivist (Hofstede, 1991; Kets de Vries, 2001a) – that is, the good of the community was seen as being much more important than the interests of the individual. A person's very identity was framed in the context of belonging to the larger social setting. This collectivist orientation was expressed in the use of land, which was owned not by the individual but by the community and was administered by the chief.

Zulu society was also past-oriented. Given all the dangers that clan members were exposed to – wild animals, war, privation and drought – the future had far less significance than the present. Moreover there was much to be learned from the past, particularly as it was remembered in the praise poems and songs that were sung at ceremonial occasions. Accordingly Zulu elders were held in great esteem, their advanced age considered synonymous with experience and wisdom. This emphasis on the past had ramifications for daily life, shaping an outlook more reactive than proactive: 'If we remember the past and are careful not to aggravate the all-seeing, all-knowing ancestors, all will be well; the future will take care of itself'.

The Zulus lived in family homesteads (known as *imizi* or *kraals*), which consisted of a collection of domed, beehive-like thatch-covered huts, arranged in a circle around a central cattle pen (or *boma*), surrounded by a stockade to protect cattle from wild animals. Zulu society was highly patriarchical, with a strict division of labor along gender lines. Daily life for men meant tending cattle, building huts and erecting fences. For women, life centered on household duties and the cultivation of vegetable gardens, activities viewed as beneath the dignity of the men.

The Pivotal Role of Cattle

Zulus were essentially pastoralists (Derwent, 1998; Knight, 1989; Krige, 1936; Laband, 1995). Their lifestyle revolved around a dependency on cattle. Cattle were their most important source of food, although millet and its by-product beer were also important. Cattle provided milk curds (*amasi*) and meat, as well as hides for garments and shields, and they were a symbol of wealth. The Zulus loved to eat cattle, although beef was usually reserved for ceremonial occasions, but the importance of cattle went far beyond being a food source. One informer described the importance of cattle to the tribal Africans as follows:

> Cattle are the money of us black people. They are the things which we cherish most. Cattle are the food of our people; we appeared with them when we appeared as people. We know how to watch over cattle, but they too know how to watch over us. From the time we are very small until we are old, until we are grown-up men, until we are gray, we are watched over by cattle. We think that we watch over them, but the doings of God here on earth are a great wonder. As one hand washes another, so it is between cattle and people. (Stuart, 2001, p. 274)

The importance of cattle in the Zulu economy was reflected in the existence of more than 100 terms for the animal, many describing physical characteristics such as color combinations and shape of the horns. Ownership of cattle was the primary physical manifestation of wealth, a major indicator of social standing. Cattle stood for independence, for power and status. Cattle exchange was a crucial part of the marriage contract. If a man wanted to get married, he had to offer an *ilobolo* (or gift of cattle) to the family of the bride as compensation for her loss and as a guarantee of her future well-being. The more cattle a person had, the more wives and retainers he was able to afford. More wives in turn meant more children, which meant more productive workers in the household. Cattle were important in the religious life of these pastoralists: because sacrifice of cattle to the ancestors was seen as necessary to ensure harmony between the spirit world and the physical world, cattle secured not only physical but also spiritual well-being. At every important ritual occasion – puberty, marriage, death – cattle were killed to please the spirit world. The cattle kraal, where the spirits of ancestors were thought to linger, became in effect the Zulu temple.

Religious Belief Systems

Traditional Zulu spirituality was based on ancestor worship and belief in witches, sorcerers and a creator god (Bryant, 1949; Knight, 1995; Mofolo, 1981). *uMvelinqangi*, or the 'Ancient One,' was supposed to have come from the reeds, and thence he brought forth the people and the cattle. According to the Zulu worldview, *uMvelinqangi* created everything that is: mountains, streams, snakes and every other animate and inanimate thing. He also taught the Zulus how to hunt, how to make fire and how to grow food. He was assumed to be above interacting in day-to-day human affairs however. That would be left to other figures in the Zulu religious constellation.

In the Zulu worldview, the living and the dead were not thought to be separate; rather, they were believed to be intimately associated with each other. Former relatives, retaining the same qualities they had when they were alive, populated the 'other' world, and they took a real interest in their progeny. The spirits of these diseased relatives were thought to guide day-to-day human affairs. When their help was needed, the Zulus contacted them through the medium of dreams.

All bad things, including sickness, drought and death, were seen by the Zulu as the result of evil sorcery or offended spirits – that is, as the outcome of disequilibrium between the worlds of the living and the dead. Because no misfortune was ever seen as being the result of natural causes alone, the populace lived in constant threat of these dark, supernatural forces – the *uMnyama* – which ruled society. The good force, *uMvelinqangi*, ruled over the dark forces, yet they posed a constant threat. Like the Zulus' emphasis on the past, this belief that external forces more powerful than themselves controlled the turn of events made the Zulu rather passive. When things went badly for a particular individual, the Zulu would observe that his ancestors had turned their back on him.

Only the *izangoma*, or diviners, had the supernatural power to communicate with the ancestral spirits on behalf of the living. These diviners (who, unlike the physical healers or medicine-men, were most often women) played a significant and powerful role in Zulu society. They were viewed as the protectors of society, because they were able to prevent disorder between the spiritual and the natural worlds. They often used cattle as go-betweens in this endeavor. These diviners (ceremonially dressed in bizarre costumes adorned with many magical charms) were also able to tell what was happening elsewhere in the present and predict what would happen in the future.

The diviners had to contend not only with angry ancestors but also with the *abathakathi* – men and women who had harnessed the powers of the universe against the welfare of society. These malicious witches, wizards and sorcerers were seen as fomenting disharmony between the spirit world and the world of the living; thus they were ultimately to blame for earthly misfortunes. The *abathakathi* could be 'smelled out' only by the diviners, which gave the *izangoma* an enormous power over life and death.

People found guilty of witchcraft – those 'smelled out' by a diviner – were impaled with short stakes thrust in succession through the rectum till they reached the neck; then they were left to die in the field, later to nourish the hyenas and the vultures. (Perhaps this dreadful punishment has its origin in the Zulu tradition of the rectal bloodletting of a newborn child to prevent it being 'overheated' by blood. Omitting this practice was expected to lead to later trouble, such as immoral sexual behavior (Fuze, 1921/1998, p. 39)). Those 'smelled out' were not generally the only victims to be executed. Because contamination was thought to extend to family and attendants, close kin and retainers were also put to death in the same gruesome manner (Lyndon Dodds, 1998). In addition, the cattle of the accused (and of their relations) were confiscated, a practice that offered a terrifying incentive to accuse wealthy people of sorcery.

A Patriarchal Society

As noted earlier, Zulu society was patriarchal and patrilineal. A man would not talk when his father was present until addressed by the older man (though he would feel no such compunction regarding his mother), and fathers and grandfathers were to be implicitly obeyed. It was typically the mother who took on the role of go-between when a child forgot that injunction and got into trouble. Mothers were not pushovers, however; they had strict expectations for behavior. In fact only maternal grandmothers were allowed to spoil children. The discipline that characterized Zulu society came from a culture in which laws of custom described in great detail every facet of behavior required at each stage of development, whether in the home or in the group. Because the power dynamics in the typical family determine the nature of relationships in a society at large, the behavior patterns learned by Zulu children toward their father and mother were the models on which all their other behavior patterns were based.

Because of the great emphasis on the collective in Zulu society, the whole kraal was considered responsible for the misdeeds of any of its inhabitants (though the greatest burden of responsibility fell on the head of the kraal). One consequence of this collective responsibility was a high degree of social control: every person in the tribe played the role of police officer, bound to report any form of transgression. In the case of serious transgressions, a whole village could be 'eaten up,' meaning that its inhabitants were killed and its cattle confiscated.

Among the chief transgressions in Zulu society were witchcraft, incest and treason. As we saw earlier, witchcraft was thought by the Zulus to underlie most difficulties of individual and tribe, and thus was punished by painful and ignominious death. Incest, a stringent taboo, could not be tolerated because it was the ultimate violation of the tribe's exogamy rules. As for treason, it was an unpardonable offense in this very hierarchically structured society, where all power emanated from the king. Although each Zulu child felt allegiance first to family and kraal, all people were taught to be totally obedient to the king and his officials. The supreme proof of obedience to the king was sacrificing one's life on the battlefield. Treason against the king was considered treason against all the people, because the king was the representative of the tribe. Minor infractions of a treasonous nature often led to a beating or the loss of lifestock, while major infractions were punishable by death. (Imprisonment, perceived by the Zulus as cruel and unusual punishment, was rarely imposed.)

Though African rulers before Shaka's time were held in great esteem, he elevated the role of the king. Once he had consolidated his power, he was simultaneously the civil, military, judicial and religious head of his people. He not only represented the authority of the entire nation – a shift from the old tribal way of looking at leadership – he also served as the primary liaison between the ancestral spirits and this world. Seen as a great sorcerer, he was the person thought most capable of approaching the ancestral spirits for their blessings; thus he was responsible for all national magic and rainmaking. Rites performed by the king on behalf of the entire nation (at planting season, or in war, drought or famine) centered on the ancestors of the royal line and invoked their power.

In particular, the king presided over the *umkhosi wokweshwama*, the 'first fruits' festival, a celebration of the new harvest that representatives from clans all over the kingdom were required to attend. Harvesting prior to this festival was forbidden, on pain of death. The king also used this ceremony to proclaim new laws, make other pronouncements and hear from the people (this being one of the rare occasions on which he permitted freedom of speech by his subjects).

Because the king represented the welfare of the nation, he was treated with the utmost care. His subjects were extremely concerned about his physical and spiritual well-being, because they believed him to be the living reservoir of forces that made the earth fertile and brought riches to the land. Without him – the major rainmaker – there would be no crops, the earth would turn to dust, nothing would grow.

He had a valet – called his *insila* (his 'Dirt') – whose duty it was to receive upon his body all nasal and throat discharges. During the day, this person would wash and dress the king; at night he would sleep at the entrance to the royal hut. He also had an *izisindabiso*, a royal anus-wiper, whose duty it was to hide away the royal stool so that evildoers could not take possession of it (royal excreta being much valued by *abathakathi* (Bryant, 1949, pp. 474–5). He also had servants who closely guarded the preparation and presentation of his food against the dangers of poison.

Before Shaka's time, African leaders were far from absolute. Most rulers had substantial controls on their power – controls that had become institutionalized over time. Consensus-building and custom held despotism in check. Chiefs were expected to rule with the help of a council of leading confidential advisors. These councilors were usually the heads of the leading families of the clans, whose rights were hereditary. Along with the diviners, whose magical powers gave them substantial political clout, these councilors played a countervailing role in the clan's decision-making.

The Zulu Life-Cycle

In Zulu society children (especially boys) were grouped together by age, each 'age-grade' spanning four or five years, and transitions from one age-grade to another were marked by ritual ceremonies. While girls took on the role of 'mother's helper' early on, for boys the first four to five years of life were relatively carefree. Boys would sleep in their mother's hut at night and spend the day playing with children of their own age-grade. When they reached the age of four to five, however, boys were given their first responsibility: helping to care for animals. They began by tending smaller animals, such as goats, sheep and calves; eventually they graduated to herding cattle, a job of immense importance in a society so dominated by lifestock. Anyone who lost a beast was severely punished. Young boys also learned the basic skills of military life through hunting and various games. With so much dangerous game around, hunting skills were a necessary survival tool. Though boys were not allowed to possess spears until they were somewhat older, they practiced fighting by sparring with sticks and by hunting small game with a throwing stick. When the warriors went on their campaigns these young boys would serve as *udibi*, or mat-carriers.

By the time the boys reached the age of 11 or 12, they moved out of their mother's hut and shared a special boys' hut with youngsters of the same age at the kraal. The time had arrived to enter into the men's world in preparation for circumcision ceremonies. Before Shaka's day, male circumcision – the first step into adulthood – was an important part of the wheel of life. Usually it was performed on males in late adolescence as part of the initiation into manhood and warrior status. This initiation was made up of a very extensive set of ceremonies, education and training (including physical conditioning), all of which lasted close to a year.

King Dingiswayo, who mentored Shaka, replaced the elaborate circumcision rituals with enrollment in the *amabutho*, military regiments that came to play a crucial part in Zulu life. The training that had been part of the circumcision 'school' was now handled by the *amabutho*. As being conscripted into an age-regiment became the new initiation ritual, Zulu society took on a more military cast. With war becoming increasingly common, this new system, which got young men into the army at a younger age, was seen as a more effective way of training soldiers. The circumcision ceremonies had not only been time-consuming, they had also involved time away from home for the young men, leaving the remaining tribe more vulnerable to attack (Omer-Cooper, 1966).

In the new *amabutho* system, when a Zulu male reached the age of 17 or 18, he went (usually voluntarily) to a garrison to *kleza*, to offer his services to the king. In the time of King Dingiswayo these *amabutho* were not a standing army but a citizen force called out when the king required them. They also made up the nation's principal labor pool, helping to maintain the king's own kraals and police his citizens. When Shaka became king, however, he changed the part-time orientation of the *amabutho*, making these regiments the center of his militaristic, totalitarian state by demanding service from his warriors for a period of 15 to 20 years.

Teenage girls also went into the king's service, again selected by age group. These girls were housed in a special part of the regimental barracks, and among other duties were required to take care of chores for the king and his family. Senior female guardians (often the wives or other family members of the previous, deceased king) were responsible for these girls.

The Zulu considered marriage a crucial rite of passage. With marriage a person reached full-fledged adulthood and was permitted fully exercised sexual relations. Because the transition from the *amabutho* (or female service) into marriage implied the lessening of the influence of the king, it occurred only with his permission. In Shaka's day this permission was usually not granted before the age of 35 to 40.

Immediately prior to marriage, men who met the king's standards for manhood acquired the *isicoco*, a fiber head ring (sometimes referred to as the 'king's ring') that was worn plastered into the hair with beeswax, symbolizing maturity. (The head ring may have been intended as a substitute for the circumcision ceremony. Some observers have argued, however, that the purpose of the head ring was to improve a maturing person's appearance by hiding bald spots. See Fuze, 1921/1998.) Married men were no longer dependents of their parents but were able to set up their own homesteads. As mature men in this new stage in life, they could now impose the duty of service on younger people, demanding help with farming, hunting and homestead maintenance. As family heads, they would spend time in the huts of their wives, although those of some importance had a hut of their own for privacy.

Although full-fledged sexual intercourse was not permitted until marriage, the Zulus were not repressive in their attitudes toward sexuality. At an early age children had considerable knowledge about sex and engaged in playful sexual activities. After puberty, however, only 'external' sexual intercourse was allowed. Although sexual play was seen as a normal part of interaction among healthy, unmarried adults, penetration during sexual play was not permitted, because it was considered disgraceful for an unmarried woman to be pregnant. The unfortunate woman who found herself in that state was usually hurried off to be married.

GROWING UP IN TIMES OF TROUBLE

Shaka – born, as we saw, about 1787 – entered a culture in crisis. The political economy of the area that came to be known as Zululand had been disrupted by European trade initiatives emanating from the Portuguese enclave at Delagoa Bay (now Maputo, capital of present-day Mozambique), and the final decade of the eighteenth century was characterized by devastating drought (known as *madlathule* – 'let them eat what they can and say nothing') and famine. Population was rising in the interior of Africa, making usable grazing land increasingly scarce (Gluckman, 1960; Knight, 1994, 1999) – a grave problem, given the importance of cattle as the mainstay of the Zulu economy. As too many cattle chased too little pasture, overgrazing depleted the soil and made it difficult for pasture to regenerate, further exacerbating the problem.

Overcrowding and overgrazing forced the many African clans in the area (and the increasing numbers of Europeans who were immigrating) to compete, generally via warfare, for this limited resource. Those clans that were peaceable by nature, ceding land to others, often fell victim to Delagoa Bay slave traders (Reader, 1998). The relative peace of the region was further threatened by the Portuguese demand for ivory, which (by offering an alternative to cattle herding as a source of wealth) put serious pressure on the existing feudal structure.

Prior to Shaka's coming to power, warfare had been a small-scale affair involving either disputes about grazing rights or arguments about the possession of cattle. But because of all of the above factors – the population explosion, the drought, the overgrazing, the slave trade and the European demand for ivory – warfare in the region gradually changed from an informal raiding-based enterprise to a serious struggle for survival, necessitating the institution of a carefully controlled politico-military system.

In this feudal society in transformation, friction had broken out between the various chiefdoms within southern Africa, and two strong, militarily important political groupings had emerged – the Ndwandwe, headed by King Zwide kaLanga, north of the White Mfolozi River, and the Mthethwa, headed by King Dingiswayo kaJobe (Shaka's mentor), along the lower Mhlatuze. Both groups had brought weaker chiefdoms under their control. The Zulus, under Shaka's father, had given their allegiance to King Dingiswayo of the Mthethwa, who was well on his way to forging a large political confederacy.

The Vision of King Dingiswayo

According to oral history, King Dingiswayo was one of the great leaders in southern Africa. His colorful early history is hinted at in his name, often translated as 'the Wanderer' or 'the Troubled One.' According to the tales told about him, he escaped his home after his father, Jobe, ordered his death, fearful that the younger man would overthrow him. Romantic tales are told about his wanderings, during which time he is said to have come into contact with white men. According to a number of accounts about his life, these contacts were his inspiration to look for new ways of organizing the societal structure of his people. He was impressed in particular by the European way of soldiering, with its drills and techniques so different from African clan warfare. He paid close attention to the trade in slaves, elephant tusks, beads and brass that was taking place between Delagoa Bay and nearby tribes, learning much about European ways from the interactions. Eventually, after his father's death, Dingiswayo returned to his home, carrying a gun and riding on a horse, neither of which had ever been seen in his country. Impressed by the power that the horse and gun represented, his people willingly accepted him as their new ruler.

According to Zulu oral history, King Dingiswayo was a compassionate, benevolent and just ruler (Stuart, 1986). He was not only capable, but also very imaginative. He had a grand vision that the fiercely independent clans of southern Africa could be coordinated into a loosely structured political amalgamation. In working passionately and effectively toward that vision, he changed the political architecture of southern Africa and created the foundation of an empire.

Various reasons have been offered to explain why Dingiswayo believed so fervently in his social experiment of creating a political federation. One explanation is economic: a political federation would facilitate the creation of a monopoly on ivory trading with the newly arrived Europeans. In return for ivory and hides, the aligned chiefs would be supplied with much-desired 'exotic' goods such as brass and beads. The possession of these goods would reinforce their power base at home, since prized goods could be held out as carrots to favorite warriors and servants. Another explanation for Dingiswayo's interest in confederation was the trade in slaves at Delagoa Bay under the Portuguese. Dingiswayo may have sought to unify the military outposts, manned with his new *amabutho*, to form a defensive boundary that would enable clans to escape from the predations of the slavers in the Delagoa Bay hinterland.

Both of these explanations point to the arrival of white settlers as the key factor in Dingiswayo's attempts at nation-building. By creating a new, broadly encompassing political entity, this visionary king would stop the incessant warfare between the clans caused by cattle raiding and disagreements about grazing rights (Morris, 1966; Walter, 1969), thereby ensuring greater strength against outside intruders. His innovations in social engineering were apparently designed to stave off the coming of more white settlers. Having become familiar with European ways during his travels, Dingiswayo understood the impact that these white settlers could have on what had been until then a very stable society. He had grasped the Europeans' military power, the revolutionary nature of their firearms, and their hegemonic ambitions. He knew that only a unified socio-political structure would be able to balance their power and bring stability and security to the region.

Dingiswayo began the unification through military conquest, gradually bringing the neighboring chiefdoms under his control. His warfare was executed with relative restraint, however (his commanders being under strict orders to limit post-conquest plunder and to avoid unnecessary destruction of property), leading many potential enemies to voluntarily submit to his regime and sign on as allies. Dingiswayo required political allegiance of each clan (through either conquest or submission) but then afterwards left the clans in peace, allowing each chiefdom under his reign considerable autonomy. Where needed, he strengthened the political bond between clans by arranging dynastic marriages, making good use (for himself and his commanders) of the polygamy that his culture favored.

Dingiswayo was also an innovator in social engineering. As indicated earlier, this visionary leader of the Mthethwa was responsible for replacing traditional puberty rites involving circumcision with a system whereby young men were organized into military regiments based on their age cohort. Under his rule, becoming a man, coming of age, meant being inducted into a regiment stationed away from home. These *amabutho* were under direct control of the king. Now every male, serving in an *ibutho*, earned his manhood by accomplishments on the battlefield rather than by lengthy circumcision rites. (Oral accounts mention that Shaka was not circumcised. In fact he prohibited the practice, considering it harmful (Stuart, 1979, p. 94).)

This new rite of passage was very successful at creating a national entity and a sense of belonging within that entity. By grouping his conscripts in military regiments away from their place of origin, Dingiswayo ensured that they bonded together not as kinsmen but as colleagues; and by giving them extensive training and combat experience, he equipped them as a formidable army. His vision of creating a melting pot that would unify Africans, and his implementation of that vision, eventually ranked him as one of the great statesmen in the history of the tribes of southern Africa.

A Leader in the Making

As we saw earlier, Shaka joined one of the *amabutho* of King Dingiswayo. As an *impi* or warrior, Shaka came into his own, finally gaining a sense of identity. While serving in the *iziCwe* regiment (which he eventually commanded), he earned the reputation of being a ferocious fighter and a talented strategist and tactician. He was an exemplary soldier and rose through the ranks of King Dingiswayo's army. Because of his fighting skills, he was nicknamed Sikithi, 'the Finisher-Off'; he was also known as 'the Hoe That Surpasses Other Hoes' (a metaphor praising his stabbing ability during battle) and 'the Heavens That Thunder in the Open'.

King Dingiswayo, who could not help but notice his subject's acts of bravery, decided to train Shaka as a future chief of the Zulu clan. The land of the Zulus was located at the periphery of his new federation (neighboring the land of his main adversary, Zwide), and Dingiswayo wanted someone strong in command there to act as a buffer against invading forces. He also needed someone with political savvy, so to further Shaka's education, Dingiswayo included this lonely, angry young man in council meetings to make him familiar with the art of statecraft.

Dingiswayo's next step in Shaka's training was to promote him to leader of the army. During his tenure in that role he developed innovative fighting techniques with which his warriors would later terrorize southern Africa. He succeeded in instilling in his warriors a fighting spirit similar to his own by subjecting them to a draconian training program; they were not just ready for war, but eager.

When the Zulu chief Senzangakhona – Shaka's father – died in 1816, his favorite son by his eighth wife (the 'Great Wife'), a young man named Sigujana, assumed the mantle of chief of the clan. Dingiswayo helped Shaka wrest that mantle from Sigujana by providing his disciple with needed military assistance. Shaka also had the support of his aunt, Mnkabayi kaJama, his father's formidable elder sister, who had encouraged Shaka in his ambitions even while he was in exile.

According to a number of sources, Shaka first sent Ngwadi, his half-brother, to tell Sigujana to step down peacefully (Stuart, 1986). Sigujana refused and was killed (supposedly by Ngwadi) during the takeover. From the day of Shaka's arrival, the life of the small Zulu clan changed dramatically. Led and inspired by Shaka, the Zulus commenced their march to greatness. His warriors would prove to be all but unstoppable. With Zululand in the eye of the storm, southern Africa would never be the same again.

2. The making of a military state: honing the *assegai*

We are not ourselves
When nature, being oppress'd, commands the mind
To suffer with the body.
    (Shakespeare, *King Lear*)

Most of the time we think we're sick, it's all in the mind.
    (Thomas Wolfe, *Look Homeward, Angel*)

It takes so much to be a king that he exists only as such. That extraneous glare that surrounds him hides him and conceals him from us; our sight breaks and is dissipated by it, being filled and arrested by this strong light.
    (Michel Eyquem de Montaigne, *Essays*)

I am Goya
of the bare field, by the enemy's beak gouged
till the craters of my eyes gape
I am grief

I am the tongue
of war ...
    (Andrei Andreevich Voznesenski, *I Am Goya*)

My hoarse-sounding horn
Invites thee to the chase, the sport of kings;
Image of war, without its guilt ...
    (William Somerville, *The Chase*)

On the one hand, man is akin to many species of animals in that he fights his own species. But on the other hand, he, among the thousands of species that fight, the only one in which fighting is disruptive. ... Man is the only species that is a mass murderer, the only misfit in his own society.
    (Nikolas Tinbergen, *On War and Peace in Animals and Man*)

Zulu fighting and warfare before Shaka's time resembled the combat of opposing sportsmen more than a battle zone. Disputes between individuals were often settled through a duel, and disagreements between clans (which generally centered on cattle-raiding) were tame, formalized affairs. In the typical script for hostile clan skirmishes, the opposing forces lined up in two long rows facing each other a little more than a spear's throw apart. Each party shouted abuse at the other, cheered on by the women and children standing behind them. The warriors, armed with small cowhide shields and light throwing spears, eventually ran toward each other, throwing their spears at their opponents, usually without much effect.

Although each man was an expert in the use of the spear, the group's action was totally chaotic, the combatants having never received training to act as a military unit. Most spears, though aimed true, could be warded off by an opponent's shield, and then thrown back to the other side. Thus battles were little more than brief and relatively bloodless clashes – hit-and-run raids that often ended inconclusively – in which the outnumbered side eventually prudently withdrew before extensive casualties occurred. Casualties, when they happened, were read as a sign that auspices were not favorable for the affected clan that day, causing the clan to retreat (often with the intention to seek a return engagement on a more favorable day).

Though people were rarely killed during these skirmishes, they were often taken captive. Women and children, never among the dead, were sometimes used as hostages. If captives were taken, the affected families typically paid a ransom in the form of cattle and received the captives back safe and sound.

All this changed, however, with Shaka. His vision of warfare was to engage in total military terrorism.

ARMY TRAINING

Shaka considered the traditional Zulu method of warfare to be completely useless. Only ineptness, in his view, would prompt a man to throw his primary weapon towards the enemy, leaving himself defenseless. Believing that such a military strategy was not only foolish but cowardly, he envisioned a much more efficient way of making war. In bringing that vision to reality, he revolutionized Zulu weaponry and military tactics.

Military Innovation

Under Shaka's guidance, warfare lost its resemblance to a game for amateurs. It became a truly deadly undertaking, leading to great loss of life. Although the *assegai* – a short, stout, heavy-bladed spear designed for close combat – may have been known before, Shaka made it the Zulu army's weapon of choice. The *assegai* had a longer blade than the usual Zulu spear – 18 inches long and 1.5 inches wide – and a short, strong haft. Shaka called this spear *iklwa*, after the sucking sound it made on being withdrawn from a deep body thrust. As a victim slid off the *assegai* blade, Shaka would shout, 'Ngadla!', 'I have eaten!'

(a common saying among the warriors). Using the *assegai* as a stabbing spear rather than a throwing spear, his men were able to retain their weapons and advance right up to their enemies behind protective shields.

Tales of magic and witchcraft surrounded the making of Shaka's own *assegai* – tales that were part of the overall myth-making process pertaining to his person. The *assegai* tales had roots in the fact that among the Zulus – as in many African societies – blacksmiths occupied a special position and the forging of metal was looked on with superstitious awe and apprehension. In keeping with the existing superstitions of the time, Shaka is said to have had a sorcerer blacksmith make his blade. To make the blade particularly powerful, it was said, this smithy used human fat – an extremely potent war medicine – in the fabrication.

Shaka also converted the shield, formerly for defense only, into an offensive weapon, making it large enough to protect the whole body. By using a larger version of the oval shield, his warriors were able to hook the small shields of their opponents, catching the warriors off guard and thus creating an opening to use their stabbing *assegai*, aimed at the ribcage or stomach. Shaka also had his warriors carry a knobkerrie – a club – that could be thrown if necessary.

While growing up, Shaka had hardened himself physically by running long distances. During those runs (the first of which were probably attempts to get away from his tormentors) he discovered that the crude cowhide sandals traditionally worn by Zulu men hampered his speed and agility. When he became an officer, he prohibited the use of such sandals, thus creating greater speed for his warriors. He forced his regiments to run barefoot over fields of thorns so that their feet became hardened and they could move more quickly in battle.

The army marched, ran and fought barefoot – on sharp stones, through thorn bushes, in deep sand and across rivers and every type of terrain possible. In the intervals between expeditions his warriors were occupied with military drills, military displays and dances. Through training and more training, Shaka honed his formidable fighting machine. Forced marches of up to 50 miles a day (carrying weapons), practice at handling weapons, and drills on the methods of dispatching the enemy were the order of the day.

The high standards that Shaka set for his men were no loftier than those he set for himself. For most of his reign he led by example, commanding his troops in person although tradition (and common practice) called for chiefs to stay out of danger. Shaka wanted to be one of the warriors, living as they did, eating their food, using the same shelter and dancing their dances, eschewing the trappings that he was entitled to as a leader.

Shaka demanded total loyalty, unquestioning obedience and the strictest discipline. Death was the inevitable reward for those who hesitated in carrying out his commands. Anyone who showed signs of fear or so much as winced in pain was accused of being a weakling and a coward, and killed. Warriors returning from battle without their *assegai* were likewise accused of cowardice and executed, as were warriors with wounds in their backs. For brave warriors, however, there was no limit to promotion, no matter how lowly the person's starting position. As a military commander Shaka replaced the traditional nepotistic practices with meritocratic rewards. Like Napoleon, he saw every soldier in his army as carrying in his backpack 'the baton of a field marshal'.

Furthermore, Shaka drilled his people to act in concert, training them to execute specific military maneuvers flawlessly. This coordination was in stark contrast to the chaotic melees of earlier years. He perfected several complex battle formations that outflanked and confused his enemies. For example he replaced the long skirmishing line with a phalanx formation known as *impondo zenkomo*, or 'bull's horns'. An encircling method of attack, this was most likely a derivative of the common method of hunting game. All available regiments were divided into four groups: the 'chest', the two 'horns' and the 'loins'. The chest – the main army, comprised of the strongest warriors – engaged the opponents immediately, striving to pin them down. The two outspread horns then raced out and encircled the enemy until their points converged. Those warriors who were the loins were held in reserve, seated nearby with their backs to the battle (so as not to become unduly excited). They could be sent to reinforce any part of the ring if the enemy threatened to break out.

The *impondo zenkomo*, executed as a synchronized mass choreography and carried out at top speed even over rough terrain, soon became the distinctive Zulu battle position. Instead of engaging in loose skirmishing tactics with light throwing spears, Zulu warriors now approached the enemy in tight formation and engaged in direct hand-to-hand battle, beating the enemy with their larger war shields and killing them with their short *assegai*. Officers supervised the battle, standing at strategic locations, using hand signals to direct the regiments.

A regiment, while on the move, lived off grain and cattle requisitioned from the kraals it passed. The men were accompanied by *udibi*, boys too young to fight (usually between six and 12 years of age), who carried the warriors' sleeping mats, neck rests, cooking pots and skin-cloaks. The hungry warriors spared their own civilian population where possible, using the food they had with them as they passed through friendly territory and camping at government residences that had stores of food. Entering enemy territory, they would resort to foraging. This system of getting supplies was not ideal: the longer a campaign lasted, the further the distance to friendly territory, the more difficult it was to obtain food in enemy lands.

The Power of Magic

Before each battle, *izinyanga*, or war doctors, engaged in a number of elaborate ceremonies to prepare the warriors for combat. Much of a regiment's success in battle was attributed to the talents of these medicine men. Through psychic means they were said to ensure the strength and the invincibility of the fighters. Among the ritual preparations for battle that they supervised, each warrior had to drink a mouthful of medicine and then vomit it into a specially dug hole. Some of this vomit was added to the great *inkatha yesizwe ya'kwaZulu*, a sacred grass coil into which were woven items of great spiritual importance. This coil, the symbol of the nation's unity and strength, was believed to bind the country together. Just before departure of the army, each warrior's front and back was spattered with a liquid that included items rich in spiritual power stolen from the enemy – items such as protective charms. After undergoing these purification ceremonies, warriors were prepared to face the enemy on the battlefield bound to each other and to the king by the ritualistic practices (Knight, 1995; Laband, 1995).

All warriors who had participated in such ceremonies were set apart from normal life and required to abstain from the normal activities of civilian society. Affected by a mystical force, they were considered to be highly contagious. Though after battle a cleansing ceremony took place, in order to stem the dangerous, contagious pollution following homicide, warriors nonetheless had to remain apart. Contact with women was seen as particularly harmful, both to warriors and to others.

Given this segregation from women, it is interesting to note that part of the purification process used intercourse to 'wipe away' the *izembe*, the contagious pollution following homicide – pollution that unchecked would cause a particular abdominal ailment culminating in insanity. Warriors who had killed opponents had to secure, by whatever means, sexual intercourse, usually with an old woman (or even herdboy) of another tribe. 'Those who have killed ... they will rape a woman; two or three may rape the same one. They may do this to a woman of any tribe a long way from their own' (Stuart, 2001, p. 344). Intercourse with this female (or boy) was thought to neutralize the *izembe*. Until a warrior had accomplished this act, he was compelled to wander about in the fields (Bryant, 1949, p. 508). This practice can be seen as an interesting way to legitimize full-fledged sexual intercourse in a society whose existing mores would not have allowed it.

Very high levels of *esprit de corps* developed among the warriors of the *amabutho*. Each regiment had its own colors, songs and war cries. The oldest regiments carried shields adorned with a lot of white, while the youngest regiments' shields leaned toward black. Between regiments there existed intense rivalry. Shaka encouraged the *amabutho* to outdo each other in acts of bravery on the battlefield, and he encouraged pre-battle dances that increased the spirit of competitiveness. In one such dance, the warriors jumped about pretending to stab an imaginary enemy and shouting ritual challenges and self-praises at each other. (Public praises in Zulu society were very important: by listing the achievements a person had accumulated over time, these praises allowed the expression of a person's identity.)

CONQUERING SOUTHERN AFRICA

In 1817, King Dingiswayo – still Shaka's overlord – was at the pinnacle of his success, having forged a confederacy, a rudimentary centralized state, among his Nguni neighbors. He had become the paramount chief of about 30 clans of what became later known as KwaZulu Natal. His dominance came to an end, however, with his capture and subsequent execution by his main rival, Zwide, of the Ndwandwe clan. The Mthethwa confederacy began to disintegrate.

The stories about Dingiswayo's capture vary. According to certain oral sources, Dingiswayo, accompanied only by a number of handmaidens, blundered into a patrol of Ndwandwe warriors. Other oral sources claim that Shaka betrayed his mentor. Still others suggest that Zwide's mother, Queen Nthombazi – a formidable woman who collected the skulls of vanquished enemies (in order to transfer the psychic power of those skulls to her son) and kept hyenas as pets – used witchcraft to bring down the great king. It is said that she attained supernatural mastery over Dingiswayo through possession of his sperm, obtained by Zwide's sister, who pretended to be in love with him. However it came about, Dingiswayo's skull does seem to have been added to Queen Nthombazi's considerable collection.

A Window of Opportunity

When Shaka heard of Dingiswayo's death, he is said to have exclaimed that Zwide killed his father, so great was his affection for the man. Despite Shaka's grief, however, he was politically astute enough to know Dingiswayo's death meant the whole of the Mthethwa confederacy was up for grabs for that person bold enough to take the helm. Shaka recognized this window of opportunity and stepped into the power vacuum with his small but extremely disciplined and effective Zulu army. With the approximately 400 Zulu warriors that he had organized and trained to a high level of preparedness, he began to score victory after victory. He first decimated the small clans in his vicinity, starting with the eLangeni, his mother's clan. As his conquests grew, so did his army: he incorporated the remnants of each clan he conquered into the Zulu fighting force.

In 1819 King Zwide, who had himself thought to take over from Dingiswayo, mounted a serious invasion of Zulu territory. Shaka, being greatly outnumbered (his army at that point estimated at 4000 men, compared to Zwide's 8000 to 10000 warriors), avoided direct battles with the main Ndwandwe army. Instead he resorted to guerrilla tactics and harassed smaller units and retreating forces. His first major victory was at Gqokli Hill, the first of a series of battles through which Shaka established his dominance. To what extent fact and fiction intertwine is hard to determine, but several oral accounts say that Shaka hid his main force in a deep depression at the summit of Gqokli Hill, surprising his adversary when his troops tried to storm it. The advantages of Shaka's new fighting techniques became dramatically apparent in this confrontation. No fewer than five of Zwide's sons fell on the battlefield at Gqokli Hill.

In spite of his relatively small fighting force, Shaka's strategic genius enabled him to withstand several more attacks by Zwide's formidable war machine. When Zwide pursued him, Shaka deliberately retreated before the Ndwandwe army, luring the enemy deeper and deeper into Zulu territory. The warriors of Zwide had expected to obtain provisions by looting Zulu granaries and cattle, but Shaka, anticipating this, had destroyed or removed all provisions. At last, exhausted and hungry, the Ndwandwe began to retreat. Shaka attacked them as they struggled across the upper reaches of the Mhlatuze Valley. After a brutal battle in which Zulu and Ndwandwe corpses are said to have piled up thickly on top of one another, the survivors among the Ndwandwe fled. As if to garnish that victory, some of Shaka's army approached the kraal of Zwide through deception, singing loudly as if they were Zwide's own army celebrating. The women of the kraal came out joyfully to welcome their warriors. What they found instead was terror: '[Shaka's warriors] impaled the children on posts; they stabbed the women; they stabbed everything at his home' (Stuart, 2001, p. 3). Shaka followed this vengeful act with a rapid sweep through Ndwandwe territory, destroying all remnants of resistance. Zwide and many of his supporters took flight; those who remained accepted Shaka's hegemony.

According to some sources, Shaka left Zwide's mother, who was captured at Zwide's kraal, to a terrible death. Because he saw her as responsible for the murder of Dingiswayo, Shaka imprisoned Queen Nthombazi without food in her dark kraal, with only a hungry hyena for company. Shaka saw the hyena as fit punishment, since hyenas were thought by his people to be witches' familiars. Only when some of the queen's limbs were eaten did Shaka, impressed by the courage of the old woman, show pity and set the kraal on fire.

The defeat of the Ndwandwe marks the true birth of the Zulu nation. In a series of annual campaigns Shaka then struck at and crushed the complex network of clans living to the south of Zulu territory and forged them into a homogeneous country. By 1820 he had taken the independence away from more than 300 clans, and most of southern Africa was under his rule. Estimates of the size of his army range from 15000 to more than 100000. (The first figure is more likely: higher estimates came from the early traders, whose judgement of numbers seems to have been unreliable.) An estimated 300000 to half a million people were subject to his rule (Knight, 1989; Lyndon Dodds, 1998). Shaka deliberately turned the region outside his sphere of influence into a total wasteland, to prevent his subjects from fleeing his rule as well as to create logistical problems for potential invaders. Only the desperate, fleeing Shaka's military machine – migrating bands living off plunder and robbery – dwelled in these regions. As one informer said, 'The Zulu country was like a pit, or a snuffbox, for you did not know where to run to; that is, if a man had to be killed it was inevitable that he would be killed, for there was nowhere to run to' (Stuart, 1976, p. 311).

3. Ruling by fear: bringing enemies and allies alike to submission

When the tyrant has disposed of foreign enemies by conquest or treaty, and there is nothing to fear from them, then he is always stirring up some war or other, in order that the people may require a leader.
(Plato, *The Republic*)

Would that the Roman people had but one neck!
(Caligula, from Suetonius, *Lives of the Caesars*)

... [F]or within the hollow crown
That round the mortal temples of a king
Keeps Death his court, and there the antic sits,
Scoffing his state, and grinning at his pomp;
Allowing him a breath, a little scene,
To monarchize, be fear'd, and kill with looks,
Infusing him with self and vain conceit,
As if this flesh which wall about our life
Were brass impregnable; and humour'd thus
Comes at the last and with a little pin
Bores through his castle wall, and – farewell king!
(William Shakespeare, *Richard II*)

Whatever crushes individuality is despotism, by whatever name it may be called.
(John Stuart Mill, *On Liberty*)

If I am unable to make the gods above relent, I shall move Hell.
(Virgil, *Aeneid*)

Shaka Zulu feared that he would not be truly paramount until he had finished off every enemy soldier and had ferreted out every potential insurrectionist from within his own ranks. He strove mightily to meet those goals.

UNFORGIVING WARFARE WITHOUT AND WITHIN

The Zulus, under Shaka's leadership, took no prisoners. Unwilling to be slowed down by weak soldiers, Shaka also put the seriously wounded among his own men out of their misery. These practices, which violated centuries-old Zulu methods of warfare, were only the beginning: according to some historical accounts, Shaka ordered the killing of all married people, children and even dogs in clans that resisted his military juggernaut. He felt that mature people were too used to the rule of their own leaders to ever become true Zulus, and he saw them as breeders of potential rebels. He is said to have asserted, 'Women that bear children must exist in Zululand only' (Stuart, 2001, p. 4). As for small children whose parents had been done away with, how were they to be cared for? Killing them was almost an act of mercy. Furthermore, if he let them live they might well seek revenge when they grew up. In the case of clans that surrendered without a fight, however, Shaka assimilated young males into his fighting force and conscripted young women to serve the regiments (Mofolo, 1981; Roberts, 1974). Shaka believed that these young people could be so indoctrinated in Zulu ways that they would forget their former homes.

This new, extreme form of warfare created total terror. As Shaka advanced through southern Africa, he made it very clear that those clans that resisted his war machine would be completely obliterated. Given the terrifying price of resistance, pledging allegiance to Shaka was the logical decision. Clans that offered their allegiance became territorial segments of Shaka's kingdom-at-large. They gained protection from raids in return for providing manpower to the *amabutho* and offering cattle as tribute. The warriors of the allied clans became a part of Shaka's royal army; they drilled and fought beside combatants from other chiefdoms. In a remarkably short time – well short of a decade – Shaka's massive program of nation-building had incorporated all of present-day Zululand and its vicinity. Clans that continued to resist Zulu rule migrated south, west or north, trying desperately to stay out of Shaka's jurisdiction.

In the Shadow of the 'Coward's Bush'

Shaka was equally ruthless and brutal with his own people, putting commoners, soldiers and those in high office to death for little or no reason (Bryant, 1929; Fynn, 1950; Isaacs, 1836). His executioners were kept busy on a daily basis. Outside of Shaka's main kraal was a tree known as *isihlahla amagwala* or 'Coward's Bush'. Here Shaka would put to death those who displeased him. (The bush takes its name from an incident when a group of warriors returned to the kraal, having failed to accomplish the task that Shaka had set for them. Shaka not only had the warriors put to death near the tree; he also had their families and their cattle killed.) These daily executions generally involved twisting the victim's neck or clubbing his or her skull. As mentioned earlier, impaling was also a common (though uncommonly dreadful) form of execution, generally reserved for situations where witchcraft was suspected. Shaka used to good effect the 'smelling out' ceremonies that were designed to ferret out witchcraft. Because anybody could be accused of witchcraft, his subjects were terrorized by these ceremonies.

As the regular use of the 'Coward's Bush' illustrates, Shaka recognized the value of terror as a tool of statecraft. He knew how to instill fear into his people, and how to use that fear to his advantage. He executed people on a daily basis for the most trivial offenses, simply to drive home to his subjects the fact that they were at his mercy. While it is undeniable that Shaka was arbitrary and unpredictable in his actions and punishments, some scholars have argued that his military state, with its army trained to a peak of violence, needed a heavy hand to keep it from running amok.

The 'Crushing'

Much of the Zulu kingdom's wealth – and it was considerable – can be traced to Shaka's campaigns during the period of 1816 to 1824. During the years 1818–20 Shaka conquered the core of Zululand; in the subsequent four years he consolidated his control within southern Africa. It was uninterrupted warfare that made it possible to conquer such a vast territory in such a short time. With every Fall season, a new campaign was underway, each more extensive than the last.

By 1827 the Zulus had become a great and powerful nation ruling over vast tracts of land in the southern coastal and interior regions of what is today known as KwaZulu Natal, and Shaka had become the chief over chiefs. By the time of his assassination in 1828, people from many different political entities had been molded into one nation. Their previous identities submerged, all thought of themselves as Zulu. And being Zulu was something to be proud of: by their depredations, the Zulus had become enormously wealthy in cattle and land.

However, Shaka's years of unrelenting warfare placed incredible strains on southern Africa. The army – the heart of the state – was a monster that had to be fed incessantly. Shaka needed to keep his warriors occupied, he needed to reward warriors of distinction, and he needed to satisfy the influential people in his kingdom. In this system of rewards, enemy cattle were the prized booty. Thus only through repeated victories – each of which brought more cattle into the fold – could the war machine's standard of living be maintained. Eventually cattle-raiding, not nation-building, became the primary objective.

Although the Zulus' depredations were limited to the coastal area, their activities had an avalanche effect, leading indirectly to what has been described as the *mfecane*, or 'crushing' – the devastation of the inland regions of the southern African continent in the early 1820s. The word *mfecane*, a Bantu term that probably derives from the Xhosa word *ukufaca* (meaning to be weak, to be emaciated from hunger), was often applied to Shaka's military and socio-political activities (Gump, 1988), but it extends much farther. While many of the chiefdoms near the Zulu kingdom accepted Shaka's hegemony, others retired to natural strongholds to resist him, and still others simply abandoned their traditional lands to move out of his way. These marauding clans, fleeing the Zulu wrath and searching for land, started a deadly game of musical chairs that broke the old clan structure of the interior and left 2 million people dead in its wake. It was a time of migration, human suffering, and a famine so extreme that cannibalism sometimes resulted. Ironically, the hunger and violence of the interior made Shaka's territory resemble an oasis of peace.

The *mfecane* depopulated an extensive portion of southern Africa, opening the door to renewed settlement. According to some historians, the Boer Great Trek of the 1830s, which passed through this area, was successful largely because virtually no one was left to oppose the new settlers. And yet, despite the turmoil in Zululand and beyond, there was good that came from Shaka's nation-building efforts: many of the socio-political communities that were brought into existence during his reign have survived into the present.

Sparta Revisited

Shaka not only accumulated wealth and citizens, he overturned the old order completely. His political maneuvering seriously diminished the power of the tribal, hereditary chiefs who had long ruled the Zulus and their neighbors. After all, a relative outsider (born Zulu but raised eLangeni and Mthethwa) was now the paramount chief, supported by favorites, many of whom were newcomers themselves. And not only did Shaka assume total political power; in addition, he reframed the role of the royal Zulu house, making himself the spiritual head of the kingdom. He elevated his ancestors to supreme positions among the spirits, asking their blessing at every major occasion. Because he was the best mediator to these spirits, he became the central figure in all the ceremonies that were an essential part of everyday life. Shaka even created new religious paraphernalia, the most important icon being the *inkatha* – the sacred coil of the nation – mentioned earlier. As long as the *inkatha* survived, Shaka preached, the nation would survive. (The British eventually destroyed the sacred coil when they burned down the kraal of the last independently ruling Zulu king, Cetshwayo, in 1879.)

The nation that Shaka created was a fundamentally military state. The regimental system initiated by Dingiswayo – the *amabutho* – gave the Zulu kingdom a large standing army of superbly trained and conditioned warriors. The political, social and economic forces of the new nation were all arranged to support the military mechanism. Historians have compared the social system Shaka created to that of ancient Sparta, the most totalitarian state in antiquity. In fact the proportion of the male population involved full-time as warriors for Shaka was substantially higher than in Greek antiquity. In Sparta the warriors were a small, aristocratic elite, while among the Zulu virtually every able-bodied male from his late teens into his forties was enlisted as a warrior (Ferguson, 1918). Furthermore although the state in Sparta made extremely exacting demands on its citizens, it was a constitutional government, and thus the citizens did not suffer from personal tyranny.

There was enormous pressure among the Zulus, especially in new regiments of young men, to 'wash their spears' – that is, to shed blood in battle. Only men who had been in battle and had killed an enemy were allowed (when their service was ended) to wear the *isicoco*, the distinctive head ring that signified full manhood and readiness for marriage. Young warriors clamored to 'wash their spears' so that they could qualify. These warriors had a vested interest in the wars of Shaka, since only war would allow them to wear the *isicoco*; only war would provide the cattle and meat that they craved, the royal herds being inadequate to feed all the people; and only war would give the rewards they needed to eventually become the leader of a household.

As noted earlier, the new nation's military outlook caused terror not only among neighboring clans but also within Zulu borders, where violence abounded. Capricious executions were the most visible form of that violence, but fights between regiments were an ever-present threat as well. In fact the various regiments were so competitive and so violent that they had to be kept separate. Some historians have theorized that the *amabutho* were sent on such frequent attacks against neighbors primarily to keep them occupied and out of trouble. With brutal warfare the warriors' obsession from training days on, they were prone to fight each other if they were not fighting enemies. This social system built on violence and terror was not well adapted to prolonged periods of peace.

GOVERNING THE EMPIRE

In the loosely bonded, decentralized confederation of clans that King Dingiswayo created, the identities and structures of the component peoples were still largely in place. The weakness of this system became obvious when Dingiswayo was killed and the confederation began disintegrating. Watching that disintegration, Shaka decided on a very different administrative model than his predecessor's. He claimed absolute authority over his kingdom, creating a law-and-order government with a highly centralized structure that lasted far longer than he himself did. Subsequent Zulu rulers retained his hierarchical leadership style and organizational apparatus, up to and including Inkatha, today's Zulu political organization.

Shaka established a hierarchy of civil and political officials subordinate to him. At the helm of this centralized hierarchy, he himself was the nation's spokesman to the spirit world, the ultimate legal court of appeal, the supreme commander of the army and the head of the civil government. He used the military apparatus, the bureaucracy and a secret service to maintain his grip over this highly centralized state.

The *Amabutho:* Protecting the Kingdom

As noted earlier, through military innovation and training Shaka created a formidable army of Zulu warriors. Though he introduced new regimental structures, he followed Dingiswayo's practice of recruiting according to common age rather than local loyalties, a fact that prevented chiefdoms from becoming centers of political opposition and kept the nation's most useful resource – manpower – directly under his control. The *amabutho* system, run by an efficient bureaucracy staffed by Shaka's key officials in regional positions of authority, was really the heart of the state apparatus.

The *amabutho* became an instrument of royal control throughout the growing nation. Because their membership was recruited from all clans that were incorporated into the Zulu kingdom, they were a melting pot, ensuring centralized power by instilling a sense of national, rather than local, identity. These *amabutho* served as an instrument both of internal control and of external defense, keeping the peace, enforcing Shaka's punishments, defending the population against raiders, providing protection for refugees and perhaps even, as some evidence suggests, trading in ivory and slaves.

Historian Alfred Bryant had great respect for the *amabutho* system:

> Life and manners in a Zulu military kraal were much as they are and ever have been in other barracks. That spirit of joviality, comradeship and *esprit de corps* ever strong in the African nature was here at its best. … While ease and freedom were abundant, stern discipline continuously reigned; but it was a wholly moral force, the young men being thrown entirely on their honor, without standing regulations and without supervision; and they seldom dishonored that trust. They were there for the sole purpose of fulfilling the king's behests. They acted as the state army, the state police, the state labor-gang. They fought the clan's battles, made raids when the state funds were low – the state funds of course being the king's cattle; they slew convicted and even suspected malefactors and confiscated their property in the king's name; they built and repaired the king's kraals, cultivated his fields and manufactured his war-shields …
>
> In such ways as this was each and every individual of the Nguni clan, boys and girls, maids and men alike, taught, first to father, then to king, to be ever obedient, docile, disciplined, self-sacrificing unto the last, unto the supreme test of offering one's life on the field of battle. (Bryant, 1929, pp. 78–9)

In Shaka's socio-political structure, his male subjects were first members of an *ibutho* and then members of the Zulu kingdom. The men felt intense loyalty toward the king, because he gave them food, arms, regalia, position, rewards of cattle and eventually their wives.

Each *ibutho* (made up of between 600 and 1200 warriors) had its own village and herd of cattle for food (though the latter was owned by the king). The *amabutho* were quartered at separate kraals near one of the royal homesteads, each distinguished by uniform markings on shields and by various combinations of headdress and ornaments. Like the cattle, the war shields of the members of the *amabutho* belonged to the king, because they were made from the hides of the royal herds. Thought to have powerful ritual properties, they were kept in a special hut at a nearby royal kraal.

Meals were eaten family-style, with meat and milk provided by the state (as was millet beer, when the occasion warranted it), while staple grains were provided by the families of the men in the *ibutho*. To further the process of socialization, during meals the warriors would shout Shaka's praises and thank him for his generosity.

A unit of unmarried females was assigned to each *ibutho* to produce food and perform other domestic duties, and occasionally to accompany the warriors on campaigns. Organizing women in this manner had the added advantage of facilitating mass marriages. Shaka insisted on 'relative' abstinence from sexual activities among his warriors, preferring his men to be celibate. He set the example for his warriors, refusing to marry although he had the pick of women. When he felt that the time had come for an *ibutho* to marry, he would order the entire regiment to do so and would specify the female unit from which they were to choose a wife. Previous alliances between men and women were not honored and could not be sustained. After marriage, the warriors would leave the *ibutho* and set up their own individual kraals. Though their primary allegiance was now their family and their clan, they remained in the *amabutho* system and could be recalled for active duty in exceptional situations.

During Shaka's rule, service in the army was continuous and long-term. Except for short visits home to see family, every warrior remained most of the time with his *ibutho*, leaving only when Shaka gave permission for the entire regiment to retire (which usually occurred only when the men had reached their forties and been successful on the battlefield). Shaka postponed the married status as long as possible for his warriors, to keep them under his control.

A number of *amakhanda*, or royal homesteads – literally 'heads' (of royal authority) – were built around Shaka's kingdom. These served as barracks for the various Zulu regiments. The *amakhanda*, visible representations of royal power, were built at strategic points in the kingdom to defend against enemies, serve as centers of administration, and offer support as symbols of royal authority. The design of each *ikhanda* (or single royal homestead) was a circle of 200 to 300 huts with a central enclosure that served both as a parade ground and as a pen for the royal cattle. Shaka probably had 13 or 14 of these royal homesteads. When not at war he would travel between them, taking residency in turn. The largest *ikhanda*, where the king had his primary residence, may have contained more than 1000 huts. Shaka's magnificent residence there – known as *kwaBulawayo* (meaning 'the place of the persecuted man' or 'at the place of the killings') – stood on the misty-blue hills above the Mhlatuze Valley.

Shaka lived in some isolation – in the *isigodlo*, a private area – at the top of the housing complex of his 'capital'. With him in this area lived a great many daughters of important chiefs given to him as tribute. (Estimates range from 1200 to 5000, the latter figure offered by Henry Francis Fynn.) These young women, known as the *umndlunkulu*, the 'Great-hut Troupe', were kept physically secluded. Anyone entering the *isigodlo* without authorization was killed. A number of his favorites among these women served in his personal harem; others were merely servants who could be given by the king in marriage, to cement ties between his clan and another. They were all regarded as 'daughters' and 'sisters' of the king, to be disposed of at his pleasure. These women were a symbol of royal wealth, because the *ilobolo* for one given in marriage went to the king, not to the woman's family – and this price was always set very high. But it was worth it: being given one of the king's *isigodlo* girls was a great honor, a reward highly coveted by Shaka's warriors.

The *Izinduna:* Administering the Kingdom

A group of men known as the *izinduna* (singular: *induna*) were central figures in the Zulu state. These representatives of the king – men who, as the king's deputies, had power over life and death – commanded the *amabutho*. They also played a key role in the central administrative apparatus of the state. They were the king's walking embodiment; as chief intermediaries between Shaka and his subjects, they were the executors of Shaka's commands. In occupying important military and administrative posts, they counterbalanced and replaced the power of the traditional clan chiefs. Dominant among Shaka's henchmen was Mbhopa, his chief *induna,* whose mother (according to legend) had been killed by Shaka.

In the earlier years of his reign, when clans submitted to the Zulu kingdom Shaka accepted the ruling family as subordinate leaders in his administrative hierarchy; this was less often the case in later years. When clans resisted incorporation, Shaka immediately put one of his own subordinates in charge; then as time passed he would add additional supporters in positions of power within the clan. If appointees were resistant to his rule, he simply had them killed and replaced them with candidates more to his liking.

In selecting headmen and subordinates for his bureaucracy, Shaka rarely looked to members of the royal family (though he had a number of half-brothers – the other sons of Senzangakona) or members of the aristocracy. He preferred commoners, often regimental leaders exceptional for their prowess in warfare, who had little or no traditional right to be chiefs, and who were therefore indebted to and dependent upon Shaka for their position. With no hereditary authority of their own, they were more likely to support Shaka faithfully.

The Secret Service: Terrorizing the Kingdom

The final element in the governance triumverate was Shaka's highly effective secret service – a network of informers, terrorists and executioners. While the *amabutho* terrorized neighboring clans, these people carried out Shaka's orders at home. Many discovered, however, that loyally brutalizing others gave no guarantee of safety to oneself inside the kingdom.

CONSOLIDATING POWER

The only threat to Shaka's absolute power came early in his regime from the *izangoma*, the diviners. Unable to oppose him directly, certain of these diviners accused some of his closest *izinduna* and counselors of witchcraft; and the accused were killed by impalement. Shaka did not take such a challenge to his power lightly, though he had to tread carefully in snuffing out the diviners' power.

To demonstrate that the *izangoma* were frauds, Shaka hatched a plot with the help of Mbhopa, his chief *induna*. According to oral history, as a dramatic provocation Shaka splattered the outer walls and ground of the royal kraal with ox blood during the night. The next morning, his people were horrified by what they perceived as blasphemy. A massive 'smelling out' ceremony was called to find out who had committed this villainous act. All the *izangoma* in the land – more than 150 – were invited by Shaka to identify the guilty, and they obliged. Working as teams, they accused more than 300 people of witchcraft. Three witchdoctors, however, guessed that Shaka was the person responsible. They said, 'It was done by the heavens above' (Stuart, 2001, p. 45). They were the only ones whose life was spared. The others were slowly tortured to death by the originally accused.

It was not only clear threats to power that Shaka dealt with so harshly. In this Sparta-like state, so different from the traditional Zululand, there was very little place for the old and the sick. Shaka had many old men put to death on the ground that they were useless. In memory of these killings he called one of his *amakhanda* Gibixhegu – 'finish the old men'.

Shaka ruled as an absolute despot, with a concentration of power that made his leadership style very different from that of the kings before him. He routinely made life-and-death decisions while taking his morning bath. Unlike previous rulers, he was not inclined to rely on the traditional tribal council. When he did ask their advice, the inquiry was more of a ritualistic nature than an honest quest for input. Certainly it did no harm to ask the councilors' advice: because he had intimidated them thoroughly, they tended to agree with anything he suggested. His military commanders were equally practical: because they held positions that previously had been occupied by tribal chiefs, they were deeply indebted to him and therefore agreed with most of his decisions. It took a very courageous member of the council or military leadership to question his policies. Perhaps the men would have been braver in Shaka's absence, but that was rarely tested. Unauthorized meetings of these groups were punishable by death.

A ROYAL ELEPHANT IN WINTER

By the end of the 1820s there were signs that Shaka was losing his grip on his kingdom. As Shaka's behavior grew bizarre, it became more difficult for his subjects to shut out the various deprivations they experienced – for the warriors, for example, dwindling food supply, delayed marriage and time away from family. In the early years Shaka had had a sense of focus, but now it was difficult for him to find – and to convince his people of – an overriding purpose. After crushing the forces of King Zwide, there were no more major wars to be fought. He had become the paramount ruler, and any unaffiliated tribes were more concerned with staying out of his way than with opposing him. Thus there was only the odd expedition against a faraway tribe to keep his war machine occupied. He used such forays to nip in the bud any restlessness he sensed in his people, but the small-scale warfare lacked the excitement of leading his war machine against overwhelming odds. He found himself spending many of his days inspecting his royal cattle, watching his soldiers dance, and hunting.

Shaka's subjects became increasingly demoralized as his erratic cruelties against real and imagined enemies intensified (Stuart, 1976, 1986, 2001). A growing number of people were horrified by his actions. Whereas once he had been viewed as a heroic warrior-king, more and more of his people now saw only a terror-inspiring tyrant. As the respect he once commanded dissipated, his rule gradually lost its legitimacy. His original constituency, pushed to the limit by his erratic actions, began to question the continuation of his reign and to think of alternatives.

The people saw – and were increasingly troubled by – behaviors such as these reported by Henry Francis Fynn, a trader who spent some time at Shaka's 'court':

> On the first day of our visit we had seen no less than ten men carried off to death. On a mere sign by Shaka, viz: the pointing of a finger, the victim would be seized by his nearest neighbors; his neck would be twisted, and his head and body beaten with sticks, the knobs of some of these being as large as a man's fist. On each succeeding day, too, numbers of others were killed; their bodies would then be carried to an adjoining hill and impaled. We visited this spot on the fourth day. It was truly a Golgotha, swarming with hundreds of vultures. (Fynn, 1950, p. 78)

As dissatisfaction increased among Shaka's warriors, a number of assassination attempts took place. One attempt was made on Shaka's life during a dance that took place while Henry Francis Fynn was visiting. Fynn delivered first aid and helped Shaka recover. Who the instigator was remained unknown, although rumor had it the would-be assassin came from the Qwabe tribe and had been sent by Shaka's arch-enemy, the fugitive Zwide. (Of course, there was also the possibility that the would-be assassin was part of a plot concocted by some of his family members.) Acting on the Zwide rumor, Shaka responded with a scorched-earth campaign in the area thought to be harboring the fugitive. No living being was spared.

The Death of Nandi

According to some historical sources, Shaka received word in 1827, while on an elephant hunt, that his mother Nandi was dying. A number of oral sources tell a very different story: they claim that Shaka stabbed his mother in a fit of rage, believing that she was concealing a child of his (Stuart, 1986; Rycroft and Ngcobo, 1988; Laband, 1997; Fuze, 1921/1998). According to one informer:

> He, Tshaka [*sic*], questioned her about a son that one of the women had had. He supposed that Nandi was hiding this son away. Some say she denied it and turned round to get some straws or wood to feed the fire with, the hut being dark, and he in his rage, stabbed her up the fundament with a sharp stick, through her leather skirt. This penetrated some inches up the anus. He told her if she divulged it he would have her torn limb from limb and eaten by the dogs of the kraal. So it was always supposed she died of enteric fever or typhoid. ... [H]ow could that be when she was supposed to be well when Tshaka left? How could she contract the disease and die in that time? After stabbing her he went off next day to hunt. This hunt had been organized before he stabbed her. A messenger was sent to say Nandi was dead. As a matter of fact she was dying. As soon as he received the news Tshaka cried, and natives said, 'the evil-doer cried like a little girl'. (Stuart, 1976, p. 57)

According to Henry Francis Fynn, Shaka arrived back home moments before 'the Great Female Elephant', as his mother was called, died from (what

Fynn thought was) dysentery. (The cause of her death will remain murky,
however.) A huge crowd gathered for the funeral, more than 60000 people
lamenting her death. Encouraged by Shaka's screams of sorrow, people tried
to outdo each other in ostentatious mourning. An orgy of killing followed for
those who did not show sufficient grief. Indeed, thousands of Zulus were
killed in the initial mass hysteria of Shaka's grief. According to Fynn:

> As soon as the death was publicly announced, the women and all the men who were
> present tore instantly from their persons every description of ornament. Shaka now
> appeared before the hut in which the body lay, surrounded by his principal chiefs in
> their war attire. For about twenty minutes he stood in a silent mournful attitude,
> with his head bowed upon his shield, and on which I saw large tears fall. After two
> or three deep sighs, his feeling becoming ungovernable, he broke out into frantic
> yells, which fearfully contrasted with the silence that had hitherto prevailed. This
> signal was enough. The chiefs and people, to the number of about 15000
> commenced the most dismal and horrid lamentations. ...
>
> But, as if bent on convincing their chief of their extreme grief, the multitude
> commenced a general massacre. Many of them received the blow of death, while
> inflicting it on others, each taking the opportunity of revenging their injuries, real
> or imaginary. Those who could not force more tears from their eyes – those who
> were found near the river panting for water – were beaten to death by others who
> were mad with excitement. Toward the afternoon I calculated that not fewer than
> 7000 people had fallen in this frightful indiscriminate massacre. (Fynn, 1950,
> pp.133–4)

Grief was apparently not the only motivation. Fynn insinuated that many
people took the opportunity of Shaka's mother's death to settle old scores.
Some sources suggest that even Shaka may have used the death of his mother
for political purposes, as an excuse to purge real and imagined enemies. He
and his followers may have taken the opportunity of Nandi's death to stifle
internal opposition to royal rule. The killings also served to signal aspiring
assassins of the intensity of his wrath, lest any of them dared to conspire
against him (Fynn, 1950; Laband, 1995; Walter, 1969). Shaka also saw the
death of his mother as an excuse to send his warriors on another expedition to
the south, invading Pondoland in an attempt to eliminate all the tribes between
his domain and the Cape Colony.

After the orgy of killings, Shaka's behavior became even more bizarre. He
demanded that his people go on a fast to commemorate his mother's death. He
ordered that for a year no crops could be planted, nor could milk – the basis of
the Zulu diet – be used. The milk of cows had to be dropped on the field. In
addition, he ordered all people to abstain from sexual intercourse. Women
found pregnant were slain with their husbands, as were the thousands of milk
cows that gave birth, so that even the calves might know what it meant to lose
a mother. After three months of these stringent regulations, with many of his
subjects already hovering near death, one of Shaka's chiefs had the courage to

confront the king with the fact that he was destroying the country. This courageous warrior, a man named Gala, is said to have walked straight up to the *isigodlo* where Shaka was residing and cried:

> Hawu! O king, thou that hast destroyed thy country. What thinkest thou, thou will reign over? Wilt thou create a new race? Shall all die because thy mother died? ... Thou hast destroyed it [the country]. Thy country will be inhabited by other kings; for it [thy people] will perish of famine. The fields are no longer cultivated, the cows no longer milked. They will be milked by those kings who will cultivate the soil; for thy people no longer eat, no longer bear, and the cattle are no longer milked. As for me O king, I say thou art dead thyself through this mother of yours. Stuff a stone into your stomach [i.e. brace thyself up, be not downhearted]. This is not the first time anyone has died in Zululand. (Bryant, 1929, p. 612)

Shaka did not fall into a fit of rage, as witnesses surely must have expected. Instead he heeded Gala's words and lifted the fast. In addition he asked his servants to give two cows as presents to this courageous warrior, and he gave Gala the right to wear the *isicoco*.

Psychopathology Rex

Although the need for warfare had diminished, the nearby clans having all been conquered, Shaka occasionally sent his soldiers out on distant expeditions that strained their capabilities to the limit. The men were tough, but there were physiological limitations on how long they could continue such grueling work. An army marches on its stomach, and times were lean. Shaka sent few provisions with this men, preferring that they forage in enemy land, but capturing cattle for food was difficult in the regions that Shaka himself had laid to waste. Capturing cattle to give to their king as war booty was equally difficult, and the warriors all knew the price of failure: death.

Shaka did not experience these difficulties himself. Although in his heyday personal engagement in military activities had had a psychologically restorative effect, he eventually stopped leading the army himself. Like many men, he did not do well in 'retirement': hunting, reviewing and counting his herds, inspecting those warriors who remained and watching them dance, and hearing the women of his *isigodlo* sing was not enough to keep him satisfied.

To keep himself occupied during the month of September 1828, when his warriors were away, Shaka decided to again demonstrate his talents as a diviner. He engaged in a 'smelling out' ceremony, accusing hundreds of women of witchcraft and calling for their execution. According to Henry Francis Fynn, the women

> were interrogated as to having magical powers or not. Finding the answer in the negative had no effect, some had the boldness to avow their being acquainted with

them, but either answer produced the same result. Dead bodies were to be seen in every direction, not less than 400 or 500 being killed during the absence of their husbands at war. (Fynn, 1833/1950, pp. 155–6)

Many more examples of bizarre behavior followed. While living at his final royal residence – a place called Dukuza, where the town of Stanger is now located – Shaka was in the habit of rising early and going down to the sea with his retainers. He required each person with him to throw a stick at the waves, to see if it returned. The owner of any stick that did not return was accused by him of witchcraft and put instantly to death (Fuze, 1921/1998). Unfortunately, once when Shaka threw his own stick into the water, it did not return, which onlookers saw as indicative of his misdeeds (Stuart, 1979, p. 168).

Early in 1828 Shaka sent the warriors south in a raid that would carry them to the borders of the Cape Colony. The warriors had no sooner returned, expecting the usual season's rest, than they were sent off on another raid – this one to the north, to fight an elusive enemy in an inhospitable land. To add insult to injury, when Shaka realized that their departure would leave him with almost no bodyguard, he ordered the older boys – those who ordinarily carried the warriors' gear – to remain at the royal kraal with him. He grouped them into a hastily formed regiment that he called 'the Bees'. Without the boys' help, Shaka's warriors would have to carry their own supplies. Shaka was stretching his subjects to breaking point, a fact that did not go unnoticed by members of his inner circle.

Unbeknownst to Shaka, at the same time he was testing the limits of his subjects' patience, members of his inner family circle were hatching a plot to assassinate him. Divisions and jealousies within the royal house had always been a source of trouble. From day one many members of the royal house had viewed Shaka as a usurper, a person of questionable legitimacy, and they now saw a window of opportunity in the army's discontent. The timing could not have been better: with almost the entire Zulu force – including Shaka's half-brothers – on campaigns out of Zululand, there were few loyal warriors who could (or would) protect him or even avenge his death, if he were assassinated.

Two of his half-brothers, Dingane and Mhlangana – the only ones willing to challenge the awesome aura that Shaka had created around himself – feigned sickness and deserted the expedition. Returning home, they entered into a conspiracy with Mbhopa. Shaka's aunt, Mnkabayi kaJama, who had supported Shaka when he first led the Zulus, was apparently part of the conspiracy too, concerned that his incessant campaigning and bizarre behavior were endangering the kingdom.

It is interesting to note that in spite of Shaka's increasingly capricious behavior, only family members were prepared to challenge him seriously. In the Zulu belief system, the person of the chief was sacred to commoners. As a result, most of Shaka's subjects were so intimidated by his mystical powers that they were scared to approach him or even to look him in the eyes. They believed that their all-knowing, all-seeing king would be able to look straight through them and perceive any mutinous thoughts. They also believed that anyone who killed a king would be doomed. Relatives in the royal clan were not so restricted. Thus it was regicide by family members that brought Shaka down. It would also be the demise of his assassin and successor, Dingane.

The Prophecy

While taking his afternoon sleep at midday on 24 September 1828, Shaka dreamed that he had been killed and that Mbhopa, his chief *induna*, was serving a new master (Fynn, 1833/1950, p. 156). The conspirators, hearing of the dream, knew that they had no time to lose. Shaka was in the habit of acting on his dreams, so they feared that executions of members of his inner circle would soon follow. That very day, the two half-brothers, with the help of Mbhopa, took advantage of a rare lapse in security to pounce on Shaka as he received an envoy. Dingane stabbed him to death. At the age of about 41, Shaka had fallen victim to a palace coup.

As remembered by his descendants, Shaka's last words were, 'What is the matter, children of my father?' In another version of Shaka's final minutes, he is said to have prophesied, 'Are you stabbing me, kings of the earth? You will come to an end through killing one another' (Laband, 1995, p. 46). Subsequently, he is said to have pleaded for mercy, begging, 'Leave me alone, sons of my father, and I shall be your menial' (Laband, 1997, p. xiv). Another account gives his last words as, 'You think you will rule this country, but I already see the "swallows" [whites] coming' (Ritter, 1978, p. 369). Still another version argues that his last words were, 'As soon as I go, this country of ours will be overrun in every direction by the white man. Mark my words' (Roberts, 1974, p. 148). Yet another testimony comes from a man whose father was killed while fighting for Shaka: 'Is it the sons of my father who are killing me? How is this, seeing I never put to death any of my brothers ever since I became king? You are killing me, but the land will see locusts and white people come' (Stuart, 1976, p. 96).

We will never know for sure what Shaka Zulu's last words were. All of the above offerings exhibit more focus and profundity than most stabbing victims can summon, suggesting editorializing on the part of the historian. We do know that his body was wrapped in the hide of a freshly slaughtered ox and then buried in a neighboring grain pit, accompanied by royal clothing and an array of weapons. A heap of stones was put on top of the grave, and the mound was covered by a mimosa bush (Bryant, 1929, p. 666).

After Shaka's murder, Dingane had few difficulties conciliating the people. Tired of violence and longing for peace, they were easily won over by

Dingane's promise of a more pacific policy – a promise that he would eventually break. The returning army, fearful of the punishment Shaka would mete out after their unsuccessful campaign, was also happy to embrace the new regime.

The end had come for one of the most remarkable leaders in Africa. Rider Haggard, in his novel *Nada the Lily*, tells it dramatically:

> In blood he [Shaka] died as he had lived in blood, for the climber at last falls with the tree, and in the end the swimmer is borne away by the stream. Now he trod that path which had been beaten flat for him by the feet of the people whom he had slaughtered, many as the blades of grass upon a mountain side ... (1882, p. 210)

Shaka left no offspring. He had not married, and those of his 'sisters' who became pregnant had been killed (though rumors persisted that he had fathered a child who had been kept concealed from him – see Fuze, 1921/1998, p. 60). In the absence of a direct heir, his murdering half-brother assumed leadership. Dingane lacked Shaka's drive and strategic genius, however, and ruled incompetently. In 1840 his brother Mpande, who proved to be somewhat more capable as a leader, overthrew Dingane. Despite the relative ineffectiveness of his successors, Shaka's legacy lasted for 50 years after his death. It took half a century, and many bloody battles, for the British to win a decisive victory over the Zulus under King Cetshwayo in 1879. Zululand came under informal British control at that time, and in 1887 it was annexed to Natal.

Although Shaka was (and still is) vilified by many, his military genius and leadership abilities led to the transformation of a kingdom of 100 square miles into a Zulu empire that extended over 1 000 000 square miles. In a period of about ten years he succeeded in building a vast kingdom and a powerful sense of national identity – an identify that remains even today. From relative obscurity he rose to become the most powerful ruler in black Africa, currying his original disorganized group of 400 warriors into a large army as disciplined as that of Alexander the Great. As a founder of the Zulu nation, Shaka passed quickly into legend. Merely uttering his name left a taste of fear in the mouths of non-Zulu southern Africans for years after the king was long dead.

PART II

The Question of Character

4. The inner theatre of the king: acting out personal concerns on a public stage

The possession of unlimited power will make a despot of almost any man. There is a possible Nero in the gentlest human creature that walks.
(Thomas Bailey, *Leaves from a Notebook*)

Nature has left this tincture in the blood,
That all men would be tyrants if they could.
(Daniel Defoe, *The Kentish Petition*)

How shall I be able to rule over others, that have not full power and command of myself?
(François Rabelais, *Gargantua*)

Every man who takes office in Washington either grows or swells, and when I give a man office I watch him carefully to see whether he is growing or swelling.
(Woodrow Wilson, speech, 15 May 1916)

I began to notice that the obligations of citizens, admonitions, restrictions, decrees, and all the other forms of pressure put on us were coming to resemble the man himself more and more closely, displaying an unmistakable relation to certain traits of his character and details of his past, so that on the basis of those admonitions and decrees one could reconstruct his personality like an octopus by its tentacles.
(Vladimir Nabokov, *Tyrants Destroyed*)

What we call the beginning is often the end
And to make an end is to make a beginning.
The end is where we start from.
(T.S. Eliot, *Four Quartets*)

When it comes to Shaka Zulu, entering the inner theatre of the king is (and must remain) a highly speculative exercise, given the paucity of verifiable information available (McDougall, 1985, 1989). The divergence of the oral reminiscences that undergird the written accounts guarantees that distinguishing reality from myth, fact from fiction, will continue to be a matter of conjecture. Because of that blurring of fact and fiction, it is equally difficult to differentiate between what in Shaka's tale is universal and what is particular. As suggested earlier, that tale is an archetypical narrative that touches a number of deep, universal psychological concerns. These include adversity, misfortune, triumphant return, excessive pride, false parentage, generational rivalry, earned recognition, revenge, vindication, group identification and temptation.

Shaka's life story – especially to the extent that it is story rather than fact – is a good example of 'family romance', the label that psychologists give to a fantasy cherished by children whose families are conflict-ridden (Fenichel, 1945). Children develop a family romance, essentially a poetic tale, in reaction to stressful experiences: they picture themselves as having been born of distinguished parents (who, through no fault of their own, became separated from their offspring) and as searching for vindication and independence. Finding the present parent(s) lacking, children fantasize that the wished-for 'absent' parents must have been better.

Exile, exposure, destitution and humiliation are common elements of the family romance, which deals with the frustration of desire by reasoning that one's 'true' parents would never be unforgiving or harsh; they would be much kinder, much more understanding. The fictitious fantasy of the family romance makes it more acceptable to a child to harbor hostile feelings against the parent (since that parent is only an interloper anyway). Oedipal elements are part of this family romance for boys, based on feelings of competition with the father for the attention and possession of the mother. In the Oedipal myth that the male family romance mirrors, the hero-son takes (real or symbolic) revenge on the father and surpasses his achievements.

The main attraction of the myth of the hero in general, and the family romance in particular, lies in the revolt of the child against the parents, a pattern that is, after all, a universal part of growing up. All young males have to find their own way, separate their attachment from their mother, and be reborn as full-grown men. Thus the Shaka story can also be seen as a metaphor for the process of separation and individuation, for becoming a person in one's own right. But the tale does not end there. There is much more to come.

The tale also symbolizes the difficulties associated with succession – that is, the trials and tribulations of taking over from the previous generation. It spells out age-old conflicts between father and son, raising questions of generational rivalry. It deals with the difficulties a father often has in choosing a successor and the urges a son often has to overthrow the previous generation.

In addition, Shaka's story can be seen as a moral tale about the value of earned recognition. The tale points out the tension between nepotistic and meritocratic practices – the triumph of capability and achievement over ascription. By celebrating Shaka's accomplishments against overwhelming odds, the tale shows us that Shaka was meant to be the rightful successor, being the most capable of his father's offspring.

The story of Shaka also illustrates the universal human feelings of hatred and revenge, of getting even. It is a story of suffering and vindication, a tale about coping with narcissistic injury. That these themes are as old as humankind facilitates recognition and identification. The wish to return injury for injury, which runs like a red thread through the dark weave of Shaka's tale, can be traced through all of recorded history.

The evolution of the Shaka story since his death is a reaction on the part of the Zulu people to the loss of their tribal, cultural and national identity. As a nation-builder, Shaka became an object of identification, a means of regaining lost pride. Read in that light, his is a story of reparation, restitution and unification. The identification that southern Africans still feel for Shaka makes the Shaka symbolism even more powerful.

The Shaka story also has a Faustian quality. A tale of temptation, it asks what price a person is willing to pay, how far he is willing to go, to obtain power. In revealing Shaka's heart of darkness, it reveals the dangerous consequences of closing a pact with the devil: hubris, violence, death. And it warns of the presence of these destructive forces in all of us. Shaka is himself in this story, but he also represents the darker, shadow side of humankind generally. We see ourselves when we watch him become so obsessed by power that he sacrifices human relationships for what the devil (in the person of malevolent diviners and witchdoctors) can offer him, and when he loses the ability to distinguish between killing for a just cause and wanton killing for killing's sake. The ending is predictable, surely: loneliness and despair. Shaka ends up on a throne of blood, isolated from his fellow human beings, struggling with depression and despondency (Haggard, 1882; Kunene, 1979; Mofolo, 1981).

PRIVATE MAN ON A PUBLIC STAGE

To understand Shaka Zulu, and to learn from his life and experiences, we have to see him not just as a man, and not just as a representative of the shadow side of humanity, but as an individual at a particular moment in time and in a particular set of circumstances. Shaka's personality, in interaction with that setting, manifested itself as political behavior. In trying to define himself, to shape his own identity, Shaka shaped a given period in history. In attempting to resolve his personal anxieties, he made his impact on society's prevailing concerns. There is an inflection point, then, at which personal identity, public identity and public ideology converge, at which individual and collective histories intersect. How Shaka handled that inflection point – how he settled personal accounts on a large scale and in a grand context (and how leaders in general attempt that task) – is our focus in this next part of the book.

Engaging in the 'reconstruction' of a historical figure – the reading of personality from his or her personal and political behavior – is a daunting task. Worse yet, it is only half the battle. To benefit from what we learn about Shaka Zulu, we have to reverse the process once again, shifting back to how personality affects behavior: after Shaka's underlying personality is revealed, we can extrapolate from him to people of similar personality type, and we can speculate about how such people might deal with various positions of power in today's society – whether in the political arena or the workplace. As we look at Shaka's personality and the challenges of the period he lived in, decoding the 'texts' that we find in interrelated factual, cognitive and affective indicators, we will be able to identify themes, forms, fantasies and images that people in power to a large degree share and that are all but universal in despots. Most of the personality themes under discussion are equally applicable to Joseph Stalin, Adolph Hitler, Mao Zedong, Slobodan Milosevic and Saddam Hussein.

The Question of Appearances

As has been stressed before, we know very little for certain about Shaka. We are not even sure what he looked like. One Zulu informant quoted in the most extensive oral-history source available claimed that he was short and very dark; another informant in that same source described him as tall with dark brown, lizard-colored skin (Stuart, 1976). Some people who dealt with him commented on prominent front teeth and a lisp or stutter, while others made no mention of unusual features. Some called him handsome, while others claimed that he had a large nose and was not very good-looking. Tall or short, ugly or good-looking, what did Shaka really look like?

A Zulu who was converted to white ways and Christianity, Magema Fuze (1921/1998), who knew contemporaries of Shaka but never met the king himself, described Shaka as follows:

> Shaka as a grown man had a good, strong, well-built body; he had good buttocks, well shaped but not large. ... He had a large body, but it should be borne in mind that he was a man of war and not sedentary. He was brown in color ... and as a king, glossy with good food. He didn't get stout ... but remained muscular and powerful. (p. 89)

James Saunders King, a trader who met Shaka repeatedly, made a drawing of the Zulu king that is supposed to have pleased him. In it Shaka is portrayed as rather tall. Henry Francis Fynn (1833/1950), another contemporary who spent quite some time with Shaka, gives the following description of him:

> Round his forehead he wore a turban [headband] of otter skin with a feather of a crane erect in front, fully two feet long, and a wreath of scarlet feathers, formerly worn, only, by men of high rank. Ear ornaments, made from dried sugar cane,

carved round the edge, with white ends, and an inch in diameter, were let into the lobes of the ears, which had been cut to admit them. From shoulder to shoulder, he wore bunches, five inches in length, of the skins of monkeys and genets, twisted like the tails of these animals. These hung half down the body. Round the ring on the head [*isicoco*], were a dozen tastefully arranged bunches of the loury feathers, neatly tied to thorns which were stuck into the hair. Round his arms were white ox-tail tufts, cut down the middle so as to allow the hair to hang about the arm, to the number of four for each arm. Round the waist, there was a kilt or petticoat, made of skins of monkeys and genets, and twisted as before described, having small tassels round the top. The kilt reached to the knees, below which were white ox-tails fitted to the legs so as to hang down to the ankles. He had a white shield with a single black spot, and one assegai. When thus equipped he certainly presented a fine and most martial appearance. (pp. 74–5)

Yes, dressed up like that Shaka must have made a very striking appearance indeed. This view is confirmed by Nathaniel Isaacs (1836/1970), another member of the group of traders who made early contact with Shaka. In his diary he noted a request from their party to see Shaka attired in his war costume, an appeal to which the king consented. Isaacs described what he saw:

His dress consists of monkeys' skins, in three folds from his waist to his knee, from which two white cows' tails are suspended, as well as from each arm; around his head is a neat band of fur stuffed, in front of which is placed a tall feather, and on each side a variegated plume. He advanced with his shield, an oval about four feet in length, and an umconto, or spear, when his warriors commenced a war song, and he began his maneuvers. Chaka [sic] is about thirty-eight years of age, upward of six feet in height, and well proportioned: he is allowed to be the best pedestrian in the country, and, in fact, during his wonderful exercises this day he exhibited the most astounding activity. (pp. 28–9)

Like all effective leaders, Shaka paid attention to the presentation of self. Clearly he knew what was needed to make a strong visual impression on people. In fact, the above descriptions suggest that his physical presentation went beyond the requirements of the position: although a colorful dress code was part of how African kings conveyed their superiority, Shaka seems to have just plain showed off. That exhibitionistic streak suggests that Shaka wanted to be noticed, that he enjoyed being noticed. Not only did he adorn himself with the most extravagant feathers, furs and beads; he highlighted his appearance by demonstrating his skills publicly – leading his warriors in their war dances, for example. Shaka had no shortage of narcissism, obviously. Freud might have been thinking of the African king when he said, 'The leader himself need love no one else, he may be of a masterful nature, absolutely narcissistic, self-confident and independent' (Freud, 1921, pp. 123–4). Appearance cannot tell us, however, whether Shaka's dramatic dressing was the offshoot of a strong sense of inner security or a defensive effort, an attempt to compensate for early hurts and feelings of inferiority.

Divesting the Persona

If we know little about Shaka's outward appearance, we know even less about
his personality. In venturing conjectures about his inner theatre, we have to
fight embellishments by the mythopoetic imagination at every turn.
Fortunately what we do know about Shaka's activities allows us to single out
themes that help us to better understand his character and his magnum opus:
the despotic, totalitarian state of the Zulus.

In attempting to understand a person's character, we need to observe the
delicate 'dance' between environment and individual. In this dance, this
mutually influential process, character is determined by such individual
factors as constitutionally granted disposition, temperament, the idiosyn-
crasies of family life, exceptional events in a person's life and general
environmental factors such as culture and religion. One or two factors alone
can never explain a person's functioning. Only a whole set of interrelated
factors is able to do so. Each infant starts life with a malleability that permits
development of character in many different directions. As life progresses into
childhood and then adulthood, and as certain avenues are cut off, future
possible outcomes narrow dramatically.

Comments made by Shaka's contemporaries about his personality are
disturbing, because they present a man of unusually sharp contrasts. Many
depictions in oral and written accounts refer both to his generosity and to his
wanton cruelty. Both Nathaniel Isaacs and Henry Francis Fynn described
Shaka as enigmatic: extremely kind and compassionate one instant, able
casually to put people to death immediately afterwards. 'Such opposing kinds
of conduct in one person appeared to me to be strange,' commented Fynn, 'but
I afterwards became convinced that both the contradictory dispositions,
delicate feeling and extreme brutality, were intimately blended in him'
(1833/1950, pp. 151–2). Another salient character trait mentioned by many
who had dealings with him was a tendency toward outbursts of extreme anger.

So what was the real Shaka like? Which of the varied sides he presented to
the world was the true self? Why the anger and the fascination with violence?
As developmental psychologists like to remind us, to understand a person we
have to start at the beginning.

NARCISSISM REVISITED

We all know about the mythological youth Narcissus, who looked at his image
in a pond, fell in love with himself, and drowned as a result. Held up as a
reminder of what happens to those who look too kindly on themselves, he
remains the archetypical representation of narcissistic behavior.

Psychoanalyst Erich Fromm encapsulates narcissism as follows:

> Narcissism can then be described as a state of experience in which only the person himself, *his* body, *his* needs, *his* feelings, *his* thoughts, *his* property, everything and everybody pertaining to *him* are experienced as fully real, while everybody and everything that does not form part of the person or is not an object of his needs is not interesting, is not fully real, is perceived only by intellectual recognition, while *affectively* without weight and color. A person, to the extent to which he is narcissistic, has a double standard of perception. Only himself and what pertains to him has significance, while the rest of the world is more or less weightless or colorless, and because of this double standard the narcissistic person shows severe defects in judgment and lacks the capacity for objectivity. (Fromm, 1973, p. 201)

Narcissism, in limited doses, is necessary for self-esteem and identity formation. And its presence in higher-than-average doses is a given in leaders, because assertiveness, self-confidence and creativity cannot exist without a strong degree of self-love. An excess of narcissism is troublesome, however: intense egotism, exclusive self-centeredness, grandiosity, a sense of entitlement and an exaggerated self-love all cause grief to self and harm to others (Kernberg, 1975, 1980; Kets de Vries, 1989; Kohut, 1971, 1977; Zaleznik and Kets de Vries, 1975). The question is, how much narcissism is too much?

Constructive versus Reactive Narcissism

In determining what makes narcissism dysfunctional, I have found it helpful to make a conceptual distinction between 'constructive' and 'reactive' narcissism (Kets de Vries, 1989). Constructive narcissism develops in response to what pediatrician Donald Winnicott called 'good-enough' caregiving – that is, caregiving that conveys love and support to a youngster (Winnicott, 1965, 1975).

Frustration is a fact of life from birth to death: we cannot always have what we want, when we want it. How parents handle the myriad frustrations of their infants and growing children has a tremendous impact on the people that those infants mature into. To be healthy, frustration must be gradual, consistent and phase-appropriate. Caregivers who monitor frustrating experiences, recognizing their children's tolerance for frustration and intervening as needed, help their offspring to arrive at mature, relatively conflict-free functioning. By providing a proper balance between soothing and stimulation, regulating play and exploratory activities as needed, effective caregivers ensure adequate affect attunement in their children. This balance is easier to achieve as children gain language skills. When working with the very young, caregivers must rely on a delicate harmonization of signals between adult and infant to help the latter shift from distress to contentment. Children whose caregivers master that harmonization are less likely, as they grow older, to become overstimulated; they are better able to tolerate high levels of excitement, regulate physiological arousal and offer appropriate behavioral and emotional responses.

Children fortunate enough to experience effective childrearing grow up with a strong sense of self-confidence. Having had caregivers who helped them to see things in perspective, offered them support, recognized and adapted to their tolerance level for frustration, and provided what psychologists call a proper 'holding environment' and 'containment' for their emotional reactions, these children are well balanced and enter adulthood fortified by a solid dose of self-worth and self-esteem (Bion, 1959; Emde, 1981; Winnicott, 1975). This constructive narcissism helps them to keep their expectations in balance (allowing for more accurate reality-testing). As a result, they need not resort to primitive defensive reactions such as denial, splitting, projection and idealization – more on these later – to keep anxiety at bay. Their inner theatre, which tends to have relatively benign imagery, follows a life-affirming script that sustains them in the face of life's adversities.

Reactive narcissism, on the other hand – the narcissism we see evidence of in Shaka Zulu – develops in people who have been 'wounded' in one way or another. Their excessively narcissistic disposition develops as a way to ward off feelings of low self-worth and depression – feelings that developed because caregivers failed at the rudiments of 'good-enough' parenting. Reactive narcissists go to great lengths to overcome the narcissistic injuries of the past. Such people can be ruthless, grandiose and exhibitionistic; extremely exploitative, they seek to dominate and control.

What, you may ask, is a 'narcissistic injury'? Overstimulation, under-stimulation and erratic, inconsistent stimulation by caregivers during critical phases in an infant's development can all wound the maturing self. In the case of parental understimulation, children do not get the attention needed for healthy development. In contrast, parental overstimulation leaves unchallenged an infant's original sense of omnipotence; as a result, boundaries are poorly set and the child has only a hazy understanding of his or her real abilities and desires. Finally, erratic treatment by caregivers prevents the child from internalizing stable imagery.

Overstimulation, understimulation and erratic, inconsistent stimulation, all of which cause extreme frustration in the child, contribute to problems of self-esteem regulation (Kohut, 1971; Kohut and Wolf, 1978) – in other words, to narcissistic injury. People who as children experienced 'mis-stimulation' grow up with a defective, poorly integrated sense of self; they struggle, often unsuccessfully, to achieve a stable sense of self-esteem and identity. Deprived of emotional 'containment' in childhood, they often enter adulthood with poorly modulated emotional and impulse control. Thus they need more than a normal dose of attention. Because of the inconsistencies in childrearing that they experienced while growing up, they do not develop the kind of trust in the outside world that is required for healthy functioning. Instead they typically feel insecure in relationships, exhibiting distrust, suspiciousness, lack of intimacy and feelings of isolation (Erikson, 1963). They are also typically prone to outbursts of rage when things do not happen according to their will.

To combat their feelings of inadequacy, reactive narcissists often create an internal self-image that is somehow special, that sets them apart from – above – the rest of humanity. This delusion of uniqueness, a compensatory, reactive refuge against ever-present feelings of failure, has a glass-bubble quality. Though fragile, this sense of uniqueness vitally affects the reactive narcissist's dealings with the environment. Discrepancies between mundane capabilities and extravagant wishes so accentuate anxiety and impair reality-testing that the person becomes unable to distinguish wish from perception, 'inside' from 'outside'. Driven by the malevolent images of their internal world, they distort events to manage anxiety and to prevent a sense of loss and disappointment.

Freud might just as well have had Shaka in mind when he noted that 'if a man has been his mother's undisputed darling, he retains throughout life the triumphant feeling, the confidence in success, which not seldom brings actual success along with it' (Freud, 1917, p. 156). Presumably, given the small family's years of exile and hostility from outsiders, Shaka and his mother were much more intensely involved than would have been the case for a typical Zulu child and his mother. Evidence suggests that as compensation for the lack of a husband, Nandi directed all her emotional energy toward her son, creating in him a sense of being special, of being the 'chosen' one who was strong enough to survive the taunting and ridicule he was exposed to while growing up. Whether she created or merely encouraged his self-deception of uniqueness, she clearly overstimulated her young son. While Shaka's secure bond with Nandi mitigated the trauma that Shaka was exposed to, and while the delusion of uniqueness that Nandi fostered protected Shaka against more serious narcissistic pathology, her overstimulation left a negative legacy.

Wanting to be treated as the special person he believed himself to be, wanting to be recognized as a chief's son, and yet being dramatically thwarted, Shaka must have been a demanding, irritating child. In fact we have to wonder to what extent he provoked the ridicule that other children meted out. Did he invite, by his superior demeanor, the youthful torture that came his way? The need to show off, to provoke, to have his own way that grew to excess in adulthood – and thrived in the royal homesteads, where no one dared to challenge him any longer – must have been evident in childhood as well.

It is not surprising that many narcissistic people, with their need for power, prestige and glamour, end up in leadership positions; and many – especially those who are constructive narcissists – are phenomenally successful. Their confidence, purposefulness, assertiveness, sense of drama and ability to influence others serve them well in organizational life. These characteristics contribute to shared vision, group cohesion, and alertness to external and internal danger signs. The more leaders are convinced of their special gifts and mission, the more they can be convincing to their audience.

Unfortunately, the darker side of narcissism – especially the excesses of reactive narcissism – brings many leaders to their knees. The self-destructive journey from effectiveness to madness begins when people create their own reality and refuse to see anything beyond what they want to see. The uninhibited behavior, self-righteousness, arrogance and inability to accept an interchange involving others' ideas impair the effectiveness of excessive narcissists and prevent adaptation to internal and external changes. Given their self-centeredness and their need for affirmation, such individuals do not welcome information that runs counter to their scheme of things; in fact they may respond to it with an outburst of rage. No wonder narcissists gravitate toward followers who are sycophants. Independent souls do not survive long in the vicinity of narcissists.

The abuse of power is closely linked to malignant narcissism. Concerned only with number one, narcissists could not care less about hurting others in pursuit of their own self-interest. Lacking empathy, they find it hard to imagine how others feel. They see friends and associates only as extensions of themselves, to be used and abused as long as it serves their purposes. They have few qualms about devaluing the people around them to underline their own superiority. When in positions of leadership, they build regimes characterized – as Shaka's was – by exclusion of others from policy-making, intolerance of criticism, disregard of followers' legitimate needs, and unwillingness to compromise.

We learn from the diaries of Henry Francis Fynn and Nathaniel Isaacs that Shaka was totally preoccupied with himself. He was interested in others only as long as they could be of service to him. Other people, other worlds, concerned him only to the extent that they fit into his schemes and desires. Other people's opinions were worthless to him, because he felt that he knew more about just about everything than did other people (as he liked to point out regularly in conversation). The world that Shaka created around him – a world that his absolute power made possible – revolved completely around him.

Body Image and the Lure of the Stage

The exhibitionistic aspects of Shaka's behavior, his constant need for attention and admiration, suggest deep-seated feelings of inferiority masked by reactive narcissism, as we have seen. Like reactive narcissists everywhere, he created fantasies of aggrandizement to protect his vulnerable self, embellishing his hoped-for future and constructing a more glorious past. At their most elemental, those fantasies dealt with physical appearance.

Feelings of insecurity often express themselves through a preoccupation with one's physical appearance. If the story about Shaka's being teased concerning the size of his sexual organs as a child is truth rather than fabrication, that teasing must have inflamed his basic feelings of insecurity. There is ample unquestioned evidence for teasing generally – enough teasing, certainly, that his body image could have become distorted. That perceptual distortion would have manifested itself in emotional and behavioral problems. Quite likely, as mentioned earlier, provocative, irritating behavior would have been part of the feedback loop – both the consequence of past teasing and the cause of further teasing (and further infuriating behavior, and so on) – resulting in a vicious circle of frustration and aggression.

Though we have to speculate about Shaka's body image as a child, and how that image developed, we are in the realm of fact when talking about his exhibitionism as an adult. As king, he participated with obvious enthusiasm in rituals that put himself – his physical self – at the forefront. For the most part these were rituals that he himself introduced, not well-established customs of the chieftains in Zulu society. He tended to be not a culture-carrier but a culture-breaker and a culture-maker, introducing new rituals that suited his character structure.

As an example, each morning Shaka had a bath in public, stark naked, in front of a large audience. After his bath he was greased by attendants with a mixture of red ochre and sheep-tail fat, in preparation for his daily rounds. This public display was certainly a dramatic way to indicate that his body shape and the size of his sexual organs were more than adequate, childhood taunts notwithstanding. In other ways too he seemed to go out of his way to display his well-developed manhood.

A preoccupation about body image tends to come to a head as a person becomes older. To narcissistic people especially, the ageing of the body is perceived psychologically as a major injury. Shaka apparently was no exception. He seems to have been downright scared of old age. His habit of making fun of and killing old men (contrary to traditional Zulu custom, which granted old people great respect) was symptomatic of that fear. We often attack in others what we most fear in ourselves.

Shaka's efforts to rid his head of white hairs also suggest a fear of ageing: he did not want to be perceived by others as an old man. No wonder he welcomed Henry Francis Fynn's administration of Rowland's Macassar oil (a hair-coloring treatment), which temporarily blackened his increasingly graying hairs. Pleased with the results of this treatment, Shaka pressured the traders repeatedly to provide him with this magical remedy, which he viewed as the secret of eternal youth. As Nathaniel Isaacs noted:

> He [Shaka] wished ... that Lieutenant King would procure some more medicines for him, and particularly some stuff for turning white hairs black ... and he wanted it very much for his aged mother. He appeared more than ordinarily anxious to obtain this latter preparation, and promised to reward Lieutenant King with abundance of ivory and droves of cattle, provided he should return with it. He begged of us, in the most entreating manner, to keep this request a profound secret, and not to betray the confidence he had reposed in us. (Isaacs, 1836/1970, p. 106)

Shaka's plea for secrecy suggests that he was not comfortable with his strong desire for rejuvenation. He seemed reluctant to admit his anxiety about getting older and about the effect his ageing would have on his people. According to Henry Francis Fynn, who also wrote about Shaka's request, the king implied that he wanted the product for his mother and stepfather, 'who were gray-headed, which did not look well in such great personages'. (Fynn, 1833/1950, p. 142)

Shaka's preoccupation with the body went even further, though some of what seems oddly narcissistic in his behavior had its roots in the cultural beliefs of Zulu society. Because any anti-Zulu medicine that was going to be used for the purpose of witchcraft had to be based on Skaka's *insila*, or body products (ranging from fingernail cuttings to excreta) – the king being the symbol and representation of the Zulu nation – these had to be dealt with appropriately by his various attendants. Shaka, a great believer in the power of sorcery (most likely remembering the fate of his predecessor, Dingiswayo), took these activities extremely seriously, punishing by death any attendant who displeased him.

Reactive narcissism can be seen as a major underlying motivational force in all that Shaka Zulu did. It was the engine that drove his intense need to prove his worth to the world. Having not been exposed at length to age-inappropriate levels of frustration, he was prone to feelings of powerlessness (and an accompanying hunger for personal power), a desire for vengeance, strong feelings of hatred, and compensatory fantasies of omnipotence. Like all reactive narcissists, he was very sensitive to personal slights, responding aggressively. Because the conflict he felt between helplessness and grandiosity was never adequately resolved during childhood, he developed a chronic inability to modulate emotional and behavioral responses. Experiencing each new setback as a reminder and reactivation of past hurts, he struck out (sometimes indiscriminately) in excessive anger. Given the power he wielded, the effects on others were often devastating. His deep sense of childhood hurt produced a pathological use – or better, abuse – of power.

THE LEADER AS A MIRROR

Leaders fulfill many functions. Some of the more salient ones are:

- Articulating a dream for the future that speaks to the collective imagination of the people.
- Creating goal-directedness that aims to make that dream for the future a reality.
- Setting up structures that further the group's goal.
- Establishing a group identity that builds a cohesive organization, clan, or nation.
- Creating meaning for the people (particularly those who are lost or are overwhelmed by anxiety), thereby articulating a clear path out of chaos.
- Being a 'container' of the people's ideas, wishes, feelings, and fantasies. (Kets de Vries, 2004)

Because no leader is an island, the many roles that leaders play are part of an interactive, dynamic, mutually reinforcing process. There is no such thing as a leader without followers. Leaders need to look back often and make sure that their followers are still with them, and they need to change tactics periodically to corral stragglers. As part of this interactive process, followers – who really want to believe in the rosy future portrayed by their leaders – tend to transform subjective into objective reality. They attribute mystical, charismatic powers to their leaders, if that is what it takes to make their fantasies come to life. In other words it is in large part the attributions of followers that make leaders special.

According to the sociologist Max Weber, the leader 'is set apart from ordinary men and treated as endowed with supernatural, superhuman or at least specifically exceptional powers or qualities' (Weber, 1924/1947, p. 358). So endowed, charismatic leaders meet the conscious and unconscious needs of their followers for 'containment' of anxiety. Often the 'false connection' of what psychologists call transference takes place in the minds of the followers (Breuer and Freud, 1893–95). As subordinates in the relationship of follower to leader, they are reminded of being a child under parental protection, and in consequence they may become confused as to person and time. In other words, followers often respond to their leader not according to the reality of the situation but as though the leader were a significant person from their past, such as a parent, other caretaker or sibling.

Idealization and its Ramifications

One common manifestation of this sort of transference is idealization.

Followers idealize their leader in an attempt to recreate the sense of security they felt in early childhood, when cared for by a parent perceived as omnipotent and perfect; they endow their leader – who, as an authority figure is a prime outlet for their transferential fantasies – with unrealistic powers and attributes. In the collective mind, the leader becomes increasingly the sole manifestation of power. Responding to that power, followers project feelings of fear, obedience, affection and admiration on the leader, and soon his or her persona develops a certain mystique. Unfortunately this 'mirroring' – this perceived change in the leader, in response to follower idealization – in turn can artificially inflate the leader's self-esteem.

Particularly during periods of upheaval, which are inevitably rife with anxiety, followers cling to their belief in the leader's powers as a way of maintaining their own sense of security and identity. Craving a response from the leader to their needs, these 'ideal-hungry' followers often go out of their way to please or charm him or her, sometimes giving in to extravagant whims or flights of fancy (Kohut, 1971). Because critical commentary quickly disappears in a climate of idealization, leaders are often surrounded by yea-sayers.

This 'ideal-hungry' behavior on the part of the followers, though often welcome at first, is not without negative consequences for the leader. Rare is the individual who remains indifferent to this form of admiration. Most leaders are alert to being the target of excessive admiration and find it difficult to manage. In leaders with a narcissistic bent, it accentuates the dangers of their self-indulgent disposition. Finding themselves in a hall of mirrors, many such leaders imagine that the projected fantasies of their followers are reality, not make-believe. They start to believe that they are as perfect, intelligent or powerful as others seem to find them. Worse yet, they begin to act on their own fantasies as well, making decisions that have no rational justification. Soon they are caught up in a self-perpetuating cycle of grandiosity: idealizing, followed by mirroring, followed by even more idealizing (Kets de Vries, 1989, 1993). Followers nourish the leader's narcissistic self through confirming and admiring responses, as idealizing and mirroring transference reactions become complementary, interwoven processes. The result: leaders find themselves in an echo chamber; the only opinion heard (though in many voices) is their own.

Leaders who let themselves be caught up in this narcissistic cycle become overly preoccupied by fantasies of unlimited success and power. Gratified by the attention they garner when successful, they seek ways to demonstrate their mastery and brilliance, abandoning caution in favor of risk (with its potential for great reward). Because leaders plagued by excessive narcissism tend to gravitate toward followers with high dependency needs – that is, followers in search of an all-knowing, all-powerful, care-giving leader – they are unlikely to be questioned by those they lead. When followers awaken from their admiring trance, however – and they usually do, eventually – they are in for a surprise. Preoccupied by grandiosity and entitlement, excessively narcissistic leaders generally become extremely callous to the needs of their disciples.

Megalomania

As mentioned earlier, leaders need a solid dose of narcissism to attain positions of power and authority. Narcissism typically becomes more pronounced once a position of leadership and power has been attained, however. Because the ability to deal with the psychological pressures of leadership reveals the real person, the acid test for the quality of leadership arrives once a man or woman is at the helm. Effective leaders keep their narcissistic proclivities in check, dealing with fame with a certain amount of equanimity. Others succumb to the temptations of leadership, letting power go to their head.

As indicated, many of the qualities ascribed to the malignant narcissistic personality are applicable to Shaka. He liked to be in the limelight, and he wanted (and expected) to be admired. However, if we measure his accomplishments, surely we must say that he really was an exceptional person. Much of the praise heaped upon him for his nation-building was arguably deserved, at least initially. So say those who believe that his behavior was completely functional, given the forces he was up against. He was a tyrant, yes; but many people believe that he took the only route to nation-building open to him in nineteenth-century southern Africa. Certainly the record time in which he consolidated the Zulu nation is a testimony to his capabilities. As indicated, however, the true test for leaders is how their reality-testing holds up once they have gained power.

For all his undeniable successes, Shaka failed that test. As his fame increased, he became more and more preoccupied by fantasies of unlimited success and power. Narcissism turned into an addiction that had to be fed constantly, for it yielded ever-diminishing levels of satisfaction. He did all he could to get his 'fix' – to facilitate the narcissistic flow. He made sure that increasingly everything revolved around him. At his command, praise singers preceded him wherever he went, and an admiring audience was on constant standby. Subjects seeking an interview with the king dropped to a reverential position on hands and knees as they approached, and they offered a string of praises such as '*Byede* [hail]! Thou who art awe-inspiring! Thou of the inmost recesses of the royal reserve! Thou of the original stem of the clan! Thou who eatest up men – by first having them and then confiscating their property!' To Shaka, this constant stream of praise became a form of psychological oxygen.

The words of Thomas Mofolo, the first important writer from what is now Lesotho, in South Africa, illustrate the adulation to which Shaka became accustomed. In his novel about Shaka, he describes poetically how people would address the king:

> *Bayede*, O Father, King of Kings!
> You who are a Lion, Elephant-never-to-be-answered!
> You who grew up while we dawdled,
> *Bayede*, Father, King of heaven!
> You, O Black One, who appeared and ruled us with compassion!
> You who are great as an elephant,
> You who devour other men;
> You whose claws resemble those of a lion!
> You who are as great as the sky above,
> You Zulu, rule us with compassion!
> *Bayede*, O King! *Bayede*, O Father! *Bayede*, O Zulu!
> (Mofolo, 1981, p. 116)

Leaders need sturdy reality-testing to stand up to such praise. Unfortunately very few possess it. Gradually believing that what is said about them is true, they fall victim to what the Greeks called hubris – excessive pride. Hubris is a recurrent theme in leadership, for the obvious reason that excessive pride and arrogance frequently accompany power. The predictable offshoot of uncontrolled narcissism, this expression of dysfunctional self-love is indicated by excessive self-reference and self-centeredness. Hubris exacts a high cost: leaders prone to excessive narcissism see only what they want to see – a process reinforced by the followers' idealization of them (Kernberg, 1975; Kets de Vries, 2001b; Kohut, 1971, 1977). They develop narcissistic myopia, their heightened desire for admiration disabling their capacity for reality-testing (Freud, 1921). Because of their great need for admiration, they eventually destroy the very relationships on which they depend.

Leaders who fall victim to hubris believe that they are so unique, so possessed of special qualities, that they can do anything. Loving no one but themselves, they see themselves as superior; they become convinced that they really are as omnipotent and omniscient as others say they are. Insensitive to the wants and needs of others, they take advantage of their followers to achieve their own ends. Vindictive, contemptuous and impatient with others, they react with disdain, rage, and/or violence when a situation is not to their liking. And as we have seen, Shaka's rage could be particularly dangerous. It often meant death, and in extremely unpleasant ways.

Victims of hubris, seeing themselves as different from common mortals, believe that rules and expectations for behavior are for others only, not for them. This sense of entitlement impedes empathy, leaving them concerned only for themselves. As self-proclaimed masters of the universe, they may also believe that they have complete sexual and aggressive license – a belief that is strengthened when their followers allow them, without question, to act out such license. Despite that sense of sexual freedom, their inability to establish deep relationships with others often contributes to sexual difficulties.

The pathological self-love of hubristic leaders is also characterized by an incapacity for gratitude. Admiration is taken for granted rather than appreciated by these leaders, who themselves dish it out only sparingly. The adulation of the praise singers that accompanied Shaka, for example, was seen by the king as only his due. Hubristic leaders not only fail to admire or appreciate others; they often begrudge others their success and possessions, feeling that they themselves are more deserving. They seek to control others (and thereby 'own' the success of others), and they often engage in envious action, trying to destroy the perceived competition (American Psychiatric Association, 1994; Millon, 1996).

That fear of competition grows out of the feelings of impotence that eat at the heart of hubristic leaders. Despite their sense of superiority, such leaders struggle with bouts of insecurity and inferiority. Although these narcissistic leaders spend their public lives self-aggrandizing, their inner theatre – for many of them – is pervaded by self-doubt and a profound sense of worthlessness. Though they may present themselves as absolutely self-confident and independent, that behavior is often a front for feelings of inferiority and the fear that, after all, they will be found to be merely average. At all costs, they want to be special. They become especially myopic, opinionated and deaf to the advice of others when in the throes of a bout of insecurity.

Shaka certainly seems to fit all of these descriptions of the hubristic leader. In every decision and act, he asserted his sense of omnipotence and invincibility, his superiority to ordinary human mortals. As time passed, he stopped listening to his valued counselors, preferring to heed the sycophants who clamored for his ear – a veritable 'Greek chorus' that echoed his opinions. And the larger his territory grew, the more his power increased, the less likely it was that formerly reliable checks and balances (such as the advice of trusted counselors) would hold secure. Eventually whatever he said – no matter how capricious or destructive – became the law of the land. (In his defense, it must be said that it would have been difficult for anyone in Shaka's position – with his history of accomplishments and in a culture that held kings in awe – to avoid becoming the victim of hubris. See Kets de Vries, 1993, 2001b, 2001c.)

Because the Zulu king was the embodiment of the nation – the intermediary between God and humanity, and God's replacement on earth – Shaka's grandiose sense of self-importance and uniqueness was seen as the natural order of things. Whatever the king did, the nation should applaud; whatever the king felt, the nation should feel – an attitude dramatized to absurdity at the death of Shaka's mother. As you will recall, Shaka's grief at his mother's demise resulted in a prohibition against sexual intercourse (with death to those who disregarded it), a requirement of visible and audible grief (with, again, death to people who failed to mourn adequately), an interdiction against planting the fields, and death to cows that had calved.

While Shaka was glorious in his prime, this pathological behavior (and the many other manifestations of Shaka's extreme narcissism) signaled that the end was in sight. What had been merely centralized, autocratic rule slipped into tyranny as indiscriminate brutality and terror increased. Shaka's subjects, who once had been glad to grant him absolute power, became increasingly restless and dissatisfied, and his inner circle stepped in to plot his overthrow.

5. Monte Cristo in Africa: seeking revenge for past wrongs

Now hear!
The elephant smashed everything; there was nothing left!
The elephant smashed everything; there was nothing left!
The branches of the tree were broken, there was nothing left,
There were only the uprooted stumps to be seen,
They were turned upside down!
As they were overturned, so men died!
    (Mtshayankomo ka Magolwana, *The James Stuart Archive*)

The way down to hell is easy.
    (Virgil, *Aeneid*)

Revenge, at first though sweet,
Bitter ere long back on itself recoils.
    (John Milton, *Paradise Lost*)

I rage, I melt, I burn,
The feeble God has stab'd me to the Heart.
    (John Gay, *Acis and Galatea*)

Heav'n has no rage, like love to hatred turned,
Nor Hell a fury, like a woman scorn'd.
    (William Congreve, *The Mourning Bride*)

Perish the Universe, provided I have my revenge.
    (Cyrano de Bergerac, *La Mort d'Agrippine*)

No more tears now; I will think upon revenge.
    (Mary, Queen of Scots, said upon the murder of her secretary)

The young Shaka must have been attuned to his mother's outrage at being treated like an outcast, and to her resulting depression and bitterness. Given the intensity of the maternal–child relationship, a mother's feelings of distress are easily transmitted and internalized by her child. Particularly in the early stages of a young person's development, there is great interconnectedness of emotions between mother and child. However, because of the child's powerlessness, his or her initial reaction to maternal distress signals is anxiety and frustration at not being able to help her. If that frustration continues (because the maternal distress is not relieved), deep-seated feelings of bitterness and anger often grow in the child, resulting in a primitive desire to hurt and destroy. Feelings of rage and the inability to modulate affect and impulse control are also common.

As mentioned earlier, both Henry Francis Fynn and Nathaniel Isaacs repeatedly mentioned the extraordinary intensity of Shaka Zulu's rage when things did not go his way. Given the poor hand his mother was dealt, she must have known great frustration herself, and we can surmise that she had limited emotional resources available to her to provide 'containment' to her young son. His limited capacity to deal with aggressive emotions – a signifier of his inability to modulate frustration psychologically – speaks of her inability to help him. The situation would have been aggravated by the absence of a supportive father figure who could comfort and could be a role model. With no strong male role model present, and his mother steeped in bitterness, Shaka had only himself to 'dialogue' with about being mistreated by the world, about having nobody to defend him – no parent to turn to, no peer group to relate to. And all that loneliness, despair and anger fermented over the years, into a wicked brew of rage.

THE MONTE CRISTO COMPLEX

People in the throes of narcissistic rage want to destroy the source of their irritation (Kernberg, 1992). At a subconscious level, they believe that eliminating that source will bring them to a state of mental equilibrium. And they want to have their way immediately, without prorogation. Because feelings of narcissistic rage lie in wait in the unconscious, ready to surface immediately when praise is not forthcoming or when criticism wounds, living or working with excessive narcissists is like living near a volcano that can erupt at any moment.

For such people, the preservation of self-image is a very delicate matter. Feelings of past humiliation are never forgotten. Rather, they are pent up – collected, as it were – needing only an explosive discharge to unleash again each humiliation's original potential for injury. That discharge typically comes in the form of yet another challenge to the excessive narcissist's belief that he or she is special and should be treated preferentially. A simple slight, and the rage erupts.

In addition to these attacks of generalized rage, excessive narcissists nurture strong feelings of hatred toward specific people they feel have done them harm. Instead of acting impulsively and indiscriminately against those people, narcissists often become obsessed by the unremitting need to destroy them, systematically and completely. Shaka, who as we have seen was often subject to a generalized rage that terrorized his people, also nursed his hatred of certain individuals. He had a very long memory, and his wrath could be ghastly.

Bitter Fruit: Revenge as a Protective Reaction

Shaka must have felt a strong need to make right the wrongs done to him and his mother. He did not want to be a *Chaka*, a poor fellow; on the contrary, he wanted to be *somebody*. He wanted to be noticed, to be taken seriously, to prove wrong all those who had belittled and mistreated him and his mother. The taunts of childhood would have been like the Greek furies, following him wherever he went, echoing the earlier ridicule he had been exposed to. And those memories of mockery drove him to action. Encouraged by his mother, he undertook a 'mission' to right the wrongs done to them – a mission that at times must have seemed impossible.

Adversity can be a source of great strength, even if it is strength of a reactive rather than proactive nature. That strength lies in the motivation to prove others wrong. If one's determination to change life's circumstances focuses on working to be valued or on making reparation, reactive narcissism can bear healthy fruit. If it turns into envy, spite, hatred and vindictiveness – the need to get even – the harvest can be very bitter indeed (Kets de Vries, 2001c; Klein, 1959).

As we have seen, Shaka certainly had adversity in abundance. That adversity, and his aggressive response to it, shaped the man he became. His later style of interpersonal relating grew out of his constant fights with other, often bigger boys: every encounter was seen as an attack. In the early years, that expectation was not cognitive distortion, or not exclusively so; it was based in reality. And because he felt an attack was always imminent, he was always coiled like a spring, ready for a counterattack. That readiness to fight was evident in Shaka as each encounter could easily turn into a fight. Such violent self-assertion, which puts a lot of stress on the body, is exhausting.

The profound sense of inferiority that ridicule bred in Shaka, combined with his readiness to return blow for blow, resulted in a strong desire to get back at his tormentors. He turned his passive hatred into action as a means of survival. In the eyes of the powerless, the only alternative to being a victim is being the opposite: a tyrant. Thus Shaka, having been tortured, wanted (at first just in fantasy) to turn the situation around and be the torturer; having been the victim of sadistic games, he wanted to turn others into the victims. This persistent urge to get even eventually transmuted into a desire to make others suffer, with youthful feelings of hatred and persistent fantasies of vengeance laying the foundation for the sadistic tendencies and callousness that he later displayed (Redl and Wineman, 1951; Socarides, 1966). However, the quest for vengeance that made him intimidating, belligerent, controlling and cruel also deprived him of the ability to trust and be close to others, thereby isolating him.

People who choose to deal with the hurts of childhood through vindictiveness and spite – and it is a choice, albeit an unconscious one – suffer from what some psychiatrists call the 'Monte Cristo complex', after the lead character in Alexandre Dumas's book *The Count of Monte Cristo*. That book tells the engrossing story of a man who has been terribly wronged and manages to get even, repaying one bad turn after the other – with interest. The count's passionate desire to get even touches a responsive chord in the fantasy life of many people (Castelnuovo-Tedesco, 1974). Indeed we all experience similar feelings, at least occasionally and fleetingly.

The good count himself would probably agree that vengeful destructiveness is not 'normal aggression'. Unlike the quick flash of a spontaneous reaction to danger, vengeance burns with intensity and duration, insatiable in its quest for fuel (Fromm, 1973). For people who suffer from the Monte Cristo complex, revenge is more than just a fleeting temptation; it becomes the major motivational force in life, an all-consuming passion. As a way of dealing with childhood wounds, revenge is ineffective in the extreme. Though in some sense it 'makes things right', it eventually consumes the person pursuing it. Though the Count of Monte Cristo exacted appropriate payment from each person who had wronged him, he felt not satisfaction in the end, but emptiness.

Shaka and the count could have been brothers, despite their differences of race and experience. Without question, the need to get even was a major motivational force in Shaka Zulu's life. It shaped his way of relating to others, formed his language of abuse and cruelty, and dictated the total destruction of people who opposed him. Unwilling to be the passive victim of abuse and unpredictability, he took control the only way he knew how: through cruelty. *He* would be the provocative one; *he* would dish out unpredictability; *he* would take control by force, putting himself in situations that invited attack so that he could counterattack.

When Shaka became the new chieftain of the then-small Zulu clan, he immediately got even with his previous tormentors. He took gruesome revenge for past hurts on the people who had made his and his mother's life miserable. Among the people killed was the uncle who had denounced Nandi's claim of Zulu fatherhood by claiming that she was only troubled by the intestinal beetle known as *ishaka*, which suppresses menstruation. It is symptomatic that as new Zulu chief, Shaka built for himself a kraal that he called *kwaBulawayo*, 'the place of the killings' or 'the place of the persecuted one', reminding everybody of the taunting he endured as a child and the expulsion of his struggling family from Zululand.

When Shaka started to build up his empire, the first non-Zulus he attacked were the eLangeni clan, the clan of his mother, though he spared people who had showed him and his mother some kindness during the difficult years. Conquering them was important to his revenge mission: it gave him another opportunity to get even – to clean the slate. According to Alfred Bryant:

> Arriving on the scene – that painful scene of untold miseries twenty years before – he surrounded the capital ... ordered all against whom he had old scores to wipe off to be brought before him; then, one after the other, had them impaled on the top of the palisades surrounding the circular cattle-fold and, while wiggling there, roasted alive above stacks of faggots and grass. ... Then near by the gruesome spot, as a monument of standing warning to all cruel treaters of children, he erected a kraal of his own, which he grimly named *enDlamate* (the place where he swallowed his spittle – supremely satisfied) (1929, pp. 126–7).

He sometimes called the *kwaBulawayo* kraal *Gibixhegu*, or 'finish the old men', in reference to his killing of men too old to go to war (and therefore useless in Shaka's eyes). This cruel killing was revenge by displacement: though his own father, who had never supported or protected him, was already dead, Shaka could kill old men as father-figures. When that was not in his political interest, he could make fun of them instead. Henry Francis Fynn recalled, 'On Shaka coming to the throne, he compelled the old superannuated chiefs to wear a petticoat similar in shape to those worn by women' (Fynn, 1833/1950, p. 285).

It was on the battlefield, however, that Shaka acted out the Monte Cristo complex on the grandest scale. In that principal theatre of violence, he sought to triumph not chivalrously but vindictively. His warfare was total, absolute and merciless, total annihilation its aim. As we have seen, he tried never to leave an enemy behind alive, killing old people, women and children to forestall their potential retribution. To him, the world was still the way it had been when he was a child: it was a question of killing or being killed.

Double Identification

As we saw earlier, not everything about the desire to get even is negative. The same pathologically combative posture that eventually made Shaka a dangerous, unpredictable ruler first made him a formidable warrior. The daily fighting of childhood and adolescence was an ideal education for a budding warrior. Shaka learned how to build up his running speed in case he had to run away from his attackers; he learned how to assess and take advantage of the vulnerabilities of others; he learned how to improvise when up against overwhelming odds. These skills, along with a strong physical constitution and determined physical training, served him well in later guerrilla warfare. Fighting became not only a method of revenge but also a way of life, a way to appease his inner demons. But no matter how much his *assegai* had 'eaten', how many lives he sacrificed, his inner demons never seemed to be satisfied.

In large part that is because Shaka may have been troubled in his search for revenge by what can be described as 'double identification'. Though now the tyrant, he could still identify (not necessarily at a conscious level) with his victims. We can speculate that his inner imagery of being wounded, of being hurt, would grow ever more vivid with each new killing, increasing the same anxiety that the killing was intended to mute. Even when he was the sacrificer, he was also at some level still the sacrificed. It was no accident that many of his sacrificial victims stood for innocence and goodness – mothers and children for example, as reported by many eyewitnesses. He destroyed these innocents because they had what he never had. In the process he attacked what he should have valued in himself: a kernel of goodness. In seeking to pacify his inner demons, he undermined his feelings of self-worth and condemned himself to isolation and a self-perpetuating cycle of rage, destruction and fear of retaliation.

MOTHER'S PROXY

Fighting was not only Shaka's way of overcoming his early feelings of inadequacy and helplessness; it was also his way of standing up for his mother, with whom, as we saw, he had an extremely close bond. Until his sister, stepfather and half-brother came into the picture, mother and child (and perhaps maternal grandmother) had only each other. During those years it was as if he were her replacement husband, addressing her need for emotional intimacy if not for sex. After he experienced that 'Oedipal victory' – taking exclusive possession of the mother through removal of the father (though through different means than the Oedipus of Greek mythology) – competitive strivings became an essential part of his character (Freud, 1933).

Children who win the Oedipal contest bear an extraordinary burden. In the absence of a supportive father, they find themselves (age-inappropriately) in a position of great responsibility. This increases their sense of being special and contributes to a false sense of omnipotence while simultaneously leading to feelings of impotence. Though empowered by the responsibility, they know that they are not prepared, physically or emotionally, to take on the varied roles of manhood. In addition to the conflict between omnipotence and impotence, which causes anxiety, such children suffer from the absence of a father's restraining, boundary-setting influence (Fernandez, 1967).

That is not to say of course that Shaka's father had no influence. Senzangakhona – the man who let him down, who deserted him – played an important role in his inner world. He came to prominence in the real world occasionally too. For example, on one visit by Shaka to his father's people, the youth is said to have refused to accept from his father the *umuTsha*, the loincloth that Zulu boys wore after puberty when visiting their father's kraal. This disobedient act led to his hasty return to his mother's people (Krige, 1936). According to another story, at one point Shaka's father paid a visit to the court of King Dingiswayo to see his son. During this visit, it is said, young Shaka took part in witchcraft intended to help ensure that he would be his father's successor. Encouraged by King Dingiswayo, the witchdoctors spared no efforts to help Shaka. For example, Shaka sprinkled charms on his father's path when the latter was going for a bath, he made his shadow fall upon his father, and he washed himself with medicines on top of the hut where his father slept – all acts thought to assure ascendancy over another (Bryant, 1929, pp. 66–7). Taking a more forthright approach, Shaka also, during a ceremonial dance that same visit, asked his father for the gift of a spear. This request conveyed symbolically Shaka's wish to be his father's successor. It is said that his father refused, claiming that the spear was not rightfully Shaka's, but his half-brother's. Apparently Shaka's father left Dingiswayo's court soon after this incident, saying that he did not feel well. According to a number of accounts, 'he was seized by great dread' and died soon after (Stuart, 2001, p. 42). Some people thought that he died of fear, or that his death was due to witchcraft.

The urge to be his father's successor must have had an early start. The more people looked down on him and his mother, the more he must have wanted to become the redeemer of his mother, to handle their tormentors as he felt his father should have. His mother almost certainly encouraged him in this, reminding him that he was the son of a chief, that it was his right to ascend to the throne of the Zulu clan. By implication if not literally, this told him that it was his mission to get even, to make right the wrongs done to mother and son. The living representation of Nandi's anger, he became her proxy. The obligation to take on her rage as well as his own fueled his Monte Cristo complex.

Strongly encouraged by his mother, young Shaka kept at his tormentors, refusing to give up. His need to succeed in his mother's eyes, to make good her wrongs, is portrayed rather dramatically in a popular novel about Shaka by Edward Ritter:

> 'Mame [Mother]!' soon I will be able to sleep more restfully like other men, for the time is now approaching when you will be a great *inKosikazi* (chieftainess), aye, perhaps the greatest in the land. For that has always been my aim from the day when Senzangakona drove us into the wilderness. You shall be the head of a great kraal, and a power in the land. Whom you frown upon will be as good as dead, and those who will live under your shadow will wax beyond all others. Whom you forgive will be forgiven. Take all of my cattle as you please, for they are yours as much as

mine. Stint not yourself and your friends, and mark well, that your true friends are all those who were kind to you in your distress and poverty, and not those who now merely come to eat your meat. (Ritter, 1978, p. 66)

The intensity of this supportive, privileged mother–son relationship, though a source of great strength to Shaka, made it difficult for any other woman to measure up. Having been marked indelibly by the early, oceanic experience of his mother's love, he could not find intimacy elsewhere.

6. The nature of relationships: being unable to establish real intimacy

Everything you do irritates me. And when you're not here, the things I know you're gonna do when you come back in irritate me.
(Neil Simon, *The Odd Couple*)

I do not want people to be very agreeable, as it saves me the trouble of liking them a great deal.
(Jane Austen, letter dated 24 December 1798)

We are so fond of one another because our ailments are the same.
(Jonathan Swift, *Journal to Stella*)

Everything great in the world is done by neurotics; they alone founded our religions and created our masterpieces.
(Marcel Proust, *À la recherche du temps perdu*)

Once we are destined to live out our lives in the prison of our mind, our one duty is to furnish it well.
(Peter Ustinov, *Dear Me*)

Explanation separates us from astonishment, which is the only gateway to the incomprehensible.
(Eugène Ionesco, *Découvertes*)

Psychology can never tell the truth about madness because it is madness that holds the truth of psychology.
(Michel Foucault, *Mental Illness and Psychology*)

We are all born mad. Some remain so.
(Samuel Becket, *Waiting for Godot*)

It has been said that Shaka was incapable of love, that he could experience only vengeance and hatred. Although Edward Ritter, in his romanticized novel about the king, has Shaka become attached to a woman named Pampata, women of Shaka's age group seem to have been of no importance to the king. Among women, only his mother and a few other, older relatives received what could pass for affection. Except for his mentor King Dingiswayo, who earned the young man's respect and affection, the males in his life fared no better.

GLIMPSES OF WARMTH

This is not to say that Shaka was totally devoid of human feeling. He supported his father's other sons, despite the fact that they were a political threat. He liked many of the warriors he worked with in his early years of soldiering, speaking of one as his 'younger brother' (Stuart, 1979, p. 6). He never forgot the kindness with which his stepfather, Gendeyana, treated him. Most important, as mentioned earlier, he was quite fond of King Dingiswayo.

Shaka also treated the first whites who arrived in his territory courteously, even kindly. Nathaniel Isaacs for example commented that during private interviews 'our reception was very different from … [that of public, official interviews]; he now cast off his stern look, became good-humored, and conversed with us through our interpreters on various subjects' (1836/1970, p. 27). Henry Francis Fynn likewise referred to 'the kind manner in which he [Shaka] received me' (Fynn, 1833/1950, p. 118). Early stories about the Zulu leader – particularly during his initial period as king – refer to his wisdom, benevolence and sense of humor.

That older women played a greater role in Shaka's life than younger women does not come as a great surprise, given the influence of his mother. Some of his older female relatives were so important to him that they were put in charge of a number of his female regiments. For example, his father's sister Mnkabaya was in charge of one of the more important *amakhanda*. As noted earlier, Shaka was apparently very attached to his grandmother and is said to have cried when she died (Fynn, 1950; Isaacs, 1836). To quote Henry Francis Fynn:

> When she [his grandmother] happened to visit him he frequently washed her eyes and ears which were in a sad state because of her age; he also pared her nails and otherwise treated her as a father might his child. We could hardly believe that a man of an apparent unfeeling disposition could be possessed of such affection and consideration of others. Further observation, however, convinced us that this was indeed the case.
>
> The following evening, while we were sitting with him, he was informed that she was dead. He remained for some moments in deep contemplation. His feelings then seemed to overpower him. He burst out crying and did so aloud. (Fynn, 1833/1950, p. 121)

After Shaka became king, his mother was the second most influential person in the land. Her kraal ranked next in importance after his *kwaBulawayo*. According to a number of eyewitnesses, Nandi was the only person who had a restraining influence on Shaka during the later years. She seemed able to temper his mood. Without her, Shaka found it hard to function, easy to careen out of control. At her death, his behavior (detailed in Chapter 3) was so bizarre that we can only conclude he must have had some kind of psychotic breakdown. Following his initial killing frenzy after her death, he apparently fell into a serious depression, lacking the energy to rule the country. The catalyst for that psychic breakdown was most likely self-reproach, since, as we saw, according to many sources he may have stabbed her following an attack of rage (Stuart, 1976).

ISSUES OF SEXUALITY

Shaka never married, and he never had children that lived. Concubines and wives who became pregnant were killed. According to the account of George Angas, a painter who spent time with the Zulus:

> One of his favorite wives, on one occasion, presented to him a son, doubtless too confident in the transports of her joy. The monster took the child by the feet, and with one blow dashed his brains out upon the stones; the mother, at the same moment, was thrust through with an assegai, and died whilst gazing on her murdered child. (Angas, 1849, p. 53)

In trying to find explanations for Shaka's behavior, we have to keep in mind that the language of the unconscious is very different than that of the conscious. In the unconscious, contradictory ideas can coexist happily without creating problems of consistency. Likewise, various motives for behavior can exist simultaneously, as we discover when we speculate about Shaka's relationships with women.

And speculation it is. There are a number of important questions that we will never have answers to. Why for example did Shaka always refer to the women in his seraglio as his 'sisters' – a term devoid of sexual connotations – rather than his 'wives'? What was the exact role of these 'sisters', and why were there so many? Did Shaka have some level of sexual involvement with them, or were they household servants only? Were they just the logical spoils of war, or were they (like his famous herd of pure white cattle) valued possessions – objects that could be shown off, that could be exchanged for something else of value? Were they one of various 'currencies' used to cement alliances with foreign chieftains and other senior officials? All these explanations for the women's role seem to be reasonable, given the culture Shaka lived in.

Self-Control and Sexuality

Because various oral accounts speak of the children of the king – and their violent and untimely death – we have to assume that Shaka had at least some limited carnal contact with his 'sisters'. But the fact that the children were few and infrequent suggests that Shaka may have had a self-imposed restriction against sexual involvement. If that is the case, perhaps he was trying to demonstrate that unlike his parents, he was able to exert self-control in sexual matters – even with an estimated 1200 women to tempt him. In that way he could best his father. He never wore the *isicoco*, the head ring signifying an end to soldiering and readiness for marriage – a deliberate choice surely, since he was king – and presumably he generally followed the injunction he gave his warriors, engaging only in *ukusoma*, 'thigh sex'. In other words, non-impregnating love play was probably his preference.

When Shaka, despite his best intentions, got a woman with child, he appeared to become furious with the hapless woman, condemning both her and the child to death. He was almost certainly angry with himself as well for failing to control himself and for taking after his father in the one area that most troubled the younger man. Perhaps, in the language of the unconscious, he was troubled by strange associations between sexuality and the capacity for self-control. After all, if his parents had shown greater sexual restraint, Shaka would not have had to endure years of torture and humiliation. An unwanted child himself, he was not about to create children who would find themselves in a similar situation.

Assuming that for Shaka the issue of sexual self-control was interwoven with control generally, it is not surprising that he opted for absolute rule. With the theme of control acted out on a public stage, he made sure that every action he took or mandated furthered control, discipline and order. Anyone who faltered – who did not obey his rules – deserved to be put to death, and was. There were no excuses, even in sexual matters. And he himself needed to set the example. If he as king could not control himself, who in his realm could?

The Hot-Button of Pregnancy

Perhaps some of Shaka's reluctance about bearing children came from pregnancy itself. Throughout his life, Shaka was obsessed with the mysteries of pregnancy. Some sources have said that among Shaka's extraordinary cruelties was the order to have a pregnant woman slit open to see how the baby was lying in the womb; he was curious to know if it was placed the same way as a calf (Stuart, 1976, 1979, 1986). The origin of this aberrant curiosity is of interest. Did Shaka's preoccupation have something to do with the fact that he was the product of an unconventional pregnancy? Was conception an unusually sensitive, psychologically loaded subject?

We can hypothesize that Shaka's mother's later two pregnancies were disturbing to Shaka. Having enjoyed her exclusive mothering for years, he may have felt a serious narcissistic injury at no longer being the only object of Nandi's attention. With his sense of self-esteem already fragile, he could not have welcomed his mother's (temporary) desertion for another man – Shaka's stepfather – and her preoccupation with a baby. Two competitors in one blow. Strong feelings of envy, one of the most primitive and fundamental of emotions, must have stirred up his already strong feelings of anger and vindictiveness. Later, when he was king, he could act out his envy and anger on a grand scale, killing pregnant women and even babies.

If he indeed had little completed sexual contact with the women in his seraglio, there is a less symbolic, more rational explanation for his killing of pregnant women. If he did not get them pregnant, who did? Pregnancy would indicate adultery: someone had broken a rule, had trespassed into the *isigodlo*, the harem. And such cuckolding warranted the death penalty for both man and woman. (According to Zulu law, conjugal infidelity was a capital offense even among commoners.)

If the stories are true, Shaka engaged in a number of serious purges to punish culprits suspected of entering his harem. Nathaniel Isaacs (1836/1970) described one such incident:

> Chaka then sat down, and desiring his people with great earnestness and precaution to be secret, stated that he had a dream which greatly concerned him. He dreamt that a number of his boys had had criminal intercourse with his girls in the palace, and that while he was teaching them songs last night, many of them were debauching his women, and had thus polluted his imperial establishment. This offence he declared himself determined to punish with rigor; his people applauded his resolution, and said, 'Father kill them for they are not fit to live'. (p. 72)

After having his harem surrounded, Shaka ordered 170 men and women slaughtered.

Shaka's concerns about pregnancy may also have been rooted in the Zulu belief that *insila*, or body products, were very powerful medicine. The *insila* of the king, especially, could be used for magical purposes that would endanger the kingdom. And what regal body product could be more powerful than semen, that source of new life? There was a precedent for that, after all: as noted earlier, it was believed that Zwide had been able to defeat Dingiswayo only because of witchcraft involving the king's semen (obtained by Zwide's mother, using a young woman as bait). Fully aware of this story, Shaka guarded his body products closely.

Some sources have suggested that Shaka refrained from sexual intercourse not from fear of pregnancy or loss of control, but to retain his physical strength (Stuart, 1986; Laband, 1997). Shaka once commented to Nathaniel Isaacs (after asking if the British king had as many girls as he had, a question to which he received a negative answer), 'that King George was like him, who did not indulge in promiscuous intercourse with women, [which] accounted for his advanced age' (Isaacs, 1836/1970, p. 51). The belief that loss of sperm will weaken a person is a very common fantasy in many primitive, and in some not-so-primitive, societies (Levine, 1980; Malinovsky, 1926).

Among the Zulus, contact with women before battle was considered detrimental to a warrior's fighting ability. It was thought that the loss of semen would weaken the fighting spirit of a warrior. Shaka's war doctors forbade the soldiers to have sex in any form, because contact with women would negate the effects of the pre-battle purification ceremonies. After battle, warriors had to participate in a cleaning ritual before they could interact with any woman they cared about. As noted earlier, the warriors could join normal society only after having intercourse with 'outsiders' (by force, if necessary) to ward off angry spirits and transmit these to the unlucky women (or herdboys) subjected to their sexual advances.

Succession Issues

Shaka may also have been afraid of having an heir. With good reason, too: succession in polygamous societies has always been fraught with difficulties. The dilemma of Oedipus is certainly not limited to Greek society, or to myth. Sons do kill fathers, and vice versa. Zulu society was famous for family discord. Regicide, fratricide and civil war had long characterized the Zulu kingdom and sapped its strength. According to a Zulu saying, 'Our kings are like male lions or leopards, killing their male offspring.' It was quite customary for new kings to kill all their brothers (and other dangerous persons) soon after their appointment, just as a precaution.

Shaka was well aware that marriage – and the children that would come with it – could split his kingdom apart. He knew from personal experience that sons could become a danger. Perhaps he recalled quarrels in his father's house – intrigues among the various wives about whose son would be the favorite. Having children, Shaka knew, would lead to strife and succession fights. A successor would almost certainly one day try to overthrow him, fulfilling a secret wish that he may have had *vis-à-vis* his own father. If feelings of ambivalence toward his own father – the urge to overthrow him, though he was already dead – were still a reality in his inner world, he would not have chosen lightly to be at the receiving end. (Remember Shaka's refusal of the symbolic loincloth offered by his father. The younger man knew from personal experience that not all sons would submit to a father's rule.) Thus Shaka had good incentive to prevent conception and, like King Laius, to kill his offspring.

Shaka's unwillingness to plan for succession might also have been associated with fantasies of immortality. Having an heir around would have made him painfully aware that he was ageing and was not as fit as he used to be. (As we have seen, getting older was a touchy subject with Shaka.) By ensuring that he would have no children, he was in fact declaring that there could be no future without him, that the future was dependent on his person – the ultimate narcissistic statement.

Marriage Policy: Mirror of Inner Conflict?

That Shaka may have experienced inner conflict regarding fully consummated sexual intercourse is one thing; that he externalized this problem onto his soldiers is something else entirely. Or is it? What is true for all of us is more obvious in the case of a king: themes in a person's inner theatre are enacted on a larger, public stage. In Shaka's empire, the king made matters of sexuality state policy. As happens with rulers of most totalitarian societies, he intruded himself into family life, exerting control over intimate affairs. As noted earlier, he went to great lengths to maintain his warriors' quasi-celibate state, making it state policy not to permit full sexual relationships before marriage. Being allowed to marry became a state monopoly: men in the *amabutho* could not marry without Shaka's permission, and that permission was usually not given before middle age. Considering himself a master in matters of sexual self-restraint, Shaka wanted his warriors tested in a similar manner.

A number of historians, writing from a population ecology point of view, have given a non-psychological explanation for the state policy of preventing marriage until military service was concluded. To them, delaying marriage was an ingenious way for Shaka to solve a knotty demographic problem. If marriage was postponed until a later age, the number of children would be decreased; and having fewer children would eventually reduce pressure on the available pasturelands (which, you may remember, were growing scarce). Some of the other sexual rituals that Shaka initiated also fit into this pattern. The need for a special kind of sexual encounter after returning from warfare, for example – which often involved sodomizing herdboys or having sex with elderly women – would not contribute to an increase in the population.

Finally, some Victorians argued that Shaka had found the ultimate way to motivate his warriors. He made extraordinary bravery on the battlefield, 'the washing of the spears', a requirement for permission to marry. Thus frustrated sexuality was channeled into warfare, a focus that led to extraordinary results. That this idea of channeling frustrated sexuality gained some currency is echoed in Nathaniel Isaacs's comment about Shaka's successor, King Dingane, who was more inclined to let his warriors marry. According to Isaacs, 'His motive for abrogating the custom of compelling them to abstain from all sexual intercourse emanated from a wish he evinced of, in some measure, tempering their natural ferocity and eagerness for war, of attaching them more to their homes, and of creating a disposition for the comforts of domestic life' (Isaacs, 1836/1970, p. 288).

Gender-Orientation

Because it is so difficult to understand the nature of Shaka's relationships with
women, some historians suggest that he was most likely a latent homosexual
and claim that he was impotent with women (Gluckman, 1960; Morris, 1966).
Such a conjecture cannot be substantiated with the limited information we
have about Shaka. In issues of gender-orientation, the nature–nurture question
is particularly difficult to resolve. Each individual's gender-orientation is the
result of a complex process of interaction between biological, environmental
and psychological factors. A person acquires a homosexual orientation when
an imbalance occurs between these specific biological, experiential and
psychological predisposing factors, each of which evolves on its own
timetable (Gadpaille, 1989).

To the extent that family factors affect the etiology of homosexuality, a
close-binding, seductive mother who devalues and dominates a rather passive,
distant and hostile father is suspect. Some researchers suggest that such a
family situation impairs a young boy's normal identification process. Boys
need a father figure to help them come to grips with factors such as rivalry,
envy and idealization. Shaka's family constellation, consisting of a rejecting,
absent father and a close-binding mother, comes close to the suspect pattern.
Without an acceptable father figure as object of identification during much of
his childhood, Shaka would have been forced into a defensive identification
with his mother.

Given the paucity of evidence available we can make only tentative
conjectures about Shaka's gender-orientation. Although some would predict
homosexuality on the basis of his family constellation, the historical record
suggests that he enjoyed associating with some of the women in his seraglio.
Nathaniel Isaacs repeatedly made reference to Shaka retiring from a
discussion and amusing himself with his ladies. What the nature of this
'amusement' was, we will never know.

Shaka's childhood games of warfare, though dictated to some extent by the
hostility of others, also suggest heterosexuality. Play behaviors and
preferences in childhood that follow the typical interests of girls are generally
considered a predictive factor (among many) for later homosexuality, and
gender non-conformity in childhood and homosexual preferences in
adolescence have been correlated with adult homosexuality. The historical
record reveals no hint of the feminine in the young Shaka.

THE MENTORSHIP OF DINGISWAYO

Though the people that Shaka was closest to were older women, King

Dingiswayo played an important mentoring role in the younger man's life. The older man was a positive role model for Shaka during his early adulthood. Having had a father who gave him scant attention, Shaka must have been gratified to have Dingiswayo – by then king of the Mthethwa clan – take an interest in him. The discipline of military service and the influence of King Dingiswayo together probably taught some self-restraint to the moody, violent young man.

As he approached adulthood, Shaka may have reached a developmental impasse centered on his feelings of hatred, distrust, control and inferiority. We can conjecture that Dingiswayo, a relatively enlightened African king, was instrumental in giving young Shaka a constructive solution to that impasse (Erikson, 1963; White, 1966). This visionary king probably encouraged Shaka to transform his anger beyond personal revenge and redirect it onto a larger stage, to nation-building (Lasswell, 1960). By having Shaka present during council meetings, Dingiswayo also helped clarify what it meant to run an empire, teaching by example some of the basics of administration. Most important, his support and encouragement must have given Shaka greater self-confidence.

Furthermore, being part of an *ibutho* must have been a rewarding developmental experience for Shaka. Isolated no more, he was now in close contact with other people of his age group – people who, because of his fighting skills, had reason to admire him. Given his previous history, he probably was not socially adept, but membership in the *ibutho* gave him an opportunity to start with a clean slate. No longer a single warrior pitted (psychologically if not actually) against members of the eLangeni or Zulu clans, he now had to learn to function in a group context. As he did so, successfully redirecting his hostile energies towards war, he gained not only self-respect but the respect of others. He was given an opportunity to pick up the threads of broken development, and he grabbed that chance (White, 1966).

Shaka, we are told, was thrust into prominence because of his intelligence and physical prowess. As he rose through the ranks, his feats of bravery and his military innovations must have gained him the support of his peers. Thus being a member of his *ibutho* enabled him to return to the track he had wanted to be on earlier: that of group activity and group respect. Being part of the regiment probably gave him, for the first time, a sense of belonging with companions of his own age, allowing him finally to construct a nucleus of self-confidence and self-respect. He was now able to make good on his childhood fantasies of success (though they would soon be soured by revenge).

It must have been interesting to watch, in person, the balance of power between Dingiswayo and Shaka, both formidable leaders. Shaka had never had a father around to help him set boundaries for his behavior, and boundary-setting is not something one can do for oneself; adult power-holders are needed to serve as counterbalance. Playing this role, Dingiswayo set boundaries that kept the intense, angry young man under some form of control. Unfortunately, at the older man's death this check on Shaka's activities disappeared. As Shaka's power increased, so did his regressive, excessively violent behavior. Executions became a routine part of court life, handed down by Shaka – now king of a territory far greater than Dingiswayo's – for a wide variety of offences and often enacted in a capricious manner. By his final days Shaka was a complete despot ruling in arbitrary fashion through fear and terror.

7. Paranoia – the disease of kings: exercising caution beyond the bounds of danger

In every tyrant's heart there springs in the end
This poison, that he cannot trust a friend.
(Aeschylus, *Prometheus Bound*)

To his friends he [Solon] said, as we are told, that a tyranny was a lovely place, but there was no way down from it.
(Plutarch, *Solon*)

At one of his more sumptuous banquets he [Caligula] suddenly burst out into a fit of laughter, and when the consuls, who were reclining next to him, politely inquired at what he was laughing, he replied: 'What do you suppose, except that at a single nod of mine both of you could have your throats cut on the spot?'
(Suetonius, *Lives of the Caesars, Caligula*)

Whoever desires to found a state and give it laws must start with assuming that all men are bad and ever ready to display their vicious nature, whenever they may find occasion for it.
(Niccolò Machiavelli, *Discourses*)

Distrust that man that tells you to distrust.
(Ella Wheeler Wilcox, attributed)

O God, save me from those who, crawling on their knees, hide a knife that they would like to sink in my back. But how can God help? All the people surrounding the Emperor are just like that – on their knees, and with knives. It's never comfortable on the summits. An icy wind always blows, and everyone crouches, watchful lest his neighbor hurl him down the precipice.
(Ryszard Kapuscinsky, *The Emperor*)

Even a paranoid can have enemies.
(Henry Kissinger, *Time*)

The word 'character' is derived from the Greek word for engraving. As that derivation suggests, character encompasses deeply etched features that differentiate one person from another, psychological traits that express themselves almost automatically in human functioning. These *character*istics determine motivation; they dictate the way a person deals with his or her internal and external world and structure the way he or she uses energy in the pursuit of goals. Given the importance of this motivational role, we might say that character is destiny.

Some people are driven by their character to lives of honesty and service; others lean toward laziness and deceit. Though we might prefer to associate with the former, we do not label the latter 'pathological'. That label is reserved for configurations of character traits that harden into inflexibility. Students of human behavior call these configurations character disorders or personality disorders. The list of character disorders includes narcissism, discussed earlier, and paranoia, the subject of this chapter.

Two features set character disorders apart: durability and pervasiveness. Thus a character disorder is defined not by extremes of goodness or badness, but by extremes of inflexibility. A behavior that is adaptive in one situation – in other words, that helps a person adjust to the environment and circumstances – can be extremely maladaptive in another. (Taking refuge in the cellar when a tornado warning sounds, for example, is adaptive, while hiding in the cellar when the phone rings is not. Washing hands before eating is prudent, while washing hundreds of times a day is not.) Any configuration of traits that turns rigid, failing to adapt to changing circumstances, has the potential to impair individual functioning and cause distress to self and others. It is the rigidity, not the configuration itself, that is the problem. Many traits exist almost universally across the population and are generally adaptive; only in certain individuals do they calcify into a character disorder.

It is helpful to think of character disorders as dimensional, not categorical, entities. In other words, a person is more or less narcissistic (or paranoid or avoidant), rather than either narcissistic or not. Furthermore there are no clear boundaries between one disorder and another. There is always a degree of co-morbidity (psych-speak for symptom-constellation) between the various disorders. Thus small changes in diagnostic criteria can easily shift the balance from one classification to another.

SUSPICION AS A WAY OF LIFE

Megalomania has been called the 'disease of kings'. That label applies equally well to paranoia, because megalomania and paranoia go hand in hand. Both are an intricate part of the worldview of people who spend their lives using power to offset a negative sense of self-esteem. Paranoid grandiosity generally develops in compensation for deep-seated feelings of inferiority and a perception of powerlessness. The more helpless an individual feels, the more defenses he or she seeks to build.

The best way to understand paranoia is to view it as a distortion of a healthy response to danger. While most of us can distinguish between real danger and safety (though we might not always choose wisely), a minority of us see danger everywhere and hostile intent in everyone. Elias Canetti, in his book *Crowds and Power*, lists as one of the salient characteristics of paranoiacs the continual urge to unmask enemies:

> These the paranoiac sees everywhere, in the most peaceful and harmless disguises: he has the gift of seeing through appearances and knows exactly what is behind them. He tears the mask from every face and what he then finds is always essentially the same enemy. He is addicted to the routine of unmasking. ... (Canetti, 1960, p. 438)

Leaders are especially vulnerable to paranoia, because they do in fact face many dangers, both obvious and hidden, in the form of opponents who would oust them, constituents who would betray them and extremists who would assassinate them. One cannot be an effective leader without rubbing some people up the wrong way. There will always be followers who feel stepped upon and dream of (or enact) retaliation, just as there will always be followers who envy leaders' power and plot to attain it. For leaders, then, ideas of persecution are a rational response to a world populated by real, not just imagined, enemies. As Shaka Zulu once said in a conversation with Nathaniel Isaacs: 'I am like a wolf on a flat, that is at a loss for a place to hide his head in' (Isaacs, 1836/1970, p. 113). With no place for leaders to hide, it is not surprising that they tend to be mistrustful, guarded, hypersensitive and hypervigilant. Sensitive to signals of danger and hostility, they react defensively.

We can conclude then that healthy suspiciousness is an adaptive mechanism for leaders. Being vigilant in the presence of perceived or likely danger is simply an extension of their wish to survive. That suspicion must always be moderated by a sense of reality, however, lest it slip over into malignant paranoia. Effective leaders ground their behavior in sound political practices that limit and test danger, and they rely on trusted associates to help them stay safe and sane.

Paranoid leaders, on the other hand, distort information and engage in delusional thinking and faulty reality-testing. In their efforts to deal with perceived dangers, they create what looks to them like a logical world. (Acute dangers require drastic measures, after all.) In fact while their reasoning may be rational, the assumptions on which their logic is based are false. Bugging the second-in-command's office and having him followed, for example, makes sense only if the lieutenant really is plotting an assassination attempt. In other words paranoid behavior is rationality run amok.

Paranoid leaders, questioning the trustworthiness of just about everybody, suffer from delusions of conspiracy and victimization. Fearing that others may do them harm, they listen for – and find – hidden meanings in even the most innocent remarks. If a cursory check disproves their particular suspicion of danger, they do not feel relief; instead they search ever deeper for confirmation of that suspicion. If that effort likewise fails, they may claim to have special knowledge of the inner experiences of the potential offender. In other words, lacking proof, they create proof. Over time, their suspiciousness becomes the prevalent, habitual mode of thinking (American Psychiatric Association, 1994; Shapiro, 1965).

Paranoid thought is typically dichotomous. All good images are retained within the self, while all bad images are projected outward. Thus malignant paranoid leaders create for themselves a world of stark contrasts, populated by 'good' and 'evil', friends and foes. Ironically, though they themselves create many of their own foes (ascribing hostile intent where there is none), paranoiacs' dysfunctional interactions with others are often convoluted attempts to build connections, to break out of the isolation that they themselves forged. Because paranoid leaders expect relationships to come to a bad end, however, they generally do: paranoia trumps intimacy every time.

SURVIVING WITHOUT TRUST

Paranoia has its origin in a basic lack of trust. This sounds simple enough, but where does a lack of trust come from? Typically it originates in an early family environment that is unpredictable and hostile. Overt child abuse and passive neglect have an influence on the young child's neurologically based capacity to regulate affective experiences. They interrupt nature's planned trajectory for emotional management, affecting the developing youngster's capacity to respond to his or her innate need for intimacy and attachment (Lichtenberg, 1991). In the absence of love, security, and consistency, distrust and suspicion thrive.

Children who grow up with the 'good enough' caregiving described in Chapter 4 internalize the comforting, reassuring maternal and paternal figures that love and support them. Children who grow up with unpredictability and hostility, on the other hand, internalize the inconstant and persecutory figures that terrorize them. The outcome of the latter form of caregiving is an adult who is extraordinarily sensitive to hostility, criticism and accusation and is incorrigibly afraid of betrayal and loss. Having learned, literally from the cradle, the need to be on guard, that adult remains vigilant long after the inconstant caregivers are out of the picture (Cameron, 1963; Horowitz et al., 1984; Lewis, 1992; Meissner, 1978; Robins and Post, 1997; Shapiro, 1965; Van der Kolk and Fisler, 1994).

Researchers of character who focus on the behavior of infants and young children have introduced the concept of the 'paranoid-schizoid position' as a normal phase of early human development (Klein, 1948, 1959). In this 'position', the young person splits the images in his or her inner world into either 'good' or 'bad'. Using a defense mechanism known as 'projective identification', the child then 'expels' those parts of the self experienced as 'bad' and 'deposits' them into someone else.

Infants, with their more limited capacity for thought and analysis, cannot understand that loving and hateful internal imagery can coexist in their internal world. They have trouble grasping the notion that the same person can be both gratifying and frustrating. Until they develop the capacity for tolerating ambivalent feelings, and for understanding that both good and bad feelings can be triggered by the same person, infants fear that one set of imagery will destroy the other, leading to a state of nothingness. The aggressive, destructive parts of the infant's own self are too painful and threatening to be tolerated within the self. Thus infants disown their aggressive imagery and retain their more loving, nurturing imagery. This latter part of the self becomes the foundation of an idealized self-concept, while the negative part – the so-called shadow side of the personality – is ascribed to others.

Over time, if development takes place with age-appropriate frustration, the infant passes out of the paranoid-schizoid position, learning to tolerate both aggressive and loving internal imagery. The developing child, gaining the capacity to tolerate ambivalent feelings, comes to realize and accept that such varied imagery makes up both self and others. At that point, the loved (but flawed) other can become internalized for the child in a stable way that guarantees security.

In cases of conflicted developmental processes, however, children (and later the adults they become) get stuck in the paranoid-schizoid position. This human capacity for splitting, projection and externalization, begun early as an adaptive defense mechanism, remains operative throughout the paranoiac's lifespan, becoming dysfunctional when it outlasts the need that spawned it. Such individuals never progress beyond a world of stark images of good and evil; they are never able to integrate good with bad. Such people – Shaka among them – continue living in a world of divided, hostile imagery, continue using splitting, projection and externalization as common ways of functioning. Believing that all bad things come from the outside and all good things from within, they cannot accept that some of the 'bad' things that happen to them are a consequence of their own actions.

Both projective identification and the tendency to split the world into good versus evil are signs of paranoid thinking. Seeing the world as incapable of compromise, paranoid leaders must constantly wage war with external enemies. Seeing badness as originating outside themselves, they look for others to blame for any setbacks they experience. And yet, despite these precautions, such leaders have an 'internal persecutor' forever present. Their own externalized 'bad' images – those images that they tried to disown – follow them like a shadow that cannot be escaped.

Shaka, growing up in a hostile, lonely world, certainly had the kind of experiences that arrest development in the paranoid-schizoid position. Knowing what we do about his background, we would expect him to have split the world into good and bad, to blame others and to have a distrustful, suspicious disposition. From infancy on, his circumstances were harsh, unkind and lonely, necessitating constant vigilance and mistrust. The quick temper, irritability and violent reactions that the adult Shaka revealed were reactivations of his memories of those circumstances. He preferred violence to helplessness, choosing the former as his primary form of relating to others. He also chose violence over loneliness, as do most victims of cruel treatment: children who have been exposed to terrifying environments generally prefer relating via violence to not relating at all. Satisfying human attachment needs is so essential to psychological survival that children will do anything to keep loneliness at bay (Bowlby, 1969).

Children who feel constantly under attack, whether from actual violence or from hostile internal imagery, may develop elaborate fantasies as a way of enhancing injured self-esteem. Eventually these secret fantasies may evolve into full-fledged delusions. The most common form of delusion is the persecutory type – delusion rooted in a pervasive, unwarranted suspiciousness and mistrust of other people. It usually involves a single theme or a series of connected themes, such as being cheated, being followed, being poisoned, being conspired against, being spied on and/or being obstructed in the pursuit of long-term goals.

People with persecutory delusions fear victimization. Because they live in a world full of enemies that need to be destroyed, they are chronically resentful and angry, always ready for a fight. The real threat – the threat that they carry with them from childhood – cannot be usefully addressed, so they substitute an external threat instead and take action against that threat, thereby gaining a modicum of control. That control of people and circumstances is necessary to shore up the shaky sense of self-esteem that typically lies at the core of paranoia.

Even when paranoiacs have control, they cannot trust it. Though they attempt to surround themselves with people considered to be loyal, they constantly test that loyalty. The only people who can survive long in the atmosphere of sycophancy that develops are flatterers, but even at their most ingratiating they cannot prove their love and loyalty, as Shaka's followers discovered. Unable to shake the suspiciousness that helped him survive as a youngster, Shaka was governed by mistrust. Knowing that mere suspicion was enough to cause execution, his inner circle engaged in complex intrigue to ward off personal victimization and to further their careers. They knew for example that they could both curry favor and get a potential rival out of the way by suggesting to Shaka that the rival in question was involved in a coup plot. Such political games created a political environment fraught with fear and anxiety.

TRANSFORMING PERSONAL PARANOIA INTO A CULTURE OF CONSPIRACY

As we have seen, a malignant paranoid disposition was an essential part of Shaka's interpersonal style from childhood on. However, the exposed position he was in as king aggravated that paranoid inclination (Kets de Vries, 1995); had he remained a commoner, he might have been able to hold his paranoia more in check. The Zulu culture in which he grew to manhood also fed his paranoia. As was noted earlier, the Zulus believed that all calamities were caused by evil spirits creating disharmony between the land of the living and the dead. In the Zulu construction of the world, *abathakathi*, evildoers, were everywhere, using their magical power for antisocial ends. These evildoers had the capacity to destroy people's health, cause death, create a drought, make the cows lose their milk and precipitate many other calamities. What fertile ground for paranoid thinking! Conspiracy to overthrow or assassinate the king would be small potatoes for the *abathakathi* – as Shaka knew from personal experience, having plotted and used sorcery to succeed his father.

Shaka took the suspicion-laden Zulu worldview and created a whole culture of conspiracy. In the turmoil of southern Africa in the early 1800s – with the influx of European settlers, the dwindling of grasslands and the frequency and growing intensity of war – his paranoid message must have been extremely attractive. Shaka sensed his subjects' fear, and he kindled it further, using the energy of that fear to build cohesiveness and accomplish huge goals. His paranoia, eventually mirrored in an entire culture of conspiracy, helped to build a nation. But unchecked, it then destroyed that nation.

Regression in Groups

Leaders who are governed by a paranoid outlook tend to be extremely talented at engaging their subjects in a cosmic battle of good against evil. Their paranoid leadership encourages the development of two of the most basic emotional states to be found in groups: the fight–flight assumption and the dependency assumption (Bion, 1959). These basic assumptions – which take place at an unconscious level – create a group dynamic that makes it much harder for people to work together productively. They encourage pathological regression in groups to more archaic (that is, primitive) patterns of functioning. Freed from the constraints of conventional thinking, groups subject to such regression retreat into a world of their own. The result is often delusional ideation – in other words, ideas completely detached from reality – which is a fertile soil for the proliferation of totalitarian ideologies.

The term 'fight–flight assumption' refers to a common tendency within groups to split the world into camps of friends and enemies (Volkan, 1988). In groups characterized by this assumption, an outlook of avoidance or attack predominates. Subscribing to a rigid, bipolar view of the world, these groups possess a strong desire for protection from and conquest of an enemy. This group tendency coincides with paranoid leaders' natural disposition, discussed earlier.

Because their inner world is already populated by conspiracies and enemies, such leaders are only happy to encourage the group tendency toward splitting. They inflame their followers against real and/or imagined enemies, using the in-group/out-group division to motivate people. The shared search for and fight against enemies results in a strong conviction among participants of the correctness and righteousness of their cause, and it energizes them to pursue that cause. It also combats emerging anxiety, channeling it outward. Furthermore it enforces the group's identity: paranoid leaders, by radiating certainty and conviction, create meaning for followers who feel lost. The resulting sense of unity is highly reassuring. As followers eliminate doubters and applaud converts, they become increasingly dependent on their leader.

Groups prone to the 'dependency assumption' are looking for a strong, charismatic leader to lead the way. The members of such groups are united by common feelings of helplessness, neediness and fear of the outside world. They readily give up their autonomy when they perceive help at hand – an unburdening process that is even easier for people living in a collectivist society like that of the Zulus. While their unquestioning faith in their leader contributes to goal-directedness and cohesiveness, it impairs critical judgment. Though they are willing to carry out their leader's directives, it is up to him or her to take all the initiative, to do all the thinking.

Shaka encouraged both the fight–flight assumption and the dependency assumption. Feeling in himself the human urge to regress to these more archaic forms of functioning, he was more than willing to take advantage of and build on the same human weakness in others. By oversimplifying his complex world into distinct 'us versus them' categories, he defined a clear path out of chaos; by making his people anxious and uncertain, he made them dependent on him. Riding these waves of regression helped him combat the demons of his inner world and build a powerful nation.

The battlefield provided an ideal forum in which Shaka could take advantage of regressive group processes. By harnessing general feelings of anxiety, he was able to transform a private war with his inner demons into an actual war. What better way to deal with aggression than by blaming an outsider – by vanquishing a foe? What better way to act out paranoia than by attacking the enemy within, killing one's own people? And if the cause of a setback was unclear, there was always witchcraft to blame.

Regressive group processes served Shaka well on the home front too. He was adept at playing people against each other, using a divide-and-conquer policy to prevent his inner circle from uniting against him. For example he often gave his senior people assignments with incomplete or overlapping authority, thereby fostering intense competition. They soon learned that one way they could garner more authority was by 'telling on' each other. As a result, Shaka had an elaborate espionage network of private and public information sources. Unfortunately, what he thought they should have said, or what he had expected them to say, was generally more important than what they actually said.

The consequence of such information (mis)management was that Shaka's followers divided themselves into factions that fought among each other constantly, thereby weakening their own positions. And that was exactly what Shaka had in mind, of course. By bestowing favors on one group, then on another, he made sure that none of the factions got the upper hand. With this delicate balancing act, he monopolized all the decision-making power, effectively destroying any internal opposition to his rule.

With the rapidity of contagion, Shaka's paranoid operational code created further paranoia. During his relatively short reign, he created a culture that left no options: one participated, or one was eliminated. And participating meant propagating yet more suspicion and mistrust, creating (and killing off) yet more scapegoats. Ironically, that shared task of finding and destroying scapegoats facilitated group identity formation among the Zulus.

Shaka's willingness to do away quickly with known enemies and suspected conspirators – the latter keeping his entourage off balance – gave him the upper hand. But he possessed the trump card as well: he was the 'chief sorcerer', after all. And he played that card often. Having a great dread of sorcery himself, and truly believing that *abathakathi* were everywhere, he was quick to accuse others of witchcraft. In the early part of his regime, he kept his war doctors busy working magic against the external enemies the clan was fighting, and he relied on his *izangoma* to smell out the enemy within. But because he did not like the power bestowed on these latter witchdoctors – their ability to 'smell out' his personal favorites was not appreciated – he eventually limited their power. When he did so, he became de facto the only real diviner in the country, and he used that designation to great effect. With a virtual monopoly on magic, he followed the route of many despots before him: total mind-control. Achieving the triumph of paranoia over reason, he made his subjects believe that he could read their thoughts and see their most secret actions.

Given the paranoia that Shaka felt and spread, one of the great surprises is that he let his half-brothers and half-sister live. Granted, he was wary about his royal brothers (knowing of course the deadly succession practices of Zulu society), and he made it a rule that his prime minister could never be a member of the royal family. And yet he was not wary enough: in spite of the paranoid dream he had the day before his murder – a dream in which his chief *induna*, Mbhopa, was serving another master – he did not take immediate action. Perhaps that lapse signifies a self-destructive streak in Shaka's personality. Alternatively, perhaps it suggests that at an unconscious level Shaka was uncertain of the legitimacy of his position, or wanted to master his inner anxiety about assassination (the latter leading him to invite danger in a cat-and-mouse game with his future assassins, wanting to see how far they were prepared to go). All it tells us for sure is that while Shaka thought he controlled all the moves and all his subjects, in the end he lost the game.

8. The terrorist mind: protecting the self by victimizing others

Tyrants seldom want pretexts.
> (Edmund Burke, letter to a member of the National Assembly)

Little by little we were taught all these things. We grew into them.
> (Adolf Eichmann, statement made at his trial)

Fear is the parent of cruelty.
> (J.A. Froude, *Great Studies on Great Subjects*)

The wish to hurt, the momentary intoxication with pain, is the loophole through which the pervert climbs into the minds of ordinary men.
> (Jacob Bronowski, *The Face of Violence*)

In violence we forget who we are.
> (Mary McCarthy, *On the Contrary*)

Of all the passions fear weakens judgment most.
> (Cardinal de Retz, *Mémoires*)

The worst sin toward our fellow creatures is not to hate them, but to be indifferent to them: that's the essence of inhumanity.
> (George Bernard Shaw, *The Devil's Disciple*)

Look out, look out, look out, that thing over there!
Long have we been eating without growing fat,
Today the house of Zulu emerges,
Long have we been gnawing on maize cobs,
Now the sun is rising, its rays are shining,
The elephant is stabbing with all its rays,
Look out, look out, that thing over there!
> (Ngidi, war song, *The James Stuart Archive*)

As was noted earlier, there is considerable overlap from one character disorder to another. We have looked now at evidence of paranoia and excessive narcissism in Shaka Zulu. Two additional character-disorder descriptions resonate with what we know about Shaka and many other leaders who rule by terror: the antisocial and the sadistic personalities (Millon, 1986, 1996). After a brief introduction to each, we will take a closer look, starting with the antisocial personality.

An essential feature of the antisocial personality 'is a pervasive pattern of disregard for, and violation of, the rights of others' (American Psychiatric Association, 1994, p. 645). Typically action-oriented, the antisocial personality acts recklessly or impulsively and shows no guilt or remorse for behavior that others deem hurtful. As Otto Kernberg (1992) has indicated, 'The antisocial personality's reality is the normal person's nightmare' (p. 82). An apparent lack of conscience is the defining characteristic of people with this character disorder. It is as if they had no internal censor to moderate their actions. Unhampered by social behavioral norms and remorse, they are extremely self-centered and show little concern for or interest in the feelings of others. They are extremely talented in rationalizing their actions. Likewise they are unable to experience empathy, though when the occasion warrants it they are able to role-play, deceiving their 'victims' with pseudo-charm.

Sadistic personalities, in contrast, *are* concerned about others, but in ways that are unpleasant and destructive. They are sensitive to others' feelings, hopes and fears – but only to the extent that domination requires. Like antisocial personalities, they have a defective conscience and feel no guilt, yet they are extremely talented at manipulating the conscience of others. This character disorder is defined by a long-standing pattern of cruel, demeaning and aggressive behavior. Sadistic personalities are driven to eliminate (either literally or figuratively) the people they have singled out as 'deserving'. They have long memories and do not easily forget past wrongs. That simmering resentment over wrongs often erupts into overt hostility. As with antisocial personalities, sadistic personalities are indifferent to both the rights and the feelings of others; they feel neither guilt nor empathy. They engage in raw brutality. Gratification is found in aggression itself, in tormenting others.

MALEVOLENT ANTISOCIAL CHARACTER DISORDER

We have all known people who show signs of antisocial personality. Although they are unpleasant to be around, they function adequately in the work world (if not the social sphere). Fortunately, few of us know, or will ever meet, someone with the extreme form of antisocialism: malevolent antisocial personality disorder (Millon, 1996).

Malevolent antisocial personalities, whose behavior reflects elements of paranoia and sadism, are the least attractive among the antisocial population; they demonstrate the most callous, vengeful, belligerent and brutal behavior. They are incapable of understanding the wrongness of their actions. They like to be in control, and because they care very little about the feelings of other people, they are ruthless in gaining mastery. They take pleasure in victimizing those they control, though they fear being controlled by others and are prepared to go to great lengths to prevent such control from happening. Because they perceive the world as a hostile, unforgiving place, they are always on their guard. Like paranoiacs, they anticipate betrayal and punishment and favor preemptive aggression. Furthermore they are driven to avenge any perceived mistreatments of the past.

Looking Out for Number One

A core belief of malevolent antisocials is that they should look out for themselves, regardless of the cost to others. Having once been the victim, they want to make sure they never again find themselves under another's control. The best way to ensure that is to do the victimizing themselves. Thus aggression, uncontrolled and intimidating, is their preferred operating mode. Lacking proper parental controls while growing up, antisocials never learned how to moderate their aggression. Now, as adults, they feel secure only when they are independent of – or better yet, in control of – those who they fear could harm or humiliate them. Having the power to live out their childhood fantasies, they gain vindictive gratification from humiliating and dominating others. When blocked in that endeavor (or any other), they exhibit a violent temper that can flare up quickly and without regard for others.

It is no surprise then that the quality of interpersonal relationships of antisocial individuals is downright abysmal. Antisocials' capacity to love, to relate intimately and affectionately with another person, is markedly impaired. Lacking the compassion, ethics and moral values that characterize most humans, they experience only superficial and shallow emotional reactions (despite their occasional empathic façade), and thus their relationships have little depth. Their only emotional 'strength' is hostility: they are champions at ignoring the feelings of others, failing to cooperate, and being irritable.

Antisocials and sadists share a lack of empathy and an inability to identify with others. Because these people cannot identify with their victims (or do so only briefly, opportunistically), the latter can be destroyed and discarded at will: it is as if the victims were merely lifeless objects, not living human beings. Antisocials and sadists have no moral qualms about destroying their victims or impounding their victims' possessions. On the contrary, they feel a sense of entitlement.

Malevolent antisocials walk a thin line between adventurousness, recklessness, impulsiveness and unruliness. Sometimes their creative, nonconforming explorations lead to novel solutions; more often these explorations transgress the limits of acceptable behavior, bringing antisocials into conflict with established mores and inflicting great pain on others. Because antisocials do not care what others think (though they do, like narcissists, enjoy the attention of an audience), they forge ahead regardless of the world's disapproval.

The nonconformist element of antisocial behavior is evident in Shaka's career. In his early years as a warrior, his ruthless, competitive, independent behavior resulted in purposeful action. Though his behavior was nonconforming, it led to new, creative solutions. The survival-of-the-fittest warfare that he advocated advanced the Zulus a major step toward nation-building. However, his intimidating style became more and more brutal, and less and less rational, as time went on – particularly when buffering figures such as Dingiswayo or his mother were no longer present.

Antisocial personalities, who are often labeled 'sociopaths', generally function adequately in intellectual dimensions, despite their socially repugnant behavior. This contrast makes the darker side of their behavior especially difficult to understand. The French label *manie sans délire* (insanity without delirium) expresses well the total contradiction this personality type presents (Pinel, 1801). Like colorblind people who cannot distinguish between certain colors, antisocial personalities cannot differentiate between acceptable and unacceptable forms of behavior. Because they have no sense of boundaries, social or otherwise, the role of tyrant comes naturally to them.

This is what military historian Donald Morris wrote about Shaka's daily routine:

> His rule was based on a fear so profound he could afford to ignore it; his subjects would no more think of resisting than a mouse would gainsay an elephant. He moved through his daily routine surrounded by a retinue that included a group of executioners, who, a dozen times daily, bashed in skulls or twisted necks at a flick of Shaka's hand. The lives snuffed out in this fashion were guilty of no great crimes; they may have sneezed while he was eating, or made him laugh when he was serious. It was no set policy that made him act like this, nor was it cruelty, which implies a desire to inflict pain. It went beyond cruelty, it ignored pain, and the people he killed meant no more to him than so many ants. (Morris, 1966, p. 67)

Any leader who can so blithely, and so groundlessly, kill his subjects has clearly rejected all external controls and is devoid of any internal controls. Having grown up in a social environment that failed to teach adaptive action – generally an environment of extreme harshness and devaluation – such leaders feel that they never got a fair deal. Eager to right this wrong, they set out to acquire what might best be described as the power of the powerless. Shaka's violent activities, as mentioned repeatedly, can be viewed as a protest against what was done to him during childhood.

Just as Shaka engaged in role reversal, taunting the weak as he himself had been taunted, so antisocials generally try to make right the injustices and restore the deprivations experienced during childhood. Believing themselves to have been victimized, they now feel entitled to be the aggressor. Their provocative behavior can be seen as a form of mastery, a way of coming to terms with what is most feared, a way of overcoming the experience of narcissistic injury and recapturing long-lost feelings of omnipotence.

Paradoxically, although they feel that *they* are entitled to transgress boundaries, they make an enormous effort to control others, setting rigid boundaries and ensuring that those boundaries are respected. Veritable martinets, they come to specialize in enforcement. Alfred Bryant (1929) said of Shaka that he 'was in no way a normal Zulu, and the Zulu people are not to be measured by his standard. He was himself the supreme being, and responsible to none. Justice, sexual propriety, mercy and all the rest of the moral code were as he ordained, and apart from him were not. He feared none, obeyed none, considered none, respected none' (p. 633). No boundaries for him, clearly. But Bryant continued:

> [Shaka] made ample amends for much vicious example by inculcating in his people many brilliant virtues. Strange, but true, this Shaka was as sublime a moral teacher as martial genius. Submission to authority, obedience to the law, respect for superiors, order and self-restraint, fearlessness and self-sacrifice, constant work and civic duty, in a word, all the noblest disciplines of life were the very foundation-stones upon which he built his nation. So rigorously enforced was the life-long practice of all these excellencies, that he left them all a spontaneous habit, a second nature, amongst his people. (Bryant, 1929, p. 641)

A Narcissistic Blend

Malevolent antisocial personalities, besides incorporating a blend of paranoid and sadistic features, also have a touch of the narcissistic disposition, discussed in an earlier chapter. An early, devastating narcissistic injury, with its compensatory self-aggrandizement, fuels the thoughts and actions of most antisocials. Results include excessive self-reference and self-centeredness, grandiosity, entitlement, exhibitionism, recklessness, a drive for retribution and vindication, a low tolerance for frustration, and narcissistic rage when thwarted. Antisocials go after what they want at all costs, and if accused of outrages, they ascribe their own vengeful, distrustful and hostile attitude to others.

Antisocial people do not want to be bothered by connections and responsibilities to others. They find it humiliating to be dependent on family or associates. If someone approaches them in search of intimacy, that person is rebuffed, because antisocials cannot believe that anyone would relate to them out of genuine concern or kindness. Unable to trust even those family members or colleagues who have a history of loyalty, they interpret all acts of kindness as ploys to deceive. Like other people with character disorders, they pay with intense loneliness for their reluctance to engage others. Although no person is an island, antisocials cannot admit that they experience a longing for some kind of connection. Doing so would be a sign of weakness. For appearances' sake, they try to keep up the pretence of total self-sufficiency.

Shaka allowed the white traders a glimpse of his isolation. Because they did not belong to his world (and were therefore not a personal threat), he could let his hair down with them in private and engage in normal human interaction. In comparing himself to 'a wolf on a flat, that is at a loss for a place to hide his head in', as quoted earlier, he may have been telling Nathaniel Isaacs that he felt not just exposed and vulnerable, but also intensely lonely.

The distrust that underlies narcissistic isolation can be narcissists' downfall. Seeing enemies in every friendly face, they are attracted to (and invite) danger. But they sometimes exceed the limits one time too many. The killing business is a dangerous venture. It invites retaliation. Assassination tends to be the reward for people who live by the *assegai*. Given the provocative behavior that antisocials typically adopt, we could speculate that, at an unconscious level, they are looking for punishment. As noted at the conclusion of the previous chapter, Shaka's laissez-faire way of dealing with his family members hints at just such an unconscious need for punishment (with assassination the inevitable outcome).

The average antisocial personality has a limited arena in which to exercise his or her conflicts. Shaka, on the other hand, could extrapolate the emotional conflicts and deprivations of childhood, his resentment toward specific children and adults, onto the social situation. His aggression found a perfect outlet in war, an activity that gave him an opportunity to test the limits of the forbidden. But because he respected no boundaries, his cruelty and callousness concerning human life became his lasting signature. In that legacy, he joins a long line of other despots, such as Adolf Hitler, Pol Pot, Kim Il-Sung and Saddam Hussein.

SADISTIC CHARACTER DISORDER

As noted earlier, sadism is a component of malevolent antisocial behavior. It is also a character disorder in its own right.

As the previous chapters have illustrated, Shaka was no stranger to sadism. But he is far from alone in his sadistic tendencies. In fact, sadistic behavior is viewed by many as part of the human condition (Freud, 1920, 1921). Certainly it has always been with us. From antiquity onward, the world has seen a succession of despots with a reputation for cruelty. Take Nero, who ruled the Roman Empire for 14 years in the first century, engaging in an orgy of murders that started with his stepbrother and mother. Or Tamerlane, the fourteenth-century Mongol conqueror known as 'the Scourge of God', who indulged a macabre passion for building obelisks and pyramids out of the severed heads of his prisoners of war. Or Ivan the Terrible, who as Russia's czar in the sixteenth century murdered thousands of people suspected of disloyalty – men, women, children, babies, and even his own son. Or for a more contemporary example, 'Papa Doc' Duvalier, president of Haiti from 1957 to 1971, who with the help of his far-flung palace army – the Tonton Macoutes – terrorized the population. And of course Saddam Hussein, president of Iraq from 1979 to 2003, a man who perfected police-state terror, even going so far as to use poison gas on his own people.

From an ethological point of view, it has been argued that aggressive acts are needed for the survival of the species. However, even if a certain level of aggression is instinctive and necessary in the human race, a case can be made for another form of aggression – a 'malignant' aggression that is not instinctually programmed but is characterological (Fromm, 1973). Malignant aggression (which is the form of aggression referred to throughout this discussion), occurs when aggressive behavior patterns are internalized in response to disturbing experiences while growing up. The salient characteristics of this form of aggression are interpersonal abrasiveness and the attainment of pleasure through intimidating and humiliating others.

In Shaka Zulu, aggressive behavior reached new, frightful and one might even say imaginative heights. Many of his contemporaries commented on his barbarous methods of domination and intimidation – and the perverse pleasure that those cruelties gave him. As is true of his life as a whole, it is hard to know what is reality and what is distortion in those reports. However, with so much smoke we can assume that there must be a fire somewhere – and a pretty big one at that. Let us see what the smoke reveals.

During a battle between the Zulus and their main rival, Zwide, some aged women were taken prisoner and brought before Shaka to be interrogated. His first comment was allegedly that they were 'good stuff for fireworks'. After he got all the information he needed out of them, he had them padded with straw and put to flames, ordering them to run home, which they did, screaming desperately, to great bouts of laughter from Shaka and his entourage (Bryant, 1929, p. 649). On another occasion, disturbed by the dress worn by a person in his presence, he is supposed to have said, 'Take him away and kill him. He makes me laugh' (Bryant, 1929, p. 648).

As was noted earlier, there was a rule that prohibited anyone from entering the *isigodlo* without authorization. When some boys peeped into his hut one day, Shaka was greatly annoyed and ordered the culprits killed. His men replied that nobody had seen who was responsible. Shaka's answer to this dilemma? He had all the boys in that particular kraal killed (Bryant, 1929, p. 648). That Shaka was prepared to commit acts of violence even against children suggests that he was still plagued by the images of the children who ridiculed him in earlier days.

Shaka's punishments were as creative as they were wide-reaching. When a cattle thief was brought before him, Shaka decreed: '"He is so fond of cattle, let him be trodden to death by them." The cattle were driven out of the gate, passing over his body. He was trodden to pieces. He was ground down to manure. His mangled remains were afterwards taken up and thrown away' (Stuart, 1982, p. 246). In an equally unorthodox decree, Shaka sought to humiliate a great warrior by treating him like a dog (again perhaps dealing with the indignities of his own childhood by inflicting indignity on others). As the man's son explained: 'Tshaka [sic] looked on my father as a dog that would not allow the enemy to get near its master Tshaka. Tshaka accordingly ordered him not to touch meat at all; it was to be put on an eating mat and he must go to it on its knees and bite off pieces as a dog. He was henceforth to play the role of real dog. This my father did' (Stuart, 1976, p. 301).

These examples give us a glimpse into the sadistic personality. As we flesh out that personality here, you will hear many echoes of the narcissistic, paranoid and antisocial personalities. Sadistic personalities are typically irritable, argumentative, abrasive, malicious and easily provoked to anger. They nurture strong hatreds (Kernberg, 1992) and experience a persistent need to destroy and dehumanize people they see as a source of their frustration. They are generally extremely dogmatic, closed-minded and opinionated, rarely giving in on any issue even when evidence supports another view. Believing that force is the only way to solve problems, they use physical violence or cruelty to establish their dominance and achieve their will. Beyond that they take pleasure in the psychological or physical suffering of others; they enjoy humiliating and demeaning people in the presence of others. Violence, weapons, martial arts, injury and torture fascinate sadistic people (American Psychiatric Association, 1987). Nonetheless they can be very detached from any awareness of the impact of their activities.

In understanding the inner theatre of the sadistic personality, we need to remember a concept discussed earlier, projective identification: sadistic people are inclined to ascribe to others the malicious motives that they feel (but repress) in themselves. Like antisocial individuals and paranoiacs, they are extremely suspicious of the intentions of others. Because of the violence they experienced in early childhood, they have no understanding that people can possess good qualities. Someone whom others experience as kind, sadists experience as weak, inadequate and unreliable. Sadistically inclined people believe only in the power of might: they identify with powerful, cruel figures and get pleasure out of the suffering and destruction of the weak. As a result they create a fearful world in which the biblical injunction is reversed to 'Fear thy neighbor as thou fearest thyself'. With a sadist in a position of leadership, always anticipating that others will act in a hostile manner, such wariness becomes a self-fulfilling prophecy: others follow suit, responding with hostility.

Just as sadistic types are unable to see the potential for good in the behavior of others, they are wary of what others say. They are extremely sensitive to perceived insults in anything from comments about the weather to comments about their person. It is as if they are expecting insults – and indeed they are. With their talent for manipulation, they distort the most innocent remark into a barb, responding with fury, scorn and vindictiveness.

Sadistic types, like some of the other character permutations discussed in these chapters, try to overcome feelings of self-contempt by expressing superiority (Horney, 1945). Craving vindictive triumph (remember the Monte Cristo complex), they attempt to counter their impotence with omnipotence. As Erich Fromm noted, the core of sadism is 'the passion to have absolute and unrestricted control over a living being' (Fromm, 1973, pp. 288–9). As each new victim – each instance of 'unrestricted control' – takes sadistic personalities closer to the omnipotence they seek, they feel the aggressive satisfaction noted earlier.

They also feel an element of righteousness. They rationalize their cruelty by saying that it is for the victim's own good. They are just laying down socially helpful rules and following them carefully, they explain. They are convinced that the weak need to be devalued and deserve degradation. Shaka often justified his behavior with a grounding in righteousness. Henry Francis Fynn noted that Shaka often used a draconian punishment to 'improve' people. Once while campaigning, for example, Shaka was irritated that one of his regiments was not moving fast enough. To move things along, 'he ordered his servants to run and stab a few of them. They did so and killed five. The regiment then ran on ahead with all possible speed'. Effective, certainly. Fynn continued by saying that Shaka, on encountering a number of herdboys resting near his royal homestead, asked them

> if they sucked the cows that had small calves [an activity that was prohibited]. They denied having done that, upon which he directed them to take the usual oath. This they refused to do, knowing they were guilty. He then told them to go to the army about a mile distant, and say he had ordered them to be put to death. They did what he told them to do and were instantly killed. (Fynn, 1833/1950, p. 152)

Alfred Bryant (1929) describes another example of Shaka's cruel enforcement of the rules – righteous behavior, in his eyes:

> It was a standing rule of discipline in Shaka's Spartan army that allsoever as showed cowardice in the fight should be rigorously weeded out and placed on the retirement list – which invariably signified death, be it by battery, by the impalement stick *per anum*, or by throwing to the beasts, preferably hyenas on the land and crocodiles in water. Further, to turn one's back on the foe and return home defeated was to

Shaka's mind indistinguishable from cowardice. ... [T]here was a luckless regiment actually so returning, having failed to achieve the impossible – eminently suitable material for Shaka's purpose. So, upon arrival, they were one and all, together with their families at home, hustled off to execution; and a Kei-apple bush ... is pointed out as the Bush of the Cowards, marking the site of their massacre. (p. 587)

How can we reconcile behavior such as this with the kindness that both Nathaniel Isaacs and Henry Francis Fynn commented on in Shaka? Certain anecdotes about Shaka suggest that his subjects believed he really cared about them. This apparent blend of kindness and malevolence is common in sadistic types, but it is only 'apparent'. The perceived kindness is actually deceit, a form of playacting designed to manipulate the 'audience'. Lacking any center within themselves, sadists play different roles, depending on the particularities of the situation. They make a compensatory attempt to show that they are capable of genuine friendliness and concern, that there is more to them than mere coldness. Such behavior often 'succeeds', in the eyes of the sadist: it puts others off guard, encouraging them to say things that they pay for – and regret – later.

Children who have been physically or psychologically abused – who have been, as psychologists say, 'scapegoated' – often find themselves incapable of genuine warmth as adults. Shaka was the object of displaced anger from many different sources in his childhood. The belittlement, teasing and humiliation that characterized his early years were a breeding ground for sadistic behavior. Although in some individuals constant belittlement leads to a depressive reaction, Shaka stood up to his tormentors and fought back (energized perhaps by his mother's support). As each successful counterattack built up his confidence, the psychological balance gradually shifted from impotency to potency. But even as Shaka's self-perception of growing power counteracted his earlier sense of powerlessness, his fear of being a cowardly nobody lingered, offering one possible explanation for his need to 'eat' (that is, kill) his regular quota of cowards.

The young Shaka, belligerent and increasingly defiant in spite of the taunts directed toward him, could never allow himself the luxury of relaxing his vigilance. Because he responded to each perceived threat as an actual, objective threat, there was always another fight around the corner. That attitude of spoiling for a fight was combined with his mother's quarrelsome ways (some of which he probably internalized), a package that aroused considerable animosity. Like all his sadistic counterparts, he was socially isolated by his fear that intimacy might lead to humiliation. Preferring to play it safe by playing it solo, sadistic personalities are untrusting and harsh in the context of intimate relationships.

Because the fear of powerlessness remains a key theme in the sadistic population even when vulnerability is diminished, there is no such thing as enough power. Given their feelings of helplessness and vulnerability, sadistic personalities grab more and more power to prevent others from obtaining it. And when they have power, they are ruthless in exerting it, often using physical cruelty and violence to intimidate and dominate others – especially those others from whom they seek retribution for past wrongs. This tendency to seek and exert power is especially strong in societies that see stern toughness, discipline and competitiveness as admired characteristics, representative of social adjustment, and see compassion, openness, trust and care as signs of weakness. We can imagine, in the culture of the Zulus in which Shaka came to power, that his aggressive ways of interaction were perceived as desirable, at least initially. If the Zulus saw their world as a rough, dangerous place consisting of conquerors and victims, a place where people needed to be kept in line by strict rules and serious punishments, they would have wanted a leader who could dominate, who could take absolute control, who would never back away from a fight.

And yet while Zulu society may have been harsh in its punishments and its quest for control, Shaka was harsher still. The Zulus wanted firm control, and they got it; but they also got the atrocities that Shaka indulged in – the dark side of his exercise of power. In addition they got his 'culture innovation'. Shaka destroyed many of the cherished symbols of the Zulu past, and he created a nation built on war, a nation that glorified violence. The glory of war made for collective euphoria in the early, heady days of success, but eventually it led to collective depression. Shaka's actions took an enormous spiritual and emotional toll on the collective psyche of his people (and on those far beyond his borders who were vanquished by him). A symphony of death was played before his terrorized audience, to be continued even after his death in activities that became institutionalized and were carried on by his successors.

PART III

Leadership by Terror

9. Following the leader: colluding in cruelty

The world has heard of monsters – Rome had her Nero, the Huns their Attila, and Syracuse her Dionysius; the East has likewise produced her tyrants; but for ferocity, Chaka has exceeded them all; he has outstripped in sanguinary executions all who have gone before him, and in any country.
(Nathaniel Isaacs, *Travels and Adventures in Eastern Africa*)

Like one that on a lonesome road
Doth walk in fear and dread,
And having once turned round walks on,
And turns no more his head;
Because he knows, a frightful fiend
Doth close behind him tread.
(Samuel Taylor Coleridge, *The Rime of the Ancient Mariner*)

Fear has many eyes and can see things underground
(Miguel de Cervantes, *Don Quixote*)

Man's inhumanity to man
Makes countless thousands mourn.
(Robert Burns, *Man Was Made to Mourn*)

A revolution is not a dinner party ... or doing embroidery; it cannot be so refined, so leisurely.
(Mao Zedong, remark, 1927)

Once a government is committed to the principle of silencing the voice of opposition, it has only one way to go, and that is down the path of increasingly repressive measures, until it becomes a source of terror to all its citizens and creates a country where everyone lives in fear.
(Harry S Truman, speech, 8 August 1950)

Persecutory paranoia and paranoid grandiosity are common ingredients in the world of power and politics. These dysfunctional processes reach a grotesque level, however, in the case of tyrants. When a despotic leader takes charge of a country, the demons of his[1] inner theatre become the demons of the society. The despot's desires, ideals and hatreds become the fears and wishes of his subjects. The despot's law becomes the law of the country; the despot's ethics, the source of all morality; the despot's grandiose fantasies, his

117

subjects' fantasies; the despot's paranoia, their paranoia; the despot's pain, their pain.

As noted in Chapter 7, regressive, archaic group processes such as the fight–flight and dependency assumptions come to the fore under despotic leadership, further darkening the shadow side of humanity as they demonstrate the lowest depth to which human beings can sink (Bion, 1959). As Sigmund Freud (1921) noted astutely:

> [W]hen individuals come together in a group all their individual inhibitions fall away and all the cruel, brutal and destructive instincts, which lie dormant in individuals as relics of a primitive epoch, are stirred up to find gratification. (p. 70)

The tyrannical leader and his followers create a common culture characterized by shared delusions of grandeur and persecution. The leader encourages his subjects in the fantasy that he loves them all equally, that each of them is especially chosen. The followers, for their part, engage in an interactive process of mutual identification. This recognition of the self in the other fosters the feeling among members of the populace that they are not alone and thus encourages the process of group cohesion and solidarity. This cohesiveness is especially appealing in a society in a state of upheaval – as southern Africa was at the time of Shaka Zulu. Heard in the chaos of political upheaval, a paranoid message disseminated by an absolute despot is particularly attractive. The despot's tendency to engage in dichotomous thinking – to present his dreams of the future in stark, black-and-white terms – introduces certainty into an otherwise unpredictable world. With friends and enemies clearly differentiated by the despot, choices can be made without hesitation.

Thus paranoia is not only the disease of kings; it is also that disease's snake-oil cure, granting both leader and subject (spurious) clarity. Paranoid thinking from the throne leaves no room for gray areas, no room for adversaries, no room for compromise, no room for reflection. Because such clarity is liberating for the insecure, despots who present the world in absolute terms are able to release from their followers a tremendous amount of energy. Paranoid thinking dictates action and struggle, which in turn fuel the group process. The despot's subjects experience a renewed sense of purpose and direction. They know where to go, what to do and whom to fight.

The reason that followers are most prone to tyrannical rule in times of crisis is that anxiety and confusion make people more susceptible to regressive pulls. Feeling lost, they give in to the lowest common denominator of emotional impressions. Caught up in that emotional whirlwind, they become less selective in both thought and action; in short, they become more gullible. When social and cultural institutions are disintegrating, the illusions of powerful leadership are tempting. Manipulative leaders, adept at simplification and dramatization (and knowing well the gullibility of their followers), take advantage of the situation and present themselves as merchants of hope. Like snake-oil salesmen, they offer 'salvation' in various forms; like the sirens of Odysseus, they lead people astray with their illusions.

Unfortunately followers who relinquish autonomous psychological functioning and buy into the collective fantasy of a despotic leader rarely recognize the destructive path they are on. They want so desperately to believe the proffered images of unlimited power, regal grandeur and awe-inspiring majesty that they fail to see what the leader really stands for. They cheerfully shake hands, cementing a Faustian bargain, not recognizing the high price that will eventually have to be paid. They are blind and deaf to their future of self-destructiveness, social disruption and economic decline.

Shaka's presence at a 'historical moment' in southern Africa's history created a situation of complementarity between the script in his inner theatre and the pre-eminent concerns of his society in transition (Erikson, 1971). The changes taking place in the physical and political landscape of southern Africa, and the death of King Dingiswayo, gave Shaka the chance to act out the script of that inner theatre on a much larger public stage. Thus the Zulu hunger for leadership, which this warrior recognized as a window of opportunity, facilitated his rise to the top; the population was predisposed and willing to transfer to him all the power he needed. Of course that predisposition alone did not guarantee despotism. Shaka's sense of grandiosity and his preparedness to engage in violent action were essential ingredients in the shift to absolute power. Because (like all malevolent antisocial types) he acted without the constraints of a strong moral conscience, untroubled by a sense of right and wrong, he had a competitive advantage.

There were two major inflection points in Shaka's life – points at which the focus of his rule by terror started to shift: the defeat of King Zwide and the death of his mother. While for many years Shaka terrorized the neighboring chiefdoms of his territory, that emphasis changed after his defeat of King Zwide. Having conquered the major threat to his absolute rule, he had less need for external warfare. And yet without the action that warfare provided, he had no way to deal with the demons of his inner world. As those demons raged, Shaka sought new enemies to tackle, enemies within his own borders. From that inflection point onward, his terror was directed primarily at his own people – at actual and perceived enemies within. He began to 'eat' his own people, executing his subjects at an accelerated pace that must have alarmed them. The second inflection point, the death of Shaka's mother, culminated in an orgy of mass violence that saw everyone as the enemy. In retrospect it seems that her death (and his possible responsibility for it) must have triggered a psychotic breakdown.

Though these inflection points heightened the violence and redirected the terror, absolute control was a goal for Shaka from the outset. When he consolidated his empire, he transformed a loosely constructed federal structure into a totalitarian, highly centralized state, keeping all the levers of power within his grasp. No appointment could be made without his approval. No decision could be made without his consent. Every official in his empire was beholden to him. Whatever happened in his domain, however slight the irregularity, it was brought to his attention and dealt with promptly. It was as if he feared that if he tolerated the little offenses, the floodgates would be opened and he could lose complete control. In changing a pastoral economy dependent on land cultivation and cattle-herding into a war economy dependent on a constant influx of cows from cattle-raiding, he built a great nation, but he grounded it on violence, terror and that paramount quest for control.

With his obsession never again to be in the role of the underdog, he pursued total centralization and absolute obedience. He made himself the senior executive, the sole source of the law, the ultimate court of appeal, the commander-in-chief and the high priest. Thus the executive, the judiciary and the religious functions were all concentrated in his hands. By opting for total centralization, the traditions (both old and new) of the royal Zulu house became the traditions of the nation, the Zulu dialect became the language of the nation, and every inhabitant of his realm was dependent on Shaka's whims.

Such a centralized structure could not have been implemented by relying on diplomacy alone. Like many despots before him, Shaka saw political repression as the answer to any threat to his regime – even the slightest form of disobedience. As time passed and Shaka grew increasingly tyrannical, he became the executioner that we saw in earlier chapters: he killed enemies on trumped-up charges (usually of witchcraft), purged dissident groups and surrounded himself with a retinue that included a staff of executioners – all in order to instill fear and awe into the populace.

THE COLLUDING MIND

Dominance and submission characterized Shaka's regime, and were recurrent themes in the only music the warrior-king listened to: intimidation. He brilliantly orchestrated his symphony of terror, knowing just which notes to play to create and sustain fear. Building on existing cultural themes, he forged a military state that exerted total control, physical and ideological; and in the process he re-educated the psyche of the population. No part of his subjects' sphere was left untouched. Everything, no matter how domestic, was under his control. Servile deference to authority was the name of the game; loyalty to him took precedence over kinship ties and personal attachments.

As described earlier, the war that Shaka waged against his external enemies was total. He completely annihilated any form of opposition, sparing no one who opposed him, women and children included. Any form of resistance resulted in gruesome death. For Shaka the word 'annihilation' meant no exceptions: no enemy building, animal or food supply could be left untouched. And his merciless war machine had the desired effect. Tales of terror about his cruelty toward enemies spread far and wide. The mere mention of his name was enough to put people into a panic.

The Tools of Thought-Control

Shaka honed many of the tools of thought-control (Lifton, 1961) for use against the inhabitants of his empire. As 'high priest', the chief diviner of the nation, he was in an excellent position to get into their minds and control their thinking. Believing him to be able to communicate directly with the ancestral spirits, secure the fertility of their land, protect their cattle from disease, and bring the much-needed rains, his subjects were in total awe of him. He was the father and the mother of the nation, praised for his magical powers in rituals, tales and songs.

Being in direct contact with the ancestral spirits certainly had its advantages. Speaking to Shaka through his dreams, these spirits provided the king with a rationale for his actions and absolved him from ordinary responsibility for his horrendous acts of violence. He could blame calamities enacted by his own hand on the *abathakathi*, evildoers who used magic to bring harm. Having wrested the monopoly of magic from the *izangoma*, the diviners, he had the final word. Whether Shaka really believed that he had special powers in dealing with the spiritual world or was just a master manipulator remains an open question, but his superstition suggests the former. So does the conviction with which he apparently made his pronouncements.

Not only the spiritual world, but also the existing pattern of family life was fundamentally changed through Shaka's military innovations. Each aspect of a subject's private sphere fell under the king's control, personal attachments giving way to absolute loyalty to the crown. And that loyalty was rigorously tested: people were asked for example to execute close family members to honor the king – and to sing the king's praises while doing so. No important decision – including decisions regarding intimate relations – could be taken without his approval. And as we have seen, one of the most important private prerogatives, the right to marry, was included in Shaka's elaborate reward structure. His social manipulation placed institutions such as the *amabutho* over other human concerns, further lessening the role of the family.

All totalitarian states thrive on the continuous search for enemies, be they internal or external. Totalitarian states are fueled by violence, war being the most common expression. When there are no enemies, totalitarian leaders invent them. They label all 'others' as either virtuous or evil, scapegoating the latter. The hunting down of those evil others – 'traitors' who do not subscribe to the tenets of the regime – diverts attention nicely from the frustrations of everyday life. Thus despotic leaders create conspiracies everywhere, using them as a 'binding' device that cements a bond between the leader and the led. Given the paranoid mindset of despotic leaders, some of these conspiracies are imaginary; given the cruelties that despots inflict on their own population and outsiders, some are very real.

Like many other despots around the world and across the ages, Shaka was a master at this form of psychological manipulation. Looking for conspiracies and identifying enemies became his way of creating structure in society, of keeping his subjects subjugated. In the name of strengthening virtue within the kingdom – on the surface a very attractive proposition – he advocated the eradication of all 'evil'. His *Weltanschauung* implied the division of the world into the forces of absolute good and absolute evil, thereby decreeing who had a right to exist and who did not. Defining the 'evil' outside helped both him and his followers in their efforts at self-definition and gave them a sense of purpose. As students of groups have observed, demonizing others can bring a lot of satisfaction and can play an important role in identity formation (Volkan, 1988). By experiencing a sense of superiority over others, people start to feel better about themselves. By 'cherishing' the enemy, people discover their own identity.

External threats are also useful as a means of asserting the leader's integrity and power. A potent enemy reinforces the leader's legitimacy, sanctions the leader's actions, helps the population accept the hardships of a stringent rule, and focuses the people's constructive energy outward. More important, it allows the leader to focus aggression outward. Tyrants have to release their aggression somehow, and if it has no external focus it turns inward, in the form of depression and emptiness. Because tyrants are quite vulnerable to depression, they learn early to fight it by finding other targets, willingly sacrificing others to save themselves.

Shaka had no trouble finding targets, and he showed no reluctance in dispatching them. Demanding total subjugation to his mind-control, he created a very dangerous world indeed – one in which any sign of independent thought could (and more often than not did) lead to death. Tremendous conscious and unconscious self-censorship grew up as a result. Blind, unthinking obedience to authority (supported by the existing patriarchal structure of Zulu society and by the existing cultural scapegoating of the *abathakathi*) became the distinguishing feature of Shaka's regime. To be good was to obey; to be bad was to be disobedient – and rewards and punishments were expected to ensue accordingly.

Information Management and the Tactics of Divide-and-Conquer

Like many despots before him, who shared his passion for total domination, Shaka was a master at creating uncertainty. He did so primarily by the tactics of divide-and-conquer.

The overall culture of terror laid the foundation for those tactics. Knowing that Shaka needed to feed his aggression with victims, people were sorely and frequently tempted to offer up others to save themselves. In addition Shaka devalued his society's traditional symbol of respect: the old men. By calling respected elders 'useless old women' and making fun of them by forcing them to wear 'petticoats', he reframed the role of those hereditary chiefs whom he did not execute, thereby breaking their power base. He replaced those hereditary chiefs – who before Shaka came along had held what power there was over life and death – with commoners who were totally dependent on his favors.

Shaka knew well the value of information, and he manipulated it astutely. As noted earlier, he rotated his key advisors, reshuffling them whenever he thought they were becoming too comfortable. This kept them from learning too much about any one thing and prevented them from building their own regional power base. In order to keep people in positions of power in his sight (and under his thumb), he summoned district chiefs to be members of his council at the royal kraal. With their family left behind, vulnerable to Shaka's long arm, they would think twice before harboring any subversive thoughts, and think many times before acting on such thoughts.

On the surface it looked as if Shaka sought the counsel of these advisors, but in reality their role was purely perfunctory. In the manner of despots before and after him, he would state his opinion up front and expect them to agree. On those rare occasions when there was opposition to his plans, he would convene another council to get the feedback he wanted. As we saw earlier, a council meeting could not be held without his presence, since that would be an invitation to conspiracy. And the advisors toed that line, and all others that Shaka drew. Since people who disagreed quickly fell out of favor or dug their own grave, the advisors knew the cost of disobedience.

Shaka not only played his civilian advisors like a violin, he manipulated his military advisors as well. He used the same divide-and-conquer technique with his generals, preventing them from arriving at a common opinion that could be used against him. As far as he was concerned, their only function was to execute his orders. Any opposition to his way of leading the nation was quashed immediately. As a result, most members of his inner circle – military or otherwise – applauded Shaka's actions and even encouraged him to be more violent.

By playing one constituency, be it military or civilian advisors, against another, Shaka made sure that no one person or group could ever get the full picture. He supplemented this strategy with a sophisticated espionage system. This system, as noted earlier, informed him of any insurrection (or hint of an insurrection). His ability to form and shift alliances depending on the expediency of the situation, his talent at eliminating actual and imagined enemies, and his aptitude for maintaining overlapping networks of spies to discover, intimidate and undermine any form of opposition served him well. The divide-and-conquer leadership style that these combined strategies comprised – the style favored by despots everywhere – put Shaka, like a spider, in the middle of a web of information. Who, knowing the venom of that spider, would choose to venture into the web? Although, as we saw in Chapter 1, the Zulus had permission to question and disagree with the king at the 'first fruits' festival, how much genuine opposition would there have been? We can only marvel at the brave *induna* who had the courage to stand up to Shaka after his mother's death, requesting that the king abrogate the edicts pronounced against the people.

UNPREDICTABLE PREDICTABILITY

Not only do despotic leaders create structures and strategies to keep their populace in check, they also specialize in random terror. Giving voice to their own vindictiveness, suspicion and hostility, they make high drama out of keeping life-and-death control over their subjects. Attuned to human weakness, they nurture anxiety, fear and dependency, nutrients that allow despotism to flourish. And they build those nutrients by creating uncertainty, keeping their subjects off guard. That uncertainty makes it difficult to foresee the future and to organize and carry out a coup.

Knowing all this, Shaka made sure that the only predictable element in his leadership style was cruelty: everyone knew that sometime, somehow, somewhere, someone's neck was going to be broken, or someone was going to be impaled, or someone's family was going to die. Who it would be, and for what reason, was yet unknown. But nobody could be exempted with any certainty.

Deliberate, unpredictable violence has a devastating effect on those who are witnesses to the brutality, and on those who hear of it secondhand. The horror of such violence plunges people into a psychological abyss, breaking their will and enforcing total subjugation on a population. Like a mouse watching an advancing cobra, they are spellbound by the behavior of their leader – so spellbound that they can do nothing to stop the advance. A review of totalitarian regimes suggests that when a certain degree of submission has been reached, the populace is prepared to accept anything. They come to believe that their leader is entitled to do whatever he wants (especially when, as in the case of Shaka, that leader is also seen as the high priest and spiritual leader). Once that submission point has been reached, saying *Bayete*! ('Hail to the king!') is the only option open to them.

Knowing that total submission required uncertainty, Shaka made terror a key element of his daily routine. As we saw earlier, a group of executioners were part of his regular retinue, their sole purpose being to bash in skulls, twist necks or arrange impalements at his command. The victims were often nobodies, but they could just as well be important figures. On many occasions Shaka selected two or three of the councilors in attendance at a meeting and ordered their necks broken on the spot.

At first glance, such behavior is highly irrational. In the context of absolute, totalitarian leadership, however, it is rational in the extreme. Shaka's seemingly random executions – and those of Stalin, Mao Zedong, Idi Amin, Pol Pot and others – served to keep the people in check. The pronouncement of death sentences demonstrated daily that Shaka was in charge, that people owed their lives to him. He was a savage god who could give, but could also take. He was a secretive, cunning leopard that could kill at a moment's notice, that had a right to kill. And if he failed to exercise that right routinely, he might give the impression that his power was waning. A king on the downswing could be held in contempt. People might disdain or even rise up against him. Thus the whimsical killing had to go on.

And so, by brutal killing, Shaka wiped out all opposition to his rule. To use the words of Nathaniel Isaacs:

Chaka ruled his people by perpetually keeping them in a state of terror, and his command over them was also greatly facilitated by his continually impressing them with the power of charms, witchcraft or necromancy, which he practiced, with inconceivable effect, on his poor, abject, deluded, and oppressed subjects. This he carried to such an extent as to excite a belief in their minds, that he had the power of knowing all their thoughts, and of seeing all their most secret actions. He pretended that he inherited this power from the spirit of his forefathers, who had deputed it to him. (Isaacs, 1836/1970, p. 153)

In ordering any of his subjects to be killed, Chaka never gave his reason for consigning them to death until it was too late to recall the sentence of execution. A sign, given by the pointing of his finger, or by the terrible declination of his head, was promptly obeyed, and as promptly executed, by anyone present. Thus a father did not hesitate to be the executioner of his own child; the ties of consanguinity availed nothing with the tyrant, his decrees must be carried into operation, and that unhesitatingly; and if after perpetrating the revolting deed the feelings of nature should predominate, and manifest themselves to the inhuman savage, the party was instantly ordered to be dispatched, with the atrocious remark, 'Take the Umtugarty [sic] [*umthakathi* – evil sorcerer] away: let me see if loving his child better than his king will do him any good. See if your clubs are not harder than his head.' The executioner was then permitted to repair to the kraal of the poor dead and mutilated creature, and there to destroy everyone who might be connected with it, to take the implements of war as his booty, and drive the cattle to the king, who orders its distribution among his warriors then present. (Isaacs, 1836/1970, pp. 150–51)

A number of anecdotes from testimonies about Shaka recorded in the *James Stuart Archive* speak to this point as well:

> Seeing vultures flying above, he cried, 'Wo! The birds of the king are hungry!' People were then killed and put out on the hill to be eaten by the vultures. And wu! The vultures were all on the hill!
>
> Then he saw a donga deep as a house, and he said, 'I wonder if this donga could be filled – filled with people?' Then people were tumbled in, and piled up in the donga until it was filled.
>
> Three of our Quabe people, Nnlanganiso, Mpezulu, and Matshongwe, had their eyes taken out by him while they were still alive. He then put them at the foot of a cliff and said, 'Look at Nnlanganiso, Mpezulu, and Matshongwe floundering about,' saying so because he had taken out their eyes. (Stuart, 1976, p. 7)

> Tshaka used to kill a man simply because he was ugly; not because he practiced witchcraft but merely because he had been born ugly. He would say, 'Hau! How ugly this fellow is! Take him away.' He would then be killed even though he had done nothing. ... That man used to play around with people. (Stuart, 1976, p. 12)

No doubt about it, Shaka knew the fear that terror inspires. Of course, he had been all too familiar with fear himself as a youngster. His brutality as an adult was probably, as suggested earlier, an attempt to master his own fear about terror. Though he could not undo what had been done to him, he could turn his passive fear into active cruelty, doing to others what had been done to him. In Edward Ritter's dramatized biography (based on material taken from many sources), Shaka seemed to talk from firsthand experience:

> Terror is the only thing they understand, [he said,] and you can only rule the Zulus by killing them. Who are the Zulus? They are parts of two hundred or more unruly clans which I had to break up and reshape, and only the fear of death will hold them together. The time will come when they will be as one nation. ...
>
> When I look up and see the vultures circling and say that the birds of the King are hungry, it gives me an opportunity of 'smelling out' those whom I consider a danger to the nation, and at the same time providing a drastic example to others. (Ritter, 1978, p. 339)

That Shaka could speak so blithely of inspiring fear suggests that cruelty came naturally to him. A true malevolent antisocial, he saw people as 'things'; they were his property, devoid of emotional value. Like cattle, they were a lower form of animal that could be disposed of at his pleasure. His words could kill them; his words could save them. Unfortunately his subjects' reactions of awe and terror, their perception of him as all-powerful, omniscient king, fed his delusions of grandeur and he became more brutal still, his early impotence transformed into the experience of omnipotence. But as Shaka learned, the experience of absolute control over other human beings is a narcotic: as time passes, larger and larger infusions of the drug are needed. And he pulled others into addiction with him. Those people who were asked to participate in executions were 'bonded' to his atrocities; they shared in the guilt, even if, like Shaka, they felt little or no guilt.

A TYRANNY OF SELF-DECEPTION

We can only imagine how Shaka's inner circle must have felt, being constantly subjected to his whimsically tyrannical behavior. Clearly, giving one's honest opinion was out of the question – too dangerous. But given Shaka's unpredictability, even flattery had its dangers. It tended to make the king suspicious and often triggered a paranoid response. That left only total submissiveness and passive dependency; and often even these were not enough. The *assegai* in Shaka's hand moved more quickly than thought, it seemed. Toward the end of his reign, that spear of death spoke as loudly in the royal kraal as it had earlier spoken on the battlefield.

Given the danger of mere proximity to Shaka, the obvious question is, Why did his subjects hang around? Why did they not flee rather than become active collaborators in his terror? Most likely, they had very little choice. If someone was asked to be part of Shaka's entourage, refusal was not an option. Any transgression of the king's wishes invited execution. Fleeing the territory as a whole was not an attractive proposition either. First, Shaka had created such a large nation that it was difficult to get beyond its range of power. Second, Shaka had created a wasteland around his empire. The barren territory that was left was populated – where there were people at all – by hungry people so desperate for food that some resorted to cannibalism.

Still, when things were at their worst, why was there not a united rebellion against Shaka's atrocities? The answer lies in human nature.

Crumbs of Power for the King's Dogs

There were of course benefits to be had by being close to the king. Shaka's activities gratified a number of psychosocial needs in those followers who earned the king's favor. The royal kraal may have been a place of high risk, but it was also a place of great reward. A hub of exciting action, it offered great contrast to the rather humdrum, pastoral existence that the Zulus had been born into.

The royal kraal was the place to be seen. There were drills, social events (including dances), courtships and other interesting activities. As in the heyday of Louis XIV's Versailles, to be somebody one had to be part of the inner circle. Not being at the royal kraal was equated with oblivion; it was as if the person did not exist. And best of all, the royal kraal housed the great king. It was the king who provided the main excitement, the king who was master of ceremonies, if you will, the king who rolled the dice of life and death. What more exciting game could there be?

With all these enticements, the royal kraal attracted a large number of people in search of power, honor, fame, glory and wealth. It also attracted those who wanted to avoid the tedious pastoral work of making a living. People of rank did not have to till the land or take care of cattle; on the contrary, they were taken care of at state expense. They were often shown enormous generosity by the same regal hand that meted out death. Shaka shared with his favorites of the moment the bounty that came to him through raids and the cattle that were seized at the executions of the less fortunate.

Furthermore Shaka was leading his people on a glorious adventure. There was terror, yes – but no longer was the tedious herding of cattle or the cultivating of land the only option. Freeing them from petty concerns, Shaka gave his men meaty roles in a great historical drama; he led them into battle and brought them out again victorious. Dangerous as war is, it appeals to basic motivational needs of humankind. It gave the struggling Zulu people a sense of purpose and meaning, a reason for living. Fighting for a just cause, they rose above the trivia of daily existence. They experienced comradeship and sexual adventure, and they felt alive. Marching against an enemy made for a sense of righteousness and dispelled any sense of alienation that individual warriors may have felt. The young men felt good knowing that they were on the side of the angels, that they were superior to the enemy, with its deceitful, treacherous behavior.

War also provided Shaka's warriors with an ideal outlet for their aggression; the ultimate definition of manhood, it tested their mettle. Flexing their muscles both literally and figuratively gave them a powerful high, a collective (and addictive) euphoria. Allowed to engage in the most violent acts without consequences, they explored their capacity for evil – a capacity that lies barely submerged in all of us. They experienced a godlike power over life and death and found it extremely seductive. They could spare lives or take them – the latter with honor rather than guilt.

Furthermore, Shaka's men were granted sexual liberty. While at war, they were given permission to rape and to engage in gang rape. Kept relatively chaste at the kraal, they were allowed to have full sexual intercourse after battle, to ward off the contagious effects associated with killing. Engaging in the violence of rape and massacre created feelings of group solidarity among the men; they shared a collective complicity that negated alienation and contributed to nation-building.

Let us not forget that Shaka's men had been trained from youth onward for killing. Although Shaka set the process of leadership by terror in motion, he had willing followers in his warriors, schooled in war during their years in the *amabutho*. In fact, their lives had been geared for war since childhood. After intense socialization in matters of war, they must have looked forward to engaging in real battle. Eager to 'wash their spears', they would have wanted to practice their learned 'profession'. Shedding blood would have been the culmination of their years of training.

Despite their training in killing, these warriors had had to keep their aggression in check for years; they had forced themselves to be respectful and obedient toward people in positions of power and authority. They must have relished the opportunity to redirect whatever underlying hostility they felt toward these authorities toward an acceptable enemy. Having been rigidly controlled during their training, they could now – on the battlefield – let go of their inhibitions and experience war as a cathartic experience.

In soldiering under Shaka, the men found a new way of life: comradeship, a sense of purpose, colorful dress, flashy weaponry and permission to indulge in violent behavior. They looked forward to raping and plundering. So Shaka was not a lonely voice in the wilderness clamoring for war. His men wanted the wealth, prestige, power and glory that battle could bring them. They wanted to advance in the military or civilian bureaucratic system and become one of the *izinduna*. They wanted to be attractive to women and hear their praises sung after battle; they wanted to 'earn' the right to marriage. Eager for all these rewards, they must have urged Shaka, during the early part of his rule, to send them on one campaign after another. Sharing his fantasies of grandiosity and majesty, they must have clamored for war. They had heeded well their indoctrination: war was a heroic ideal that would build a great nation.

This kind of collusion between leader and followers is the despot's major source of power. After all, totalitarian rulers cannot act alone; they are not islands unto themselves. They need others who are prepared to participate in their cruelty. As Hannah Arendt remarked in her essay *On Violence*:

> No government exclusively based on the means of violence has ever existed. Even the totalitarian ruler whose chief instrument of rule is torture, needs a power basis – the secret police and its net of informers. ... Even the most despotic domination we know of, the rule of master over slaves, who always outnumbered him, did not rest on superior means of coercion as such, but on a superior organization of power – that is, on the organized solidarity of the masters. Single men without

others to support them never have enough power to use violence successfully. (1969, pp. 50–51)

As mentioned earlier, a collectivist society such as that of the Zulus facilitates passive subjugation to the will of an autocratic leader. Order, discipline and absolute obedience to the king were qualities ingrained from childhood onward in Shaka's people. Youngsters were taught to conform, to obey. Their socialization in unquestioning obedience was intense and relentless, especially once Shaka had gained power. In describing Zulu society, Alfred Bryant emphasized the importance of obedience:

> The one great law that governed there was the law of complete submission to parental authority; and that authority was drastically enforced. Unquestioning, unanswering obedience to the supreme power was demanded without distinction, of all alike, of mothers, of sons (some of them already middle-aged men with families of their own), of every child. Every failure to obey was immediately followed by a penalty inflicted without mercy; while persistent subordination might lead to the disgrace of expulsion, and open revolt might even terminate in death. And what each inmate of the kraal saw practiced by the father, he in turn practiced in his own regard, demanding of all his juniors the same measure of obedience as was demanded of him by those above. Alongside, or out of, this practice of complete submission was gradually evolved something more than mere respect, almost a holy awe – *ukw-esaba* or to fear, as the Zulus call it – for those above one. (Bryant, 1929, p. 76)

On top of that Zulu tendency toward obedience, Shaka overlaid ideological training that enhanced the mindset of total obedience to authority. As we have seen, the *amabutho* system subordinated the will of the individual to that of the institution; it accentuated the leader's influence while it fostered the suppression (if not outright destruction) of previous loyalties and identities, loosing even the strong family ties between parent and child. Given that indoctrination, it is not surprising that obeying commands became a reflex reaction among the Zulus. I suspect that they came to appreciate the simplicity that obedience brought them – with no need to think or plan for oneself. As one informer said after Shaka's death, 'The old regime was good, even though the king killed off frequently. We used to think the king was having sport and we thought little of it. He never seemed in earnest' (Stuart, 1979, p. 248).

Indoctrination into Violence

The *amabutho* system also desensitized Shaka's warriors to violence, making them better able to tolerate the cruelty that they were asked to inflict. The training to become a Zulu warrior involved a process of gradual brutalization and glorified violent killing, a process that moved from watching more experienced colleagues commit violent acts to participating in ever more violent acts oneself. This desensitization also involved divesting target groups of human qualities (as for example when Shaka belittled old men and cowards). Researchers have shown that violent socialization of this sort makes people more prepared to commit atrocities (Athens, 1992; Grossman, 1996; Rhodes, 2002; Von Lang and Sibyll, 1983). We have seen ample evidence of that fact in concentration camps in Hitler's Germany, Stalin's Russia, Mao Zedong's China and Radovan Karadzic's Bosnia.

In fact, the socialization of the *amabutho* was so effective that Shaka and his *izinduna* had to work hard to keep a lid on the violence; they had to orchestrate activities, specifying that violence was permitted only at certain times and certain places. How explosive this form of brutalization could become is well illustrated by the mass violence that erupted when Shaka's mother died.

Though the men lived with violence every day, they felt protected in a way by the cruelty that they inflicted on others. Shaka convinced his men that 'washing their spears' would help them overcome their own fear of death – would even in a sense free them from death. Thus violence and terror became the warriors' guardian angels. The men were helped in this belief by Shaka's role as supreme spiritual leader. When Shaka rationalized mass killings by invoking predestination and divine mission, the warriors believed him, accepting their assigned tasks as sacred duty. What he thought was right, must be right – so said their patriarchal, superstitious worldview. In validating Shaka's construction of reality, the Zulu people increased his influence, thereby weakening the individual dissenter's hold on reality.

THE INNER THEATRE OF THE FOLLOWERS

We have looked at why people stay with and do the will of a despot. Now let us look at how those subjects of a despotic regime cope with the situation. How do they deal with experiences of horror and terror? What does thought-control do to their minds? What kind of coping patterns do they develop?

Vladimir Nabokov, in his reflection on tyrants, allows one of the victims, a schoolteacher who has led a hard and lonely life, to speak his mind. This man, obsessed with hatred of his country's dictator (whom he had known personally during his youth), engages in a rather contorted monologue. During the course of it, he becomes aware of how much thought-control he has been exposed to:

> [T]he assassination of the tyrant now turned out to be something so simple and quick that I could accomplish it without leaving my room. The only weapons available for the purpose were either an old but very well preserved revolver, or a hook over the window that must have served at one time to support a drapery rod. ...

> By killing myself I would kill him, as he was totally inside me, fattening on the intensity of my hatred. Along with him I would kill the world he had created, all the stupidity, cowardice, and cruelty of that world, which, together with him, had grown huge within me. ... (Nabokov, 1975, pp. 33–4)

This passage points out the degree to which totalitarian societies invade a person's private, inner world. Nabokov's reflections indicate the psychological difficulties associated with such an invasion, as a person struggles to maintain a modicum of individuality. Many people lose that struggle, swept away by the leader's charisma and tactics of intimidation, and perhaps welcome their own death.

Interpersonal Sources of Power

People go along with the practices of despotic regimes due to persuasion, coercion, and/or the expected rewards when co-opting with the regime (Kets de Vries, 1980). Which factor has the greatest force depends on the leader's tactics and the individual follower's needs and vulnerabilities. People who are completely converted by the leader to the set of values the regime represents tend not to consider that there might be contorted psychological group processes involved. People who come to compliance not through ideology but through coercion or to gain promised rewards are more likely to question privately the legitimacy and correctness of the regime's actions.

With the first category of people – the true believers who fall under the leader's spell – a symbolic merger occurs between leader and led. Accepting what the leader stands for, these followers strongly identify with the values and ideology that the leader espouses. They give up their own sense of identity to become part of the leader's vision. Whatever confusion they felt formerly is obliterated; whatever gaps they formerly perceived between where they were and where they wanted to be are filled by the leader's expectations for them. This coming together of need and solution often generates an almost religious experience of ecstasy. These 'converts', who have found both their calling and their messiah, make up the backbone of despotic, totalitarian regimes. They keep the regime's machinery running, supporting the leadership by praise and by doing whatever dirty work the regime requires. Happy in their conversion, devoted to the new belief system, they are always eager to convert others to their way of thinking.

In contrast, people who comply with the party line only out of the fear of sanctions are not invested in the regime's ideology. Having seen what happens to nonconformists, they are afraid of the brutality that will result if they do not follow the leader's commands. Lacking the courage to resist, they stifle their doubts and just go along. Still other people – the opportunists or careerists – comply with the regime primarily for the benefits that compliance will bring.

Having seen how much the 'in-crowd' profits from their wholehearted endorsement of the regime, they subscribe to the leader's way of looking at the world solely out of greed and ambition.

As suggested, people in these latter two groups – the coercive and reward categories – participate not out of a strong sense of inner conviction but out of convenience. They are willing to suppress their doubts and pay lip service to the demands of the regime in a form of 'pseudo-loyalty'. In other words, they present to the outside world a false self (Winnicott, 1965). Though they may gain security and material rewards, they pay greatly for this choice: presenting a false self suffocates a person's desire to grow, to develop and to be authentic. Having a chameleon-like 'as if' personality, they have no inner core (Deutsch, 1965).

In the beginning phase of any despotic regime there are typically many true believers. That number drops, however, when disenchantment with the regime sets in, when people realize that they have been following a false prophet, have been pursuing an illusion, and that original promises have not been kept. As that disenchantment grows, more and more people are only pretending to subscribe to what the leader stands for. The result is a nation populated by play-actors and hypocrites, as in present-day China and the Soviet Union during its final days. As the authenticity of true belief is replaced by pretense and manipulation, the driving ideology becomes simple: hold on to power, whatever the costs.

Group-Think

Persuasion, coercion and the hope of reward all factor into followers' decisions to support a despotic regime. There are also peculiar intrapsychic psychological dynamics at work, especially when it comes to persuasion. You may have heard of the now-famous 'Milgram experiment', a social psychological investigation that explored obedience to malevolent authority (Milgram, 1975). In this experiment, unsuspecting subjects were made to believe that they were giving electric shocks to a test-taker, who pleaded desperately (but fictitiously) for the shocks to stop. Many of the subjects continued to give the electric shocks despite the test-taker's distress. The results, based on a random sample of the population, showed that people are remarkably willing to yield to authority. They also revealed that the people who did so felt alienated from their own actions. The 'collaborators' abandoned their humanity and abdicated responsibility for that choice. Allowing the authority figure to absolve them for their actions, they delegated their guilt to others. Although they knew that what they were doing was hurtful and unnecessary, they lacked the will and courage to act on their convictions. Going along with the authority figure, relaxing their conscience, rationalizing their behavior – this was easier than taking a stand and protesting the shocks.

When reflex-like obedience to authority becomes a way of life in a given society, a collective mindset emerges and what psychologists call 'group-think' takes over (Janis, 1971). As noted in Chapter 7, collective pathological regression makes people revert to more archaic patterns of behavior and more absolutist forms of thinking. We have all seen, in group settings, how individual judgment and behavior can be influenced by the forces of group dynamics. People in a group typically do not feel responsible for the decisions made by the collective, and they are reluctant to question the appropriateness of any given decision. Because the group is working toward a common goal, there is an illusion of unanimity regarding the means to that end. An unquestioning belief in the morality of the group's actions allows individuals to overlook or even support atrocious acts. Sometimes there are people in a group who play the role of 'mind-guards', preventing adverse information from coming to the fore and resorting to rationalization when things do not go as planned.

The Process of Dehumanization

As noted earlier, dehumanizing the enemy paves the way for leadership by terror, because it allows ordinarily humane people to become active participants in the regime's atrocious acts (Des Pres, 1976; Erikson, 1963). This complex psychological process, which combines defenses such as unconscious denial, repression, depersonalization, isolation of emotions from cognitive thoughts and compartmentalization (that is disconnecting related mental representations and walling them off from each other), facilitates the use of terror. To perceive another person as human requires empathic or vicarious reactions based on perceived similarity. Dehumanization shuts off empathy by implying that the victims are not individuals in their own right. They are not like us – people with feelings, hopes, fantasies and concerns. Instead they are subhumans or demonic forces bent on destroying that which the perpetrators hold dear. And clearly something that evil requires different treatment, unusual methods. Any atrocity that addresses the problem is permitted. Defenses such as these help bypass the moral inhibition against killing. When the enemy is a subhuman or nonhuman – an inanimate object, event – its destruction need not be hampered by the restraints of conscience.

As the Milgram experiment demonstrated, people are eager to please those in authority. Psychologists talk of the 'idealizing transference' and submission to an overpowering, uncompromising force, but what it comes down to is this: when we please the leader, we feel a sense of oneness with him or her. There is an illusionary merger between leader and led that allows the underlings to feel a temporary sense of omnipotence. For a moment, they know what it is to have the power of the leader. They feel absolved of any moral responsibility – that lies with the leader – and they feel bonded to both the leader and the other group members by their shared action, even if that action is both cruel and deadly. When the leader is a despot, the identification that followers feel leads them to imitate his violent acts. What he did to them, they can (and should) do to others.

In any totalitarian structure, a group of key players surfaces around the leader. This group does everything it can to demonstrate political solidarity. These players encourage and support the leader, realizing that it is in their self-interest to change roles from passive bystander into proactive participant. They may have a feeling of righteousness about their participation, but their motivation is typically selfish: as a reward for their loyalty, they hope to obtain power, prestige and protection from the leader's wrath. They want to become so important to the leader that he will never see them as expendable, and to that end they take whatever preventive action they can, such as informing on others. If they play their role well, they tell themselves, it will be those others who are sacrificed on the altar of terror.

DEFENSES AGAINST THE ANXIETY OF TERROR

Psychological defenses do not offer much protection against tyranny, but sometimes they are all that the victims have to rely on.

Identification with the Aggressor

Some people, in an effort to cope psychologically with despots, resort to the defensive process known as 'identification with the aggressor' (Freud, 1966). When people find themselves in situations of great distress, they feel a basic need to retain an element of psychological security. A tyrannical regime, especially in its more advanced stages, certainly qualifies as distressing. The violent and unpredictable behavior of the leader, and his coercive use of power, strikes terror and paranoid anxiety into the hearts of his followers. To cope with these feelings, they develop an ambivalent relationship with the leader. They feel frightened by him, but attracted too, and lured by the protection he seems to offer. Perhaps awe, with its blend of dread and admiration, best captures the follower's ambivalence. And if people have the choice they generally choose admiration over dread.

In full-fledged identification with the aggressor, individuals impersonate the aggressor, assuming the aggressor's attributes and transforming themselves from those who are threatened to those making the threat. These victims (or victims-to-be) hope to acquire some of the power that the would-be aggressor possesses. The more extreme the actions of the leader, the more aggressive the self-defense must be – and thus the more tempting it is for subjects to gain strength by becoming part of his system and sharing his power. Victims become informers, for example, or sub-guards in concentration camps, and in those 'aggressive' roles they sometimes act more barbarically toward their fellow prisoners than the real guards do, resorting – though they know well the pain – to psychological and physical torture.

Violence and submission are closely intertwined in identification with the aggressor. The victims of a despot's violence hold their hostility in check by excessively subservient behavior toward the aggressor. Turning the aggressor into a 'good' person, they reduce their feelings of fear and helplessness. This defense is an illusionary effort at gaining control over an uncontrollable situation. The hostility does not simply go away, of course; it comes out eventually, transformed and displaced towards people out of favor (Adorno et al., 1950). We see evidence of the victim's desire to elevate the aggressor among Shaka's followers. Nathaniel Isaacs recorded an example of pathologically submissive behavior at Shaka's court (though in this example the victim had no opportunity to redirect his hostility toward a less powerful candidate): Shaka's chief domestic servant, who was knocked down and dragged away by the king's executioners, distinctly thanked Shaka while being beaten to death (Isaacs, 1836, p. 74).

Identification with the aggressor is a sinister pact between a 'mirror-hungry' leader, who never can receive enough admiration, and 'ideal-hungry' followers, who clamor for an all-wise, all-powerful leader to guide them out of the 'desert'. Because of the anxiety created by social unrest and the violence of tyranny, the despot's subjects are prepared to suspend independent thinking and go along with the whims of the leader. They are willing to participate in whatever atrocity he chooses to enact, knowing that resistance will be met by violence; what he does (or did) to them, they will do to others. Their principal rewards are survival, solidarity and social cohesion.

Dissociative Thinking

Given that throughout history there have been abundant volunteers for the posts of assistant despot and deputy conqueror, we can surmise that we all have a dark side capable of cruelty. Likewise we all possess defenses against cruelty. Our arsenal includes, but is not limited to, identification with the aggressor.

As Vladimir Nabokov's earlier-quoted comments about despots indicate, some people resort to dissociative thinking to handle the violence and terror of a totalitarian regime. Dissociation is a common mechanism by which people cope with overwhelming, stressful experiences. It is a way of coping that has run wild. As an occasional tool it can be lifesaving: when faced with a tiger in the wild, a person needs to stand back and assess the situation without emotion. As an everyday coping device, it is excessive: people who rely on dissociation not as a one-time fix but as a way of life disconnect themselves from the world, looking at themselves as an outsider would. Like the walking dead, they are there, but not really there.

Dissociation can be viewed as a schizoid resolution to the human condition. It is effective at defusing anxiety, but it results in feelings of uncertainty or conflict regarding one's being and purpose. It also makes for a sense of unreality, a subjective experience of deadness, disconnection from others and internal disintegration. Dissociative people carry out a charade, putting on a bland mask in public to cover the turmoil within.

Fleeing into Despair

While some victims of tyranny take refuge in dissociation, others flee – but not far enough to do any good. The best example of flight behavior is withdrawing, becoming depressed, giving in to feelings of helplessness and hopelessness. People who take this route engage in non-stop self-recrimination. Despairing of a life free from violence and cruelty, they become morose, tearful, joyless, fatalistic, hopeless about the future. Devoid of their former vigor and focus, and seeing themselves as worthless and inconsequential, they are unable to initiate action. They expect the worst, and that is usually what they get. Eventually they either become resigned to the situation, withdrawn and apathetic, or they welcome violent acts by the regime against them as a way to stop the work of worrying.

Fighting for Freedom

Yet the best defense is a good offense, as we so often hear in the world of sports. In a society of sheep served by a government of wolves, there are generally a few citizens who are unwilling to baa. Knowing that human liberty is lost when people become sheep, they stand up to the demagoguery of the despot. They take a stand, refusing to accept any deterioration of individual freedom and human rights. Rather than painting the despot in pretty colors, distancing themselves from the violence, or fleeing into despair, they take a combative posture, refusing to participate.

People who take the 'fight' position understand exactly the Faustian bargain they have been asked to participate in – material advantages in exchange for dishonesty, hopelessness, cruelty and destruction. Some freedom-fighters are swayed initially by the sirens of a utopian ideology but stand up for freedom once they see the excesses of their leadership; others recognize the new order for what it is from the outset. However they come to their determination, they stick with it: at great risk to self and family, they defend their convictions. Many heroic examples – most of whom died for their efforts – can be found in Hitler's Germany, Stalin's Russia and Mao Zedong's China.

People who are willing to fight for what they believe, regardless of the cost in personal suffering, are needed if despots and their regimes are to be overthrown. Such people resist exploitation, defend the right to liberty for all, and believe that all people should be able to follow their own dreams. People with this mindset are catalysts for the creation of new, more democratic societies out of the rubble of tyranny. By defending principles of personal responsibility and individual liberty, they bring human dignity to all.

NOTE

1. Because most despotic leaders of nations are in fact men, I have chosen in this section to use the pronouns 'he' and 'his' generically, thereby avoiding the clutter of 'his and her'. Many despots of the business and cultural worlds are women, however. Despotism is not limited by race or gender.

10. Lessons in leadership: teaching by example and omission

Mankind has been created for the sake of one another. Either instruct them, therefore, or endure them.
(Marcus Aurelius, *Meditations*)

When kings the sword of justice first lay down,
They are no kings, though they possess the crown.
Titles are shadows, crowns are empty things,
The good of subjects is the end of kings.
(Daniel Defoe, *The True-Born Englishman*)

Power is not revealed by striking hard or often, but by striking true.
(Honoré de Balzac, *La Comédie Humain*)

A leader is a man who has the ability to get other people to do what they don't want to do, and like it.
(Harry S Truman, *Key Management Ideas*)

A leader who doesn't hesitate before he sends his nation into battle is not fit to be a leader.
(Golda Meir, *As Good as Golda*)

The opportunist thinks of me and today. The statesman thinks of us and tomorrow.
(Dwight D. Eisenhower, speech given at Lafayette College)

Surround yourself with the best people you can find, delegate authority, and don't interfere.
(Ronald Reagan, *Fortune*)

The art of leadership is saying no, not yes. It is very easy to say yes.
(Tony Blair, *Mail on Sunday*)

Having deconstructed aspects of Shaka's despotic leadership style, we can now make our own judgment about what he stands for. We can view him as a warrior-king of epic proportions who brought the Zulu nation to greatness, or a ruthless psychopath and despot in the manner of Hitler, Stalin, Pol Pot and Saddam Hussein. The verdict will vary, depending upon the reader, but perhaps most of us would recognize elements of both greatness and despotism in his personality. Shaka was ruthless, certainly, but leadership by terror helped him to get things done. The writer Magema Fuze believes that Shaka was a man of destiny who 'arrived expressly for the purpose of bringing unity to the country instead of disunity, and rule by one person instead of everyone doing as he pleased' (1921/1998, p. 59).

Looking back on history, we can learn a great deal from 'good' leadership, but we can also learn from 'bad' leadership. The study of dysfunctional leadership has great pedagogical value, since it teaches what *not* to do. Whether we are in government or in business, there are a number of lessons we can learn from Shaka's leadership style – from his excesses as well as his successes. In spite of all his shortcomings, in spite of all his human frailties, he was an unusual leader, a political visionary, an inventive military commander and an astute political survivor.

Shaka offers us the following lessons in leadership:

- Develop a clear and concise vision.
- Recognize the importance of strategic innovation.
- Know the competition.
- Act quickly and decisively.
- Empower subordinates.
- Promote entrepreneurship.
- Engage in effective symbol manipulation.
- Select and promote with care.
- Set a good example.
- Hold people accountable.
- Reward people fairly.
- Devote adequate resources to training and development.
- Be prepared for discontinuous change.
- Guard against hubris.
- Create a culture of trust.

Let us look at each lesson in turn to see what Shaka can teach us about effective leadership, whether by positive example or negative.

LESSON 1: DEVELOP A CLEAR AND CONCISE VISION

- Effective leaders see the big picture; they have a 'helicopter view'.
- Effective leaders seize opportunities.
- Effective leaders engage in active dialogue to establish direction and define strategy.
- Effective leaders are farsighted; they focus on the future.
- Effective leaders have the courage and tenacity to defend unpopular decisions.

- Effective leaders enlarge their subjects' horizon.
- Effective leaders know how to simplify complex situations.
- Effective leaders give clear direction and guidance.

King Dingiswayo's rule was a liberal and enlightened one, its fundamental purpose being the creation of a federalist state. It was Dingiswayo's statesmanship, supplemented by Shaka's brutality in warfare, that planted the first seeds of the impressive Zulu empire. When Shaka came to power, he built on his predecessor's vision, concluding that complete centralization was necessary for a truly unified nation. His vision of a future empire called him to destroy the existing tribal organizations and incorporate people from all clans into a single Zulu kingdom – *his* kingdom. He imposed a whole new state superstructure over the confederacy, obliterating the goals, aspirations and power structures of the various chiefdoms. People from many different political entities were now molded into one.

The perfection of the *amabutho* system, combined with the construction of *amakhanda*, created a military infrastructure that supported Shaka's grand scheme of a unified nation. His terror tactics and take-no-prisoners policy toward clans that resisted his war machine proved to be extremely effective: most clans preferred to join his empire voluntarily rather than fight and die. The deal was clear: clans that pledged allegiance to his empire would fall under his protection; in turn they would provide him with new warriors to support his impressive war machine.

In Shaka's vision for the Zulu nation, obedience to authority, respect for law and order, fearlessness, self-sacrifice and civic duty were the order of the day. He spelled this vision out clearly at the outset. Unfortunately, after the consolidation of his rule, his vision faded. Rather than focusing on nation-building, he became distracted by lesser goals. He sent his people out on campaigns not for nation-building but to keep the men occupied and to obtain the cattle he needed to keep his key power-holders satisfied. He became nothing more than a cattle-raider on a grand scale – a pirate on land – leaving chaos in his wake as tribe after tribe tried to escape his war machine. Furthermore in later years he was unable to adapt his vision to changing circumstances. For example he failed to recognize the implications of the arrival of the Europeans on the scene.

LESSON 2: RECOGNIZE THE IMPORTANCE OF STRATEGIC INNOVATION

- Effective leaders always challenge the status quo.
- Effective leaders know the value of innovation.

- Effective leaders know the power of improvisation and surprise.
- Effective leaders are eager to learn new things.

Shaka was a talented strategist and an inspired tactician. From an extremely young age, he challenged the existing conventions of his time. Never afraid to question the status quo or reject old traditions, he enjoyed innovation and adventure. During his tenure in the military and on the throne, he revolutionized the Zulu army's weaponry and military tactics. As noted earlier, it had been the custom for Zulu warriors in battle to throw their spears and retreat. Believing that this method of warfare was both cowardly and inefficient, Shaka developed the stabbing *assegai* and redesigned the Zulu shield, making the latter larger and shaping it so that it could hook the opponent's shield and pull it away, exposing the opponent's body to a thrust from the *assegai*.

Shaka also created several complex battle formations that outflanked and confused his enemies. In the tactical formation known as *impondo zenkomo*, or 'bull's horns' (described in Chapter 2), the attacking Zulus would break into four groups: the two 'horns' would go racing to surround the enemy force, the 'head' (at the center) would advance slowly for the kill, and the 'loins' (sitting with their back to the warring parties so as not to get overexcited) would wait to fill in as reserves as needed. Used in conjunction with the *assegai* and the redesigned shield, this formation gave him an enormous competitive advantage.

Shaka was a master at strategic improvisation and attack by surprise. A great guerilla fighter, he used commando raids and deception to great effect. He typically sent scouts, specially selected for their courage, in advance of the main force. Their task was to trick the enemy into thinking that they made up the main body of soldiers. When that advance group was attacked, the main body of the army would emerge to startle the enemy.

Surprise also applied in the way Shaka dealt with military information. Before battle, he told no one what his exact battle plans were. In later years, when he no longer accompanied his warriors on their campaigns, he entrusted only the commander-in-chief (and perhaps his next in command) with the details of the battle plan. Limiting the dissemination of information lessened the chance that word of the strategy of the expedition would leak out to the enemy.

Shaka's talents at improvisation showed themselves especially clearly in his war against Zwide. He was successful, in spite of overwhelming odds, because he was able to adapt his strategy to the changing situation:

- When Zwide's troops entered his territory, Shaka used a scorched-earth technique to prevent them from obtaining provisions.
- When Zwide's warriors were deep in Zulu territory, Shaka had

volunteers infiltrate the Ndwandwe army after dark. Because both armies spoke the same language and were dressed similarly, it was difficult to tell them apart in the dark. Shaka's men crawled among the sleeping Ndwandwe, pretending to be sleeping themselves, and killed many men under cover of darkness, creating chaos and spreading fear.

- Shaka employed surprise to good advantage at Gqokli Hill. Using the terrain masterfully, he kept part of his fighting force out of sight to encourage carelessness by the enemy.
- Shaka tricked Zwide's commanders into dividing their army into sections. He drove a huge herd of cattle across a ridge, suspecting that the greed of Zwide's generals would overcome their good sense. Sure enough, they sent a portion of the army after the cattle, weakening their force and giving Shaka the advantage he needed.
- After winning the battle, Shaka tricked his opponent once more by appearing at Zwide's royal residence singing the Ndwandwe national war song. The inhabitants let him come closer so that they could cheer their supposed victors. This tactic enabled Shaka's men to approach at very close quarters and massacre the inhabitants.

Shaka has been called the most capable battle commander in southern Africa. He breathed, lived and dreamed of war. Anything having to do with the art of war was of interest to him. During Shaka's interaction with white traders, he appeared to be extremely eager to learn about their methods of warfare. According to Henry Francis Fynn and Nathaniel Isaacs, warfare was the favorite topic of his conversation when they met. He even forced some of the white traders to go on a raid with him so that they could demonstrate their fighting skills. Paradoxically he did not recognize the advantage of using firearms. He felt that the *assegai*, having the advantage of speed over the guns of the day (which required slow and clumsy reloading), was far superior.

Shaka had a great thirst for knowledge generally, not just about warfare. No opportunity was lost to gain new wisdom. That curiosity was sometimes perverted however. As mentioned earlier, when he was studying human anatomy he had pregnant women opened alive to see how the fetus was placed. To assuage his curiosity, he had people's eyes taken out to see how they would adapt to these new circumstances (Stuart, 1979, pp. 161–2).

LESSON 3: KNOW THE COMPETITION

- Effective leaders put a great emphasis on competitive analysis.
- Effective leaders assess the strengths and weaknesses of their opponents.
- Effective leaders invest in good information systems.

Competitive analysis was a major feature of Shaka's strategic model. He was a great believer in military intelligence, seeing it as the first line of a nation's defense. He never went on a campaign before thoroughly assessing his adversary's situation, gathering as much information about strengths and weaknesses as possible. As Nathaniel Isaacs said: 'It is not the Zoolas' [sic] system of warfare to meet their enemy openly, if they can avoid it: they like to conquer by stratagem, and not by fighting; and to gain by a ruse what might be difficult for them to achieve by the spear' (Isaacs, 1836/1970, p. 113).

Believing that one could never know too much about an enemy, Shaka devoted ample resources and energy to information-gathering. He relied on espionage to assess the condition and strength of every tribe that surrounded his nation. In every campaign, he dispatched spies well beforehand to explore the lay of the land and to infiltrate the enemy camp and figure out their plans. He also introduced a sophisticated system of military scouts – brave men who went on missions to locate and evaluate the enemy, and who served as decoys, giving the main army the advantage of surprise.

Shaka made a point of knowing not just each enemy, but also the terrain where that enemy would be met. He knew the value of being more familiar with the battlefield than the adversary, a reconnaissance effort that showed its value in the battle against Zwide. Because of his familiarity with that terrain, Shaka's much smaller army was able to use the geography of Gqokli Hill to their advantage, gaining an astounding victory.

After using his information-gathering system effectively against enemies and battlefields, Shaka turned it against his own people. He used spies to control his subjects and used his personal retainers to monitor the pulse of his kingdom. The king's 'eyes and ears' were everywhere, eager to report on any irregularity. That system of intelligence also helped Shaka in making key appointments and identifying troublemakers. Placing loyal subordinates in key administrative and military positions, he was ready to snuff out any resistance to his regime at an early stage. Furthermore, these key advisors were required to spend time in the capital, serving on the council of the king. That enabled Shaka to keep an eye on them and increased his familiarity with more remote parts of his empire.

LESSON 4: ACT QUICKLY AND DECISIVELY

- Effective leaders know that they are either quick or dead – and they opt for the former.
- Effective leaders demand speedy execution throughout the organization's hierarchy.

Shaka knew well the advantage of speed. When he gave an order, he expected it to be executed immediately. Since the punishment for delay was death, he was rarely disappointed. Given that extreme sanction, his warriors were exceedingly fast. For example his army could move up to 70 kilometers a day, a phenomenal distance in a pre-mechanized age. (As mentioned earlier, Shaka's warriors had little or no baggage while on the move; rather than carrying provisions, they pillaged local kraals.) That speed often granted them the advantage of surprise. When the British fought Shaka's successors in later years, they were astounded by – and dangerously ill-prepared for – their speed of attack.

The military emphasis on speed started while Shaka's warriors were still in training. Young men who could not keep up during long practices or real marches – and did not have a good excuse for falling behind – were instantly killed by the rearguard or executioner.

LESSON 5: EMPOWER SUBORDINATES

- Effective leaders work hard to create commitment within their group or nation.
- Effective leaders minimize secrecy and keep their subjects informed.
- Effective leaders are willing to delegate important tasks.
- Effective leaders create a sense of ownership.
- Effective leaders give people a voice.

Shaka teaches us this lesson not by commission but by omission. Empowerment of subordinates did not fit his Machiavellian vision of government. To Shaka, power was a zero-sum game. With a fixed pie of power, he saw giving to others as having less oneself. Failing to understand that power multiplies in the hands of committed followers, resulting in a bigger pie, he interpreted empowering others as relinquishing personal power and thus kept the levers of power close to his chest.

That is not to say that Shaka did not shift power when it suited his purposes. He was a master politician, skilled not only at protecting his personal power base but also at taking power from others and playing people against each other. For example he broke the power of the hereditary chiefs by executing many, replacing others with loyal commoners, and confiscating the cattle of all. Any local chiefs lucky enough to survive had to share their minimal power with the *izinduna* in charge of the military barracks. All warriors were under the jurisdiction of the military, not of any pre-existing local government.

Although Shaka was good at information-gathering, as we saw earlier, information-sharing was not his forte. On the contrary he believed in the 'mushroom treatment' – that is, keeping his people in the dark. He meted out morsels of information to propagate deception, cause terror and further his goals of internal espionage. Quick to form and shift alliances to his personal advantage, he did not hesitate (with the help of his elaborate spy network) to eliminate potential enemies and undermine incipient rebellion. Nathaniel Isaacs and Henry Francis Fynn commented on the regularity with which Shaka killed his closest advisors.

Shaka's miserly distribution of information out was carefully calculated to increase the flow of information in. As mentioned before, Shaka often gave different key administrators the same assignment without telling either one of the overlap. When they found out that they shared the same task, they were generally so eager to outdo each other that they brought Shaka more information than he would have gained otherwise. This system also allowed Shaka to compare his advisors' diligence in providing information. By engaging in 'fuzzy' delegation – delegation that was ambiguous regarding authority, responsibility and jurisdiction – Shaka kept his advisors on their toes and tricked them into revealing their hand. In keeping with that policy of playing people against each other, he constantly reshuffled the senior posts in his administration, forcing his advisors off balance. Given these strategies, none of his subjects ever got the whole picture and therefore could not plot effectively against him. His Machiavellian style made it extremely difficult for them to unite against him.

Moreover, by taking total control of the most productive part of the workforce – the warriors – through the *amabutho* system, Shaka further reinforced his power base. His use of this system helped in creating a common identity and establishing a special loyalty to the king. Members of the *amabutho* looked to Shaka as the source of patronage and advancement, and in return they helped him break the power of the local chiefs. And because each *ibutho* consisted of people from many different clans, the military system reduced the possibility of rebellious activity within any given clan.

Shaka's achievements on the battlefield, combined with a smoothly functioning system of patronage and an emphasis on law and order, made for a strong initial power base. Later in the regime, the combined force of the bureaucracy, the espionage network and the military created an aura of invincibility that was heightened by Shaka's role as ultimate legal court of appeal and principal representative to the spirit world. He was so formidable in the latter role that he succeeded in neutralizing the role of the *izangomas*, the diviners – the only real threat to his absolute power.

So Shaka had power, and plenty of it. The question is, did he use that power to get the best out of his people? Obviously the answer is no. Although many of the power-hoarding practices described above achieved the goals Shaka set for them, only his policy of selecting military and political leaders based on merit could be described as empowering. All of his other leadership practices were centered on maintaining his personal power base. Was he ineffective? No. Could he have been more effective if he had empowered his people? Most definitely.

LESSON 6: PROMOTE ENTREPRENEURSHIP

- Effective leaders encourage entrepreneurial activity.
- Effective leaders tolerate mistakes.
- Effective leaders recognize the value of due process.

Again, Shaka teaches us by omission. As we saw in the previous lesson, Shaka had no interest in sharing power. Neither did he want to encourage independent thinking. He wanted followers who would brainlessly execute orders, warriors who were well-trained but mindless killing machines. Strategy, tactics and improvisation on the battlefield were his prerogative (and occasionally that of key battle commanders); he wanted no entrepreneurial action from his warriors. Most military leaders would agree that obedience on the battlefield is key, but effective leaders solicit advice and creative solutions from their advisors and subordinates before engagement – and they incorporate that creativity into their battle plans.

Shaka's primary tools in discouraging independent thought were the previously mentioned practices of secrecy and disinformation, along with an intolerance for mistakes. Effective at preventing organized dissension, the first two tools also effectively stifled creative problem-solving. The third tool, intolerance for error, discouraged people from trying to find a better mousetrap. Shaka's followers knew that any violation of rules and procedures could prompt a death sentence, with no fair process or possibility of appeal. True enough, Shaka provided a reason for each gruesome execution he ordered – purportedly the violation of some rule but often only a result of his irritation. Thus what he offered was fair process in form only, not in substance. The resulting climate of fear crushed even the hardiest kernel of creativity.

LESSON 7: ENGAGE IN EFFECTIVE SYMBOL MANIPULATION

- Effective leaders are able to energize and inspire their people to direct them toward specific goals.
- Effective leaders radiate enthusiasm and self-confidence.

- Effective leaders are action-oriented.
- Effective leaders are good at 'impression management'.

Shaka was very effective at 'impression management' – that is, the use and manipulation of symbols, both physical and verbal, to motivate and energize the people. He was for example a master of rhetoric and storytelling, adept at using similes, metaphors and irony. Despite anecdotal evidence of a stuttering problem in childhood, Shaka radiated self-assurance when addressing his people. He couched his message in simple, understandable language, and he used repetition to help that message sink in. He always spoke to his army before battle, using poetic language to fire up his warriors, and he led his men in war dances.

Not only was he a capable orator, he also had a great capacity for dramatization. He liked to mimic the gestures and speech of others, and he was good at composing songs and praises for his people. An expert at singing loudly in public, he also enjoyed performing the songs he wrote. He dramatized his emotions as well. He used rage, for example, to great effect, throwing what could only be called temper tantrums. The hatred that he expressed against his enemies felt so authentic that it was infectious; it persuaded the people of the righteousness of his cause. Shaka also used ceremonies, symbols and settings to dramatic effect. This talent at the management of meaning was a great asset to the nation-building endeavor.

Although many of the official ceremonies and religious invocations that Shaka used were not his creation, he reframed and celebrated these ceremonies on a more imposing scale. He made the most of being the spiritual head of the Zulu kingdom, the ideological high priest. A warring party embarking for battle was happy to receive all the help it could from magic and the gods. The Zulus were helped by their ancestors as well, through help communicated via Shaka's dreams. He made clear to his subjects that his ancestors were continuously in communication with him, telling him what had to be done. Such messages were very convincing to a susceptible audience. When Shaka had to announce a decision or execution that he knew the people would find hard to accept, he simply declared it not to be his, but imposed on him by their ancestors, a fact that made the outcome more palatable. He also announced the ancestors' blessing – again through the medium of dreams – at the start of each military campaign, giving the men a perceived competitive advantage.

The specific rituals that Shaka ordered before a campaign – another form of symbolism – bound the warriors together and instilled in them a sense of invincibility. As both stage manager and performer, Shaka was unsurpassed at boosting an army's fighting spirit. So much so in fact that when a battle started, Shaka's warriors were in a fighting frenzy; if unrestrained, they killed everything that got in their way, including noncombatants and livestock.

Shaka could turn even negative portents into signs of imminent victory, so inspiring was he while campaigning. The Zulus tell of a time when one of his warriors rushed up to tell him that 'one of the men had been bitten by an *iMamba* [one of the most deadly poisonous snakes]. "Bitten by an *iMamba*?" queried Shaka. "Not he. *I* am the (only) *iMamba* who is to bite; and he whom I shall bite is the son of Kondlo [his adversary]"' (Bryant, 1929, p. 198). Another time, when Shaka's army was preparing to do battle against the Ndwandwe, attacking 'in the horns of the morning' (that is, at first light – the favorite Zulu time of attack), a gust of wind blew the prominent crane feather – a symbol of royalty – out of Shaka's headdress. The men saw this as a dreadful omen. 'The army cried out, "We are full of fear! The king's plume has fallen just as he is sending us out to fight."' But before one of his attendants could pick up the feather, Shaka cried out, 'Leave it! There is another that will fall' (Stuart, 1976, p. 284) – in other words, that of his opponent.

In addition to making the most of traditional Zulu religious symbols, Shaka helped create new ones. As noted earlier, he introduced the *inkatha* – the sacred coil of the nation – which symbolized his sovereignty and the unity of the chiefdom. Building on his father's idea of creating an object that would magically protect the Zulus from enemies and misfortune, he took a thick grass coil of around 80 centimeters in diameter and made it potent by adding bodily excretions of his own and his enemies, along with secret medicines. He used the *inkatha* at all great occasions, calling upon his ancestors to protect him and the nation.

A tiny but effective tool of symbol manipulation was Shaka's remarkable ability to remember names and faces. He had an extremely well developed visual memory, and he used it to convince his warriors that he took a personal interest in each of them. Those men who were singled out and recognized, who faced the king and heard him utter their name, were greatly inspired.

LESSON 8: SELECT AND PROMOTE WITH CARE

- Effective leaders choose their key players based on merit.
- Effective leaders select people with 'edge' – that is, people who get things done.
- Effective leaders build on the strengths and weaknesses of their people by creating an executive role constellation.

Shaka paid a great deal of attention to the selection and promotion of his key administrators and officers, though we would not agree with all of his criteria. He wanted go-getters who would get things done, but he also wanted people who would execute his commands unquestioningly. As mentioned earlier, he promoted based on merit rather than nepotism (as was the traditional Zulu practice). This was positive for several reasons. First, the fact that any capable person could reach a high position was good for morale. Second, because appointments to higher office depended on success at the battlefield, men were motivated to high achievement. Third, people in key positions were loyal to Shaka because they knew that it was he, not an accident of heredity, that kept them at their post. Fourth, the selection of outsiders over family members limited the potential danger of insubordination by Shaka's half-brothers, other family members and the various hereditary chiefs. Finally, the practice of incorporating people from different backgrounds into positions of leadership reinforced Shaka's melting-pot strategy. Selecting and promoting based on merit rather than heredity helped him fuse the various clans into a single national identity.

Using this merit-based system, Shaka built a committed team around him – an 'executive role constellation' in which key players built on each other's strengths and compensated for each other's weaknesses (Hodgsdon et al., 1965). Although Shaka was reluctant to delegate in matters of state, and in later years played his advisors against each other, he believed in delegating on the battlefield. He gave his military *izinduna* major roles during battle, though he held tightly to the reins of decision-making and information flow. The extraordinary coordination that this delegation resulted in made for success on the battlefield.

While Shaka may have had a good eye for selection and promotion initially, he lost that edge as time passed. Eventually he was looking to hire not leaders but sycophants. By the end of his regime, moderating counsel was rarely offered (and more rarely heeded). That lack of countervailing powers eroded Shaka's already shaky reality-testing.

LESSON 9: SET A GOOD EXAMPLE

- Effective leaders lead by example; they are strong role models.
- Effective leaders back their words with action.

When Shaka was first a military leader, he did not take advantage of his position. He led by example, serving as an important role model. He made an effort to interact with all layers of his military organization. He lived his warriors' life – ate the same food, endured training and fought beside them. Because he knew what it meant to be a warrior, because he 'walked the talk', the men could identify with him. Even after he had attained kingship and power, he could still be found at the front in both training and battle, could still be seen personally assessing the enemy force and checking the reports of his scouts and spies for consistency. Eventually though, as we have seen, his preoccupation with internal enemies kept him from leading the army into battle himself.

Henry Francis Fynn gives a striking example of Shaka's leadership as the army returned home from the front. Concerned that they would lose both herdboys and livestock as they drove their captured cattle through a river, Shaka personally saw to their safety:

> On our crossing the Umzimkhulu, where the tide was high, many little boys would have been carried down with the stream. Shaka, foreseeing this, plunged into the river, with only his head-dress on, and remained one and a half hours in the water, giving the boys to the care of the men, who otherwise would have left them to their fate, and collecting the calves, which were nearly drowned, ordering fires to be made to assist in their recovery. (Fynn, 1833/1950, p. 151)

LESSON 10: HOLD PEOPLE ACCOUNTABLE

- Effective leaders set clear performance standards.
- Effective leaders hold their people to commitments and deadlines.
- Effective leaders build alignment between values, attitudes and behaviors on the one hand, and systems on the other.

Under Shaka, people were held accountable to an unprecedented extreme. The Zulu leader spelled out clearly what he expected from his subjects – respect for the basic cultural values of his new nation, particularly as defined in the *amabutho* – and he demanded compliance. As military leader and king, he was astutely aware of the fact that the devil is in the detail. He subscribed to the philosophy that what is not measured does not get done, so he was explicit in his demands and vigilant in his enforcement. And every citizen of the land was fully aware of the high price of disobedience. He made sure that this deadly message came across wherever he went, his executioners (who at a nod of his head would break necks or crush skulls) following directly behind him. Accountability taken to this extreme results in a culture not of responsibility but of blame.

Shaka's devotion to accountability was nowhere more evident than on the battlefield. He began by setting the bar for accomplishment high. Frequently, before battle a few favored *amabutho* (groups of nearly the same age and number) were invited by Shaka to visit the royal cattle enclosure. In a ceremony known as *giya*, which continued until sunset, selected warriors performed athletic feats and challenged warriors of the rival *amabutho* to better them. In a tradition Shaka introduced known as *ukuxoxa impi*, or discussing battle, individual warriors praised themselves, recounting stories of their exploits while singing and dancing. Other warriors then built on the dancer's praises, a dialogue that served as a great morale booster. Shaka would join in periodically, sometimes daring the men to certain specific accomplishments during battle. These *izibongo*, or praise songs, were the Zulu equivalent of medals. The objective of this day-long exercise was to encourage great acts of bravery during battle. When things got tough on the battlefield, commanders would remind their men of the promises made during the *giya* ceremony.

Having established beforehand (in part through the *giya* ceremony) his expectations for battle, Shaka then later, after each battle, discussed with his generals the performance of each regiment while the warriors were assembled on the main parade ground. Regiments that had challenged each other in *giya* were scrutinized, their challenges recalled and their performance assessed. The chief of each regiment was then asked to pick out the cowards, who were treated with the greatest contempt by leadership and peers alike, publicly humiliated, and executed. The warriors present at assembly listened to Shaka's words, 'Pick out the cowards', with trepidation (Stuart, 1982, p. 87). One eyewitness recounts:

> On coming back from this campaign … he said that the cowards should be picked out. The cowards were then separated. After this their left arms were held up, and they were stabbed under the armpits like goats, Shaka saying 'Let them feel the assegai!' They were then stabbed. These men would then be killed as if they were cattle. (Knight, 1994, p. 25)

The chosen candidates for execution were those warriors whose spears had been captured by the enemy, those who had thrown away their spears, and those who had wounds in their backs (a supposed sign of cowardice); all these warriors were exposed to the wrath of the king. Henry Francis Fynn tells of one regiment that had been beaten by the adversary. All the warriors who fled and returned home were put to death (Fynn, 1833/1950, p. 129). Many such cowardice killings occurred in full view of the regiments. According to an informant:

> They would be picked and a semi-circle formed. They would be put inside and [made to] stand up. They would then be given assegais and told to stab one another. They would fight two at a time, and even if a man won two or three times, i.e. killing his man, he would himself presently fail and be killed, or he would be put to death by order of the king if he were the only one remaining. (Stuart, 1982, p. 87)

In Shaka's opinion, such executions stiffened his warriors' resolve in battle. They were a warning that people needed to give their best. The execution site known as the 'Coward's Bush,' mentioned in Chapter 3, was a stark reminder of what would happen to people who failed to deliver. Zulu warriors had two choices: to be massacred by the enemy or, if accused of cowardice, to be massacred by Shaka.

Over time, however, this system of selecting cowards, always cruel, became perverted. Shaka was of the opinion that there would always be cowards in battle, always be warriors who did not give their best effort. Thus he expected a quota of cowards to be killed after each battle. Commanders who knew of no cowards had to invent them to please Shaka. No doubt much injustice was done in this manner.

LESSON 11: REWARD PEOPLE FAIRLY

- Effective leaders make sure that outstanding performance is rewarded.
- Effective leaders use various types of incentives to reward their people.
- Effective leaders ensure the fairness of all incentives, sanctions and rewards.
- Effective leaders give effective, constructive feedback in an ongoing manner.
- Effective leaders celebrate achievements.

Just as Shaka supervised the execution of cowards after battle, he personally attended to the handing out of rewards after each campaign. Those regiments that had demonstrated excellence in battle were rewarded with cattle. Shaka even distributed cattle to the kin of warriors who had distinguished themselves in battle but died, an unheard of gesture. He promoted a select few to the *induna* position, a step in a chain of promotion that could lead to the command of an *ibutho*.

Any cattle taken in battle were considered to be the property of the nation, as noted earlier, but Shaka (especially in the early days) was generous in sharing the spoils of victory. Even when as a young officer under Dingiswayo he was given cattle for his valor on the battlefield, he shared the spoils with his men, an unusually generous gesture. As king, he continued to be generous to those whom he favored.

Shaka also distributed *iziQu*, necklaces made of interlocking wooden beads, to warriors whose regiment had particularly distinguished itself in battle. These ornaments were extremely valued, largely because the king awarded them personally. In his later years he also gave European trade goods such as beads. The most valuable present Shaka could give, however, was an *isigodlo* girl from his harem.

Even when there was no tangible reward, Shaka offered his men constructive feedback. Especially when he was just starting to build his nation, he walked the battlelines chatting with his soldiers before combat. He pleased them by remembering their names and recalling their brave deeds during previous battles. This public praise had an extremely positive motivating effect. When the battle started, Shaka often asked for volunteers eager to distinguish themselves, offering rewards to those who survived.

LESSON 12: DEVOTE ADEQUATE RESOURCES TO TRAINING AND DEVELOPMENT

- Effective leaders recognize the value of training and development.
- Effective leaders spend time coaching and mentoring their people.
- Effective leaders use training programs to build collaborative relationships among their followers.
- Effective leaders create a unifying organizational culture.
- Effective leaders ensure that their people put the interests of the group above their personal interests.

As we have seen, Shaka was a strong believer in the intensive training of his warriors. The success of the Zulu army can be attributed in large part to that iron discipline. From the moment the adolescent boys moved into an *ibutho*, they were involved in daily drills. People who observed Shaka's warriors at close quarters (including the British adversaries in the post-Shaka days) marveled at their discipline on parade and in battle. Seeing them in action was like watching a well-synchronized ballet. The men were an awesome sight.

Shaka accomplished more than just skill acquisition in this training. He turned his men into killing machines, so indoctrinating them in violence that they learned to slaughter people as they would slaughter their cattle; but he also created unified regiments out of amorphous groups. Binding individuals into an *ibutho* and binding the *amabutho* into an army, he created a unifying organizational culture centered around war. In a process of total indoctrination that hardened his warriors against any adversity or adversary, he conveyed the clear message that physical bravery on the battlefield was the only thing that mattered. He socialized his warriors so thoroughly that they waited with joyful anticipation the moment when they could 'wash their spears' in blood. They needed combat to attain self-affirmation, admiration and a sense of identity.

Through the *amabutho* system, Shaka molded groups of individuals into high-performance teams. He went to great lengths to make sure that his warriors put the interests of the group above their personal interests. Zulu warriors of the past had been experts with the spears, but they worked individually. Now Shaka wanted seamlessly coordinated units trained to act in concert, collaborating as they executed synchronized maneuvers such as the 'bull's horns.' Thus in perfecting his war machine he became a master team-builder.

Training happened even when the men of the *amabutho* were at leisure. As has been indicated, Shaka enjoyed composing songs and dances for his regiments to perform. These songs and dances were more than whimsical entertainment however. Executed with extreme precision, they were part of the military training effort. By dancing together, the warriors learned to move in precise formation and to perform specific tasks at exact moments; they learned to react quickly to difficult commands. Shaka also used hunting as a way to accomplish military preparedness and keep his warriors in fighting shape.

LESSON 13: BE PREPARED FOR DISCONTINUOUS CHANGE

- Effective leaders are open to change.
- Effective leaders are able to handle continuous as well as discontinuous change.

Although Shaka initially was very open to change, prepared to adapt to changing circumstances and embrace new ideas, this outlook evolved over time. After his early military innovations, he failed to adapt his fighting strategy and became stuck in a time warp. Though in one account of his final words he prophesied the ruling of the 'swallows' (or whites), he did not grasp the impact the Europeans would have on the landscape of southern Africa or understand the ramifications of the developments at Delagoa Bay and in the southern Cape region. To the detriment of the consolidation of his empire, he could deal with continuous change, but not with discontinuous change.

Shaka eventually acquired guns (as did later Zulu leaders), but he never understood their potential or learned how to use them effectively. The confidence he felt in his warriors and their method of warfare kept him from seriously considering alternative approaches. He continued to believe that an energetic Zulu charge could overpower any group of men with firearms. Unable to look ahead and anticipate improvements in the relatively primitive firearms that he was familiar with, he laid no groundwork for defense against canons and machine guns. The Zulus' *élan vitale* – the burst of energy that they demonstrated in fighting – was eventually outgunned, as later battles led by his successors would demonstrate.

LESSON 14: GUARD AGAINST HUBRIS

- Effective leaders support good corporate governance through a system of checks and balances.
- Effective leaders actively seek out feedback about their leadership style.
- Effective leaders use constructive feedback to improve themselves.
- Effective leaders learn from their mistakes.
- Effective leaders recognize the power of humility.

In the political landscape of nineteenth-century Africa, Shaka Zulu, with his despotic totalitarian leadership, was an exception. Many of the African chiefs behaved more like constitutional monarchs, with considerable checks on their power. Some were merely figureheads, deferring on most things to their council of advisors. Most chiefs, however, were found somewhere in the middle. Most had to consider and act in accordance with the wishes and expectations of their people.

In abolishing the traditional, participative decision-making process in not having effective organizational governance, Shaka lost the benefit of the wisdom of the clan's elders, formerly the keepers of custom and law. He all but forbade feedback from the very people who were best equipped to advise him, ridiculing and even killing men past their fighting prime. He discouraged feedback from others as well. By his design, his entourage answered only to him, and those subordinate chiefs, generals and ministers soon learned that what their leader really wanted was not answers (and certainly not contrarian thinking), but praise, praise and more praise. When true feedback disappeared, Shaka lost touch with reality and no longer learned from his mistakes.

King Dingiswayo, while he was alive, was willing and able to give Shaka feedback. As mentor he had a balancing influence on the impetuous young man. After Dingiswayo's death, however, the picture changed. As Shaka consolidated his power, also breaking the influence of the *izangoma* in the process, he did away with everyone willing to really challenge him. Eventually only his mother was able to exert any moral influence on him. Near the end of his life, his entourage – totally cowed by Shaka's use of terror – would tell him only what they thought he wanted to hear. The messenger had been killed too often. And yet, as history has shown repeatedly, leaders who fail to take account of the people and their wishes – who have no effective corporate governance in place – find themselves in serious trouble. With no checks and balances, their paranoia, grandiosity and sadistic behavior have a free hand, with dire consequences for themselves and their people.

The pride that every leader should feel in a job well done became exaggerated in Shaka: the confidence that developed as he grew into adolescence ballooned into unfettered hubris – the quicksand of leadership effectiveness. Enjoying the perks of power, he could not see that hubris and wisdom cannot coexist. Lacking a grasp of history, he did not know that truly great leaders possess a sense of humility. Fearing his own humanity and vulnerability, he could not understand that leaders who stoop venture into greatness, while leaders who soar burn their wings against the sun.

LESSON 15: CREATE A CULTURE OF TRUST

- Effective leaders generate trust.
- Effective leaders show respect for and interest in their people.
- Effective leaders welcome disagreement.
- Effective leaders work to dispel fear.

If we had to single out the one lesson on leadership that Shaka teaches best, it would be this one, although it is another that he teaches by omission. Just as light objects are more clearly seen against a dark background, we learn the need for trust from the Zulu culture's total lack of trust. We have seen again and again that Shaka demanded total, unquestioning obedience. Discipline started with complete submission to parental authority and culminated in total obedience to the king. Respect for 'those above' was an essential part of the Zulu socialization process. The fact that ordinary people were called 'the king's dogs' says it all. All rituals, tales, songs, gestures, hopes and fears that made up the culture of the royal kraal reinforced this pattern of subordination and obedience.

In the same way that Shaka encouraged his men to dehumanize the enemy, he dehumanized his men. He meted out punishments not out of concern for the individual or even the state, but out of pathology. When he held 'performance appraisal' sessions after battles to identify the heroes and cowards, he was not respecting individuals, even if he took the trouble to remember names and deeds. After all, if no cowards were identified, he demanded that victims be produced anyway.

The terror on which Shaka relied for his power – terror that would produce victims for victims' sake – destroyed not only trust in leadership but trust in humanity. Zulu citizens knew that the killing machine had to be fed and that they could increase their own chances of escaping it if they offered up a victim or two themselves. Who could trust his neighbor in that climate?

When trust is dead, so is the humanity that makes people different from animals. The spark of creativity that distinguishes our species is extinguished by despotism. Many failed human experiments have taught us that there is an inverse relationship between totalitarianism and creativity or entrepreneurship. As we noted in an earlier lesson ('Promote entrepreneurship'), a culture of despotism cannot get the best out of people because it does not allow creativity to flourish. Robot-like behavior replaces improvisation in a culture where people live in perpetual fear, where 'yea-sayers' prevail, where there is no constructive dialogue, and where reality-testing fails (Kets de Vries and Miller, 1984). Although a terror-based leadership style offers the despot short-term gains, in the long run it results in ritualistic, static behavior. It froze the Zulu nation in a time warp and precipitated its decline.

CONCLUDING COMMENTS

All leaders have both strengths and weaknesses. The above lessons on leadership, drawn from Shaka's tenure as Zulu king, show us how permeable the border is between the two: weaknesses can be turned into strengths, and strengths can corrode into weaknesses. The anger that Shaka felt as a youngster for example hardened into admirable discipline, while the pride that helped him endure childhood torments eventually grew into hubris, blinding him to the worth and humanity of others. Shaka was not the final despot, nor will today's tyrannical leaders end the chain. Despotism will flourish, off and on, until followers learn the preceding lessons on leadership and demand that their leaders master them too.

PART IV

Deconstructing Totalitarianism

11.   A throne of blood: deploying the tools of tyranny

A tyrannical sultan is better than constant anarchy.
(Egyptian proverb)

Any excuse will serve a tyrant.
(Aesop, *Aesop's Fables*)

I have almost forgot the taste of fears.
The time has been my senses would have cooled
To hear a night-shriek, and my fell of hair
Would at a dismal treatise rouse and stir
As life were in't. I have supped full with horrors;
Direness, familiar to my slaughterous thoughts,
Cannot once start me.
(William Shakespeare, *Macbeth*)

Twixt Kings and Tyrants there's this difference known;
Kings seek their Subjects' good: Tyrants their owne.
(Robert Herrick, *Kings and Tyrants*)

A tyrant ... is always stirring up some war or other, in order that the people may require a leader.
(Plato, *The Republic*)

Where laws end, tyranny begins.
(William Pitt the elder, speech, House of Lords)

[W]e are apt to forget that the vast majority of men and women who fell under the totalitarian spell was activated by unselfish motives, ready to accept the role of martyr or executioner, as the cause demanded.
(Arthur Koestler, *The Invisible Writing*)

It takes two to make a murder. There are born victims, born to have their throats cut.
(Aldous Huxley, *Point Counterpoint*)

A profile of Shaka has emerged from the preceding chapters. He was an extraordinary individual – no question there. A complex man capable of feelings of affection and tenderness, he attained renown because of his brutality. His pride in self and nation, his rhetorical ability, and his skills at

161

influence, manipulation and intimidation made him an unprecedented leader. As a martial genius and strategist he had no peer in southern Africa. He created a powerful nation with a populace distinguished by submission to authority, obedience to the law, self-restraint, preparedness for hard work, engagement in civic duty, fearlessness and self-sacrifice. Abandoning the traditional agricultural economy, he brought into being an economic model built solely on military conquest.

The choices that Shaka made in harnessing both creative and destructive forces were the logical outcome of his personality. In his kingship – more particularly, in his reliance on terror – Shaka found a solution to his existential problems. Just as violence determined his identity, so it determined his interpersonal and leadership styles. Because killing permeated his being, killing was his main tool in nation-building. Thus Shaka's peculiar way of creating the Zulu nation can be seen (to be somewhat reductionistic) as a projection of his individual psychopathology. He transformed his own lethal addiction – killing, the inhumanity of war – into a heroic ideal in the minds of his people. He presented widespread killing in such a way that it offered purpose and meaning to his subjects. His attempts at cure and recovery determined his country's destiny.

Shaka's persecutory paranoid state, his megalomania, his antisocial behavior and his sadistic predisposition lent themselves well to the cultural system of his time. This psychologically wounded man used these personality traits to deal with the vicissitudes of the world as he knew it, simultaneously doing good and wreaking havoc. This pattern is not unique. Many recent tyrants sprang from similar insecure backgrounds. Well-known despots such as Joseph Stalin, Adolf Hitler, Benito Mussolini, Mao Zedong, Saddam Hussein and Slobodan Milosevic all experienced serious hardships while growing up. Most were exposed to violent or detrimental treatment: teasing by other children, beatings or even sexual abuse. All of them grew up distrustful of others and were fascinated by destructive pursuits, both in fantasy and reality. All of them rebelled against their fathers or substitute fathers. All of them ended up loners, 'outsiders' to the social system they would come to dominate. And all of them presented and acted out their personal problems for a larger audience. As leaders they saw an opportunity to master the demons of their internal world by externalizing those demons on a public stage. In that attempt at mastery, they reshaped the world of their contemporaries.

Not – as has been said before – that there will be a direct causal effect between traumatic childhood experiences and psychopathology. There will be a number of mediating factors that can ameliorate what happens as the child passes through maturational sequences.

This is not to say that traumatic childhood experiences inevitably result in psychopathology. Human development is a complex interface of genetic predisposition, birth order, family status, the history of a child's successes and failures, serendipity – and, for the unfortunate few, trauma. Development follows an innate timetable that determines successive maturational sequences depending on the above-named factors.

But in Shaka's case, childhood trauma did lead to psychopathology. And like many tyrants before and after him, Shaka transferred that trauma to his people, inducing into the populace regressive behavior patterns that led to subjective dependency. The result was a vicious circle of projected aggression and a good-versus-evil Manichean worldview (along with other archaic individual and group processes discussed in earlier chapters). A loose confederation of clans became a violent state colossus (with Shaka at its center) that fed on the bodies of external and internal enemies.

In consolidating his power, Shaka used the tactics of terror and divide-and-conquer to manipulate and intimidate all other potential power-holders. He was the paramount ruler; he was the law; he was, as religious leader, the chief ideologist, the keeper of the cultural flame. He echoed, in deed if not voice, the statement of Louis XIV, the French sun king: 'L'état c'est moi' ('The state, that is me'). As time passed, human life meant less and less under the reign of Shaka. Executions eventually drove the state apparatus and maintained order in the empire. As the Zulu nation consumed its own people, the threat of being singled out for execution followed each of Shaka's subjects like an inseparable shadow. This threat was the only democracy the Zulus would know: it touched everyone, leaving no one exempt.

Having destroyed the original Zulu culture and ripped to shreds the moral fabric of Zulu society, Shaka was eventually brought down by the same terror that built him up. He learned the lesson of all tyrants: the limits of tyranny are determined by the endurance of the victims they suppress. Tyrants can push their people only so far. At some point – finally, after deaths in the thousands or millions – every regime of terror becomes so ineffective that assassination is the only logical outcome.

SORCERER'S APPRENTICES

According to Niccolò Machiavelli, any creator of a new nation has to act like a tyrant for a while (Machiavelli, 1966). Machiavelli viewed the adoption of the despot's role as a natural phase in nation-building – one that would of necessity last until the nation-builder had achieved his or her primary goals. While Shaka took on the role of tyrant without hesitation, he failed to temper his violence or modify his rule by terror after he had consolidated his power base. Because of that intemperance, the Zulu kingdom never became a society based on the rule of law, and the populace never had a say in how that rule of law should be applied. Unable to make the transition that Machiavelli believed possible, Shaka – like the mythical sorcerer's apprentice – unleashed powers that he ultimately could not control.

Why is it that some societies can pass through an initial despotic phase into freedom (if, in fact, Machiavelli was right), while others become mired in despotism? What creates fertile ground for the cultivation of despotism? How does the process of despotic rule evolve?

From Alienation to Belonging

In general, despots are leaders who take personal advantage of a chaotic situation. As noted earlier, they tend to flourish in societies in transition. If we review history, we see that the greatest despots have emerged in situations of war or class war. Consider Germany after the First World War, dealing with a sense of national humiliation and a class struggle verging on civil war. Consider China, still haunted by the affront of Western powers intruding in their sovereignty, a process that started in the nineteenth century. The lingering presence of the memory of such indignities is typical of the world's breeding grounds for tyranny. Societies in which democratic traditions and institutions are still lacking or are poorly developed, societies with weak political systems and/or an ineffective judiciary, and societies in severe economic distress are especially vulnerable. These social conditions, especially occurring together, facilitate a power grab by a power-hungry despot. They allow such a leader, generally with the help of a gangster-like regime, to exploit the lack of organization, alienation and bewilderment of the citizenry.

Notwithstanding the twentieth century's much-vaunted progress in the scientific and economic realms, that period witnessed the rise of some of the most brutal and oppressive regimes in the history of humankind. Nations just emerging from colonial or communist rule seemed to be particularly vulnerable. Such nations have had institutions imposed on them – institutions not rooted in their original culture – making them susceptible to despotism. Many such examples can be seen in the history of Africa, Asia and the Middle East. The proliferation of recent, new dictatorships in countries formerly belonging to the Soviet Union also suggests this vulnerability.

When formerly colonial or communist countries become independent, people generally have sky-high expectations about the future. These expectations are followed by deep disappointment once the gap is seen between hope and harsh reality. Deep contrasts between wealth and haunting poverty, both within nations and between nations, and the prevalence of corruption that is made more visible through the media, add to this state of discontent.

All of the above social conditions create alienation within a society, and that alienation paves the way for tyranny. When social institutions disintegrate, when there is little to hold on to, people are more willing to subject themselves to despotic regimes. They are more inclined to search for messiahs who promise economic and political salvation from the hardships the population is experiencing. Those individuals who are insecure and lonely are looking for a safe harbor, searching for the 'containment' that they hope a strong leader offers; they are looking for a 'holding environment' that will contain their existential anxiety and deal with their sense of alienation, dislocation and aloneness. They can find all those things in one mass movement or another. Mass movements, whatever their ideology, typically offer solidarity, an end to loneliness and anxiety, and hope for a better future.

In Praise of Tyranny

Let us return for a moment to Machiavelli's view, shared by many political scientists, that dictatorship is a transitional phase that many countries have to go through on their way to democracy. Those who support that view argue that non-democratic political configurations do not deserve the harsh condemnation they receive from democratic idealists. Like it or not, they remonstrate, simplistic Western political formulas do not suit certain societies at an early stage of development. Given the mindset of the people in these developing societies, democratic structures would turn out to be highly ineffective – worse, in the end, than a transitional tyranny. The people in these societies are simply not ready to deal with the freedom that democracy not only offers, but demands.

Proponents of Machiavelli's position, while acknowledging the darker side of dictatorship, are quick to point out the advantages of being ruled by an autocratic government. Although despots repress their citizens, they may also (as we saw in the case of Shaka) protect the population from outside dangers, reknit a society torn apart by violent upheaval, put an end to internal strife, introduce law and order, and eradicate certain forms of corruption. Some despots even create a new prosperity (or at least the illusion of prosperity) by embarking on great public works and by providing such services as schools, housing, hospitals and roads.

What these Machiavellian proponents fail to acknowledge is the likelihood – the all-but-certainty – that autocratic leadership will become all-out tyranny. Positive contributions notwithstanding, the shadow side of power-based leadership almost inevitably comes to the fore. As time passes, most leaders with despotic tendencies increasingly feel entitled to do whatever they want, however inappropriate their behavior may be. Most of them sink into a narcissistic 'soup', believing without question that societal boundaries of acceptable behavior no longer apply to them. As excessive narcissism raises its ugly head, feelings of entitlement sway behavior. Gradually, the perks and privileges appropriated by the ruling elite become increasingly glaring. The leader and his henchmen engage in regressive activities, the arbitrary use of power, the grabbing of scarce resources, the repression of free will and the violation of human rights, all of which mean misery for the populace and decline for the economy.

While dictatorships are one-way streets, democracies are two-way streets: in the latter, the people have a voice. That does not mean that democracy is perfect. Life in freedom is not always easy. After all, having choices implies having responsibilities. Moreover democratic decision-making can be cumbersome and slow. Democratic leaders are often unwilling to bite the bullet and make unpopular but necessary decisions, because they are concerned more about being re-elected than about the good of the country. Furthermore compromise and coalition politics do not always lead to the best outcome. The latter for example sometimes results in a paradox of voting whereby the least attractive candidate wins the election.

And yet the alternative to democracy is not really an option. While benevolent autocracy is a theoretical possibility, rule by a solitary leader typically ends in servile obedience to authority and abuse of human rights. In contrast, democracy (though flawed) safeguards human dignity, protects individual freedoms, assures free choice and gives people a voice in decisions that affect their destiny, allowing them to work for a better future for their children. Humankind's desire for justice and fair play makes democracy possible. Humankind's capacity for *in*justice makes democracy necessary. Given the shadow side of human behavior, we need democracy, with its many checks and balances on power, such as the judiciary, varied political parties, independent administrative bodies, a free press and a comprehensive legal system. These elements help prevent leadership and followers alike from falling into a regressive abyss; they serve as boundaries against humankind's excesses.

But a political system that grants fairness to all should never be taken for granted. Given the ever-present potential for individual and societal regression, democratic practices must be continuously defended. As noted earlier, *we all have a Shaka Zulu in the attic*. We all have a darker side, a violent streak ready to erupt as circumstances dictate. Shaka is not just a quaint illustration of perverted leadership of bygone years. He is a reminder of what every leader, every individual, can become.

Like Shaka, modern tyrants hang on to ideologies whose dogma they interpret according to their own needs, not the needs of their people. They resort to repressive measures. They engage in demagoguery. They oppress their people, depriving them of freedom and hope. They prevent their people from developing their capabilities to their fullest potential. They taint their rule with fear, misery, degradation, and poverty. Like Shaka, they create an outwardly passive, subjugated populace dead to critical inquiry. And like Shaka, they eventually eat their own.

The Enchantment of Ideology

Beyond the obvious tool of violence, what do tyrants use to remain in power? What levers of action do they pull? The answer varies, depending on the society and its circumstances, but the strongest weapon of the despotic regime is ideology. In most totalitarian states, virtue and evil – the forces of light and of darkness – become bound into the state ideology, which presents the pursuit of virtue as a universally accepted ideal. Ironically, in the process of universalizing that pursuit, despotism destroys the moral fabric of a society. To use Robert Jay Lifton's words:

> [I]deological totalism does even greater violence to the human potential: it evokes destructive emotions, produces intellectual and psychological restrictions, and deprives men of all that is most subtle and imaginative – under the false promise of eliminating those very imperfections and ambivalences which help to define the human condition. This combination of personal closure, self-destructiveness, and hostility toward outsiders leads to the dangerous group excesses so characteristic of ideological totalism in any form. It also mobilizes extremist tendencies in those outsiders under attack, thus creating a vicious circle of totalism. ...
>
> Behind ideological totalism lies the ever-present human quest for the omnipotent guide – for the supernatural force, political party, philosophical ideas, great leader, or precise science – that will bring ultimate solidarity to all men and eliminate the terror of death and nothingness. (Lifton, 1961, p. 436)

Frequently the leaders of such totalitarian states create huge bureaucratic machines to institutionalize their allegedly virtue-based worldview. The existence of such institutions goes a long way toward creating a submissive, obedient populace that reiterates the party's propaganda. As Hannah Arendt observed, however, the degree of intrusion by despotic leadership can vary. She distinguishes between totalitarian domination and less extreme forms of 'mere' tyranny or dictatorship:

> The decisive difference between totalitarian domination, based on terror, and the tyrannies and dictatorships, is that the former turns not only against enemies but against its friends and supporters as well, being afraid of all power, even the power of its friends. The climax of terror is reached when the police state begins to devour its own children, when yesterday's executioner becomes today's victim. (Arendt, 1969, p. 55)

To Arendt, totalitarianism implies an ideology with supreme values – a political religion, if you will, that replaces traditional religion. That ideology claims to have the answer to all important social and historical dilemmas. Frequently the promise is a laudable, utopian-like solution to the human condition, but the ideological goals of totalitarian systems vary. While the Soviet Union under Stalin and the People's Republic of China under Mao Zedong sought the universal fulfillment of humankind through the establishment of a classless society, Germany under Hitler's National Socialism attempted to establish a Thousand-Year Reich based on the superiority of the so-called Aryan race.

As has been noted, the urge to surrender to some form of idealistic belief system is most prominent in fragmented, divided societies plagued by stress and uncertainty. Although what the outside world sees of despotism is the merciless leader, the belief system that supports him is often in place before he steps up to take the reins. Alienated and frustrated intellectuals and/or theocrats in such a society are often the ones who first develop and speak of a particular vision of utopian society. They typically establish a pseudo-scientific or extremist religious base for their theories, thereby undergirding their 'formula' for the perfect society. Through their convoluted ideology, they offer a form of 'salvation' to a select group of true believers – those who are chosen to attain the 'promised land'.

These ideologists paint a stark world of good and evil, truth and falsehood, and stake an absolute claim on the former. As a test that will determine their entry into the 'promised land', followers are challenged to overcome a number of obstacles posed by 'nonbelievers'. These opponents, as we saw earlier, are depicted at best as evildoers, at worst as 'sub-humans'. The ideologists encourage their followers to fight these 'evil' adversaries with whatever force is necessary. As time evolves and the group of followers grows, a political party (either established or new) embraces the ideology, with believers unquestioningly parroting its tenets. And out of that party emerges the leader, the 'high priest', who will turn vision into tyranny.

Leaders of ideology-based totalitarian states will do anything to win new converts. They want to spread their creed – but only to people 'worthy' of conversion, of course. They are convinced that sharing their ideology, whether secular or theocratic, will bring enlightenment to the masses. There is a sect-like intensity to this need to convert others: the fragility of the ideology demands constant validation from others, to bolster faith in the worldview, create solidarity and reinforce the righteousness of the cause. In contrast, people who resist conversion threaten the ideology and make the converted uncomfortable. They remind true believers of the shakiness of their belief system, often triggering anger and violence.

Whichever party adopts the totalitarian ideology generally attempts to give the appearance of propriety. For example it typically makes participation in politics, especially voting, compulsory. As we all know, though, in totalitarianism the right to vote does not mean the right to choose. The only real choice is the party and the party's leader. The lack of choice is enforced through political repression. The ruling party and its leader restrict the rights of citizens to criticize the government, the rights of opposition parties to campaign against the government, and the rights of certain groups, associations and political parties to convene (or even exist). They try to shape the thoughts of their subjects through control of educational institutions and the media. In fact they seek to dominate all economic and political matters, including the attitudes, values and beliefs of the population, thereby erasing the distinction between state and society. The citizen's duty to the state is thus the primary concern of the community, and the goal of the state is the replacement of existing society with the utopian society depicted by the favored ideology.

Despotism's total control over the armed forces and the police help ensure survival of the regime's ideology. Typically, a terrorist-type police force and omnipresent informers monitor and enforce the despotic leader's monopolistic control over the economy and the media. These military institutions are used to terrify the populace, ensuring that the people toe the party line – whatever prevailing theological or ideological belief system defines itself as the embodiment of goodness and light. We have all heard how the Gestapo and the SS in Hitler's Germany, the NKVD in Stalin's Soviet Russia and the Khmer Rouge in Pol Pot's Cambodia used terror to paralyze the populace. People who protested the limits to freedom imposed by these regimes were threatened, tortured, interned in concentration camps and/or executed. The Ministry of Intelligence and Security, the Ministry of Interior and the Revolutionary Guards in Iran have used similar tactics to shore up an unpopular theocratic regime; and in Iraq when Saddam was still in power, his elite forces – his Special Republican Guards – maintained an iron grip over the population.

Distorted mass communication is a hallmark of any despotic, totalitarian regime, propagating the prevailing utopian goals and official ideologies through thought-control. Ideological propaganda and morality-education permeate such regimes. While in ancient societies the indoctrination by despots was rather crude, contemporary totalitarian leaders use modern propaganda techniques to brainwash their subjects into the 'right' way of thinking, forcing a mendacious ideology down their subjects' throat. In today's totalitarian states, information flowing from the party is severely censored, with distorted discourse and 'news-speak' sanitizing corruption and abhorrent acts. Absolutely no honest, open debate is permitted; any moral or spiritual authority independent of the leader or contrary to party doctrine is prohibited. Rote memorization of the party line is encouraged, and people who engage in critical inquiry or speak out against the party line are arrested or worse. Ideological jargon and magical celebrations replace open discussion as the party and its leader engage in verbal acrobatics to hide the reality of the situation.

The Illusion of Solidarity

Another important element that fosters the continuation of tyranny is the isolation that despots enforce. The very idea of totalitarianism implies the breaking of lateral relationships between individuals – the original sense of community – in favor of strong ties to the state. This dissolution of the original ties between people creates helplessness, dependency and loneliness. There are those familiar words again – the very traits that encourage people to look for a savior and to hope for salvation. It is a vicious circle: helplessness breeds a need for strong leadership, and excessive leadership breeds helplessness.

Despots understand intuitively the psychological vulnerability of humans. They are aware that people are more easily manipulated when they feel isolated and powerless. Lacking reference points, lacking other people to exchange opinions with, isolated individuals gradually lose their common sense and their ability to think independently. Regressing to a state of passivity, they become increasingly helpless. And in that dependent state, they are open to a salvific ideology and a leader apparently endowed with superhuman, omniscient, omnipotent qualities – qualities touted by the state propaganda department. In the person of the leader, the power of the state, the people and the ideological movement become unified.

Thus tyrants look for ways to keep their subjects isolated. They go to great lengths to break up traditional relationship patterns. Further, they prohibit all associations between citizenry that could lead to free debate, knowing that the loss of 'voice', the inability to speak one's mind and talk with others who cherish similar 'apostate' ideas, enhances feelings of isolation. To ensure that the populace cannot coordinate any form of political opposition, tyrants suppress or destroy all organizations and individuals that espouse views diverging from the main secular or theocratic ideology. To that end they rely on an elaborate network of spies and informers (many of whom are happy to turn in friends and associates in the hope of saving themselves), and they use police terror to prevent lateral communication.

Having destroyed existing relationship patterns, tyrants can then transform their fragmented society so that it better achieves their purpose. They do so by replacing connectedness with magical thinking, human intimacy with the pursuit of an illusion – that same illusion that lies at the heart of the regime's ideology. Propped up by their propaganda machine, these leaders encourage their subjects in the fantasy that they are wise, noble, kind and understanding. They offer evidence that they are doing whatever they can to create a perfect society – one in which, according to the propaganda machine, there will be justice for all, everyone's needs will be met, there will be meaningful work for everyone, and hunger and poverty will be eradicated. The result, they promise persuasively, will be a just, humane society, a society in which children can grow up safely.

The Search for Scapegoats

Rarely do things work out that way however. In the process of striving for their utopia, tyrants create injustice and misery. And whose fault is that? Well, not the tyrants', certainly. They can always find someone else to blame. The typical tyrant might, when 'learning' of an incident of cruelty or injustice, announce that he did not know of the problem; if he had, of course, he would have handled things differently. It was some key person or group that was really responsible for people's privations. This is a nice fairy tale, but it lacks even the smallest kernel of truth. Of course the despot is responsible. He knew exactly what was going on (or if he did not, it was because he chose not to know). The very definition of a totalitarian state is that nothing can be done without the leader's knowledge and say-so. If the inner circle or the military behaves cruelly, it is because he tells them to. He selects his henchmen; he dispenses orders and permission; he rewards obedient behavior. And the henchmen oblige. They follow his wishes, sometimes even exceeding his demands to show their loyalty (especially if they 'identify with the aggressor', as discussed in Chapter 9).

Because the leader sets the tone for the whole society, his unwillingness to take responsibility creates an entire culture of blame. Each henchman passes on blame to his or her underlings, who in turn do the same to theirs. But somewhere in that cascading blame the responsibility has to finally come to rest. Thus scapegoating comes into play in every tyranny, the inevitable result of dichotomous thinking. The 'nonbelievers' described earlier – forces of evil (so designated by those in power) – are seen as posing a great threat to the purity of society and the well-being of 'believers', and thus are deserving of 'elimination'. The Jews in Nazi Germany, the kulaks and capitalists under the Soviet regime, the educated elite in Pol Pot's Cambodia, the Tutsi in Rwanda, the non-Arab Christians and animists in southern Sudan, and the Muslims in Kosovo were all victims of scapegoating. They were the source of all the problems their countries were experiencing.

We have seen in earlier chapters how essential enemies – real or imagined – are to tyrannical regimes. With the help of propaganda, despots inspire intense hatred for their chosen scapegoats, creating a primitive level of commitment to the cause. In the process, as noted earlier, they create a sense of belonging in their followers, give them a sense of purpose, and distract them from the real issues of the day. Indoctrinated by a constant stream of virulent propaganda, people become willing to inform on neighbors, friends and family members. But there is an even uglier side to scapegoating: it has a genuine attraction to people. Violence repels most people, yes; but it also intrigues and draws them. In addition, as with participating in violent spectator sports, engaging in scapegoating is a way of overcoming one's own fears. As I indicated in the description of 'identification with the aggressor', violent participation is, for many, a way of dealing with their own anxiety and feelings of doubts about the regime. It is a form of insurance as well: people hope that by showing commitment to the regime and its policies of violence, they can save themselves. Even those who only stand at the sidelines are affected. Those who watch this macabre 'spectator sport' are bound together by shared guilt over not putting an end to the violence.

The Creation of a State Colossus

In totalitarian societies, nobody has any individual rights. Every aspect of human activity is dominated by the prevailing ideology; all spheres of life are under the control of the state and its leadership. To make such total control truly effective, all legally recognized buffers between the leader and his subjects need to be eliminated. No reliable, independent authoritative body can stand between the leader and the masses. This means that tyrants need to subvert existing institutions, particularly the judiciary, to make their control absolute. Traditional groups such as labor unions, political parties, an independent press and other associations of any kind need to be destroyed. Meaningful participation in a vibrant political community cannot be tolerated, though participation (or better, 'imprisonment') in ideologically 'correct' institutions and in front organizations is allowed, encouraged or even mandated.

Because divine authority is a particular threat, totalitarian regimes typically combine spiritual and secular guidance, gaining a monopoly on correct interpretation of both secular and religious thought. The totalitarian state's ideology then becomes the nation's religion, as it did in Nazi Germany, Stalin's Russia and Mao Zedong's China, often claiming to represent the 'general good' or the liberation of some oppressed group. Totalitarian regimes also, as noted earlier, deprive individuals of the sense of community that lateral relationships bring, severing those ties in favor of stronger ties to the state. The resulting loss of personal identity is compensated for by shared identification with the powerful leader, who has all the answers as proclaimed through his ideology.

Under despotic systems, ordinary people are nothing more than cogs in a merciless political machine. The leader uses the police, the military and other specially designated henchmen to spread fear in the general population and to impose the extreme sanctions of imprisonment, internment in hospitals and camps, torture and execution on those people who oppose the government. Such is the imprimatur of a dictatorship. In the case of truly despotic regimes, the secret police often becomes like a state within a state, suppressing freedom in the name of law and order but holding its own actions above the law, free from accountability. As despots use a segment of the population to keep the other people under their oppression, terror gradually becomes not only a means to an end but an end in itself. In this vicious circle, the ones who carry out purges one day may be purged the next. The consequence is be a totally cowed, subdued population.

As discussed earlier, ideology is everything in totalitarianism. It serves the leader's narcissistic fantasies, and it creates a 'fusion' of leader and led. By facilitating conscious and unconscious dreams of togetherness, of shared purpose, it creates a false sense of group solidarity. Maintaining this delicate mental equilibrium implies the abdication of autonomous functioning. Thus any attempt at individuation, at independent thinking, is seen as high treason, an attack on the state. Because individuation starts early, the family is important as a training ground, a forum for building patterns of obedience to authority. Someone who knew no freedom in childhood is less likely to protest a lack of freedom later on.

Given the importance of early indoctrination, many totalitarian governments use pre-school and later schooling to eliminate undesirable attitudes that the parents may have passed on. Some totalitarian regimes have even taken children away from their parents and raised them in communal houses. The Soviet Union for example experimented with communal houses in the 1920s and 1950s. Likewise, during the war with Afghanistan during the 1980s, the Soviet government forcibly took tens of thousands of young Afghani children to the USSR to be raised away from their families. The Hitlerjugend, the Pioneers, the Komsomols, the Red Guards, the Khmer Rouge and the *amabutho* can all be seen as tools to brainwash young people, gain their support for the prevailing ideology, and even make them spy and inform on their parents.

THE ULTIMATE COST OF TERROR WITHIN

It seems self-evident to democratic Westerners that parents and families, not governments, should be responsible for rearing and educating their children. While that may be a cultural bias, history shows us irrefutably that enduring great societies are built on freedom of spirit and freedom of expression. Such freedoms cannot flourish in the absence of basic standards of morality, civic virtue and justice for all, fairly administered. Creating special rights for some people, as despotic regimes do, undermines individual freedom and civil rights, and thus undermines civilization itself.

Far-reaching restrictions on freedom inevitably result in economic decline. Freedom in the economic sphere makes for individual initiative and entrepreneurship, creates employment and helps eradicate poverty. In this way, it supports all the other freedoms. Someone with a job and three square meals a day feels freer to express her opinion than someone dependent on others for survival. Totalitarian governments, on the other hand, with their gigantic bureaucracies, are not conducive to the spirit of entrepreneurship. Bureaucracy, corruption and uncertainty, combined with the lack of individual freedom and human rights, sap the energy and rend the moral fabric of a country. A government that does not hold itself accountable cannot create a foundation for economic growth. As totalitarian states mature, their practices are greater and greater obstacles to economic development. Unemployment, poverty and hunger typically result, as in the regimes of Mengistu Haile Mariam of Ethiopia, Joseph Désiré Mobutu of the Democratic Republic of Congo and Robert Mugabe of Zimbabwe. Despots, though they may enjoy a temporary honeymoon period, bring on economic decline.

They also destroy a country's cultural institutions and sense of national pride. The discontent that grows up in a populace around inequities and lack of freedom eventually turns even an environment of creativity and free thought into a breeding ground for the disenfranchised. In their anger and desperation, seeing enemies and conspiracies everywhere, citizens begin to commit desperate terrorist acts. Unable to touch the leader, they strike out wherever they can, destroying their own society in the process.

Once people embrace a theological or secular belief system that has no room for compassion, goodness and hope, it is only a matter of time before violence sets in. And once violence takes hold, civilization itself is condemned. Dictatorships and totalitarian governments kill civil society; it is as simple as that. Post-Saddam Iraq has become a prominent example. Thus people have to combat despots before totalitarian states are established. They need to be able to dream, to imagine a better society for their children and for future generations, and to incorporate their dreams into positive goals, both individual and collective. They need to remember this old Chinese saying: 'Happiness is something to do, someone to love, and something to hope for.' Without meaningful work, close ties to family and friends, and reasonable hope of a positive future, people quickly become alienated. That alienation becomes universal when totalitarianism deprives people of these essential rewards, and an entire population loses its sense of humanity and compassion.

12. Dancing with vampires: preventing tyranny through effective governance

He conquered every country,
Where can he conquer now?
He! He! Eya Eee!
He vanquished chiefs,
He vanquished nations,
Where can he conquer now?
> (Magema Fuze, Shaka war song, *The Black People*)

We have buried the putrid corpse of liberty.
> (Benito Mussolini, speech, 1934)

A single death is a tragedy; a million is a statistic.
> (Joseph Stalin, attributed)

Kill a man, and you are a murderer. Kill millions of men, and you are a conqueror.
Kill everyone, and you are a god.
> (Jean Rostand, *Pensées d'un biologiste*)

Under a government which imprisons any unjustly, the true place for a just man is also a prison.
> (Henry David Thoreau, *Civil Disobedience*)

An eye for an eye makes the whole world blind.
> (Mahatma Gandhi, *Non-Violence in Peace and War*)

Liberty is the hardest test that one can inflict on a people. To know how to be free is not given equally to all men and all nations.
> (Paul Valéry, *On the Subject of Dictatorship*)

No matter what part of the world we come from, we are all basically the same human beings. We all seek happiness and try to avoid suffering.
> (Dalai Lama, *Speech on Acceptance of the Nobel Prize for Peace*)

Shaka's life story reminds us that all leaders are susceptible to the darker side of power and warns us that no single individual should ever be in complete control of an organization, community or society. That human susceptibility to cruelty and violence turns people in high positions into villains with alarming frequency. The statement *Homo homini lupus* ('Every man is a wolf to every other man') is all too painfully true. However admirable leaders may be when

175

they first take the scepter, however enlightened they may be, however much they may resemble Plato's philosopher-king, they are not exempt from the pull of psychological regression.

Perhaps the best test of a person's character is to put him or her in a position of power. That's the hardest test, certainly. Unfortunately most leaders fail the test miserably. Even the most 'normal' human being can become cruel and callous when given too much power. Power is so intoxicating, so addictive, that only the hardiest individuals can survive it without psychopathology. Even those on the receiving end of power feel its psychopathological effects: they often become dangerously overdependent.

Power and reason cannot coexist peacefully, and reason is always the loser. Excessive power blurs the senses, triggers delusional paranoia and corrupts reality-testing. As we have seen, paranoiacs do not take their delusions lightly. Many a reign has been steeped in the blood of enemies more perceived than real; many a ruler, from Roman emperors to modern despots, has been more executioner than diplomat. And in every case, those who are carried away by power eventually self-destruct – but not before sacrificing countless victims on the altar of their ambitions.

Having seen what happens when paranoid leaders who are malevolent antisocials take the helm, using their vast wealth of resources to shape a society based on their inner imagery, we stand forewarned. Shaka's story is a cautionary tale, reminding us that every culture needs to build and maintain strong checks and balances against the abuse of power. Without these safeguards, any regime, no matter how benign, can give way to despotic rule. Thus power retained should always be a check to power conferred.

Democracy requires well-entrenched social systems that protect against the destructive potential that lies dormant in humankind. As I have reiterated, only political diversity, a well-established legal code, and freedom of expression and economy can ensure democratic rule. But these things alone are not sufficient. In addition, individuals must have a civilized personal code of conduct and endorse a civic mindset that supports democratic social structures. In other words, the populace has to internalize a civic culture that protects against the abuse of power. That internalization comes from learning the fundamentals of democratic government at home and in school, seeing democratic government at work in daily life, watching open and honest elections, and hearing respected adults support human rights (and question authority when it restricts those rights). Only through the combination of supportive social structures and an internalized civic culture can the relinquishing of power follow the assumption of power.

It is bad enough when a 'normal' person becomes intoxicated by power (as victims of child abuse can attest). But when that intoxication strikes a national leader – someone delivering his or her lines on a world stage – the consequences can be devastating. The paranoia that such intoxication spawns makes despots trigger-happy: fearing that others are seeking to overthrow them, they resort to what psychologists call 'protective reaction' – that is, they take the aggressive initiative, attacking before they can be attacked. If their protective reaction gains a base in reality (if, for example, dissidents from their own regime form an alliance with external forces), it is as if oil had been thrown on their paranoid fire. Even when paranoia does not argue for war, despots are motivated into combat by the sense of purpose and solidarity it gives the people, and the distraction it offers from the despot's own doings.

What makes despots so dangerous for the world community is not so much their tendency toward violence as the ease with which that tendency can be indulged. Starting a war – engaging in *any* violence, for that matter – is so much easier for despots than for democratic leaders. Despots do not need to ask permission from various executive and legislative bodies. Despots do not have to convince the populace. The most they have to do – if that – is get an official-sounding agency to rubber-stamp their war effort. They have the power to do pretty much as they wish.

It goes without saying that wars come at an incredible price in human suffering for the citizens involved. But the visible costs of war – death for soldiers and civilians, homelessness, privation, economic disaster – are only the tip of the iceberg. There are hidden effects of war that can take generations to rebuild – for example, the loss of self-respect and national pride, and the obliteration of culture and creativity. These desolating consequences are a persuasive argument for humankind to rid the world of dictatorships – even if, paradoxically, it takes war to do so. If the cause is just, it is much better to have a short preventive war than years of stretched-out agony. Certain regimes are so corrupt and destructive that they have to be restrained, no matter what.

After a career of villainy and deception, many despots are brought down, regime in tow, by victors in battle. Others survive a losing war only to be brought down by segments of their own population who, seeing the devastation that accompanied defeat, decide that enough is enough and mount a successful insurrection.

Sometimes what brings a despot to ruin is rot within the regime. The idealism that flourished when the regime was first put in place gradually becomes cynicism as the ideals lose their meaning. Those true believers who once fought for an ideal now fight only for the perks that loyalty brings. The lure of those perks is strong: in a society built on favoritism, corruption is inevitable. And with the onset of corruption, the regime loses two of its most powerful sources of control: moral authority and political legitimacy. Furthermore corruption breeds dissension among the exploited masses, who nurture thoughts of revolution as the only answer to their disenfranchisement.

A good illustration of a regime brought down by inner rot is the decades-long reign of despot Nicolae Ceausescu of Romania. His secret police, known as the Securitate, maintained rigid controls over free speech and the media, tolerating no internal opposition. He encouraged an extensive personality cult and appointed his wife, Elena, and some members of his family to high posts in the government. His regime, despite the glowing promises of the early years, was marked by disastrous economic schemes that led to great suffering for the populace. Over time, his regime became increasingly repressive and corrupt. After years of agony, that regime finally collapsed. The catalyst was his order, given to his security forces, to fire on antigovernment demonstrators. A December 1989 uprising of the people, in which the army participated, led to his arrest, his trial and sentencing (by a hastily assembled military tribunal), and his execution. His wife and other key figures were also put to death.

DETERRING TERROR

The execution of Nicolae Ceausescu is a rare exception; few despots are ever held accountable for their evil acts. The tragic paradox of history is that those individuals who murder one person are more likely to be brought to justice than those who plot the genocide of millions. Despots who commit crimes against humanity far too often go into quiet retirement instead of being brought to justice. A small sampling of the many examples available:

- More than 9000 people disappeared during the 'Dirty War' in Argentina that started at the end of the 1970s to end at the beginning of the 1980s. The perpetrators are living happily ever after.
- Syria's late dictator, Hafez al-Assad, also had a happy ending to his life, although he ordered the death of at least 10000 people in the city of Hama after an insurrection, and then bulldozed over the city.
- The late North Korean dictator, Kim Il-Sung, who kept a tight rein on his totalitarian state, advocated what he called a self-reliance policy. The net effect? He caused the starvation of millions of his people. He also lived happily ever after, and died in his bed.
- Few people recall the holocaust inflicted by the Ottoman Empire against Armenians in 1915, though more than a million people died. Nobody was ever held accountable for this troublesome mass murder. In fact, the Turks never even acknowledged that it happened.

This pattern of denial is changing however. Since the milestone International Military Tribunal at Nuremberg in 1946, where war crimes and crimes against humanity were prosecuted, the world has been taking increasing notice of despots. That tribunal, and the subsequent tribunal in Tokyo (which reviewed war crimes committed by the command of the Japanese Imperial Army), established a precedent for holding the leaders of a country responsible for crimes committed by that country. Unfortunately these trials did not lead to the establishment of a permanent international court that would be especially empowered to deal with crimes against humanity. In the decades just after these two large tribunals, the prosecution of war criminals lessened significantly again – most likely due to the effects of the Cold War – and power politics froze meaningful decision-making. During (and because of) this passivity, Pol Pot, a criminal responsible for the death of over 2 million Cambodians, was never brought to justice.

Since the breakdown of the Berlin Wall and the end of the Cold War, however, the United Nations has been taking a more active position against despots. Shamed into action by the tragic events in former Yugoslavia and Rwanda, the Security Council established two specialized ad hoc tribunals. The first, the International Criminal Tribunal set up in The Hague, began by bringing to justice the instigators of various crimes against humanity in former Yugoslavia, convicting a number of the key players, the most important one being Slobodan Milosevic. Similar steps were then taken to bring to justice the people responsible for the genocide in Rwanda. The second International Criminal Tribunal, convened in Arusha, sentenced Jean Kambanda, former prime minister of Rwanda, to life imprisonment (the harshest penalty available) for supporting and promoting the massacre of some 800 000 Tutsi when the Hutu briefly held power. Though these results were encouraging, even more needs to be done. This means that the serious political, practical, linguistic and financial difficulties presented by the international tribunals need to be overcome, and quickly.

Difficulties notwithstanding, these tribunal convictions – further milestones in the effort to bring high-level perpetrators of crimes against humanity to justice – are a warning to dictators everywhere that the world is changing and that they can no longer expect to escape consequences. Another positive step is the willingness of many national courts to bring charges against dictators. The court in Chile for example acted against Augusto Pinochet, former president of that country, for human rights abuses that occurred during a period when many members of the political opposition disappeared. Such indictments are a signal by and to the world community that nobody stands above the law.

These changing attitudes toward instigators of crimes against humanity, including mass murder and the repression of various freedoms, allowed for open discussion of what more could be done to prevent despot genocide. The United Nations, accused by many of doing too little too late in both former Yugoslavia and Rwanda, entered that discussion with serious soul-searching concerning its proper role in the twenty-first century. One of the primary objectives of the United Nations is securing universal respect for human rights and fundamental freedoms of individuals throughout the world. Its reluctance to intervene against war crimes and other crimes against humanity – to halt them immediately rather than condemn them later – has come to haunt the institution. Many politicians and military strategists believe that if the UN had taken preventive action in hot spots around the world, considerable violence could have been avoided, millions of lives could have been saved, and many countries could have avoided political and economic ruin.

Such discussions have contributed to a greater preparedness on the part of the UN and the world community generally to deal with situations of tyranny. The world community today is reluctant to ignore leaders and regimes that engage in civil war, mass murder, ideological intolerance and murderous repression. The mass media has played a huge role in that shift, awakening the conscience of the world. In this day and age, atrocities are difficult to hide. The work done by a despot's henchmen today may be broadcast tomorrow on CNN or BBC World News. That visual awareness of human atrocities, projected by television into billions of homes, helped many of the world's key decision-makers – always attuned to the pressure of their citizens – to recognize the exponential costs in human suffering of standing by as spectators. These leaders saw that preventive action would be a bargain, in cost-benefit terms, compared to an after-the-fact salvage operation.

The lessons learned from the events in former Yugoslavia and Rwanda have made the United Nations increasingly prepared to engage in military intervention. The disastrous attacks of 9/11 were another wake-up call to the world. Those attacks, which announced that acts of terror do not honor national boundaries, succeeded in weakening the isolationist position of the United States. It is now clear to the world – and to the United States in particular – that certain regimes consider terrorism one of their finest export products. Though we have long known that despots will not hesitate to alienate whole segments of their society, destroying their civil, civic culture in the process, it is now clear that those alienated citizens – unable to find a level playing field in their own society – will readily look for scapegoats outside. We now see that if we want to prevent further 9/11s, we have to go to the root of the problem: alienation and brutalization of any population must be stopped at all costs.

The activities of the Taleban, Al-Qaeda and Iraq's ruling elite have made it clear that sometimes the only way to get rid of despots and totalitarianism is through outside interference. Controversial as it may be, force is often the only way to change such regimes. In the past, the world community has been reluctant to violate any nation's territorial integrity, believing that war should be instigated only for defensive purposes. The questions of territorial integrity and defensive war become less significant, however, if the price of inaction is the terrorization and impoverishment of an entire population, or the imprisonment or murder of opposition groups. Territorial integrity is even less an issue when a despotic regime itself ignores borders, exporting terror by threat or action.

Having just ended the bloodiest century in human history, the international community is now more prepared than before to send UN troops, or troops from specific countries, to prevent or stop civil war or mass murder fostered by despotic regimes – in other words, to take pre-emptive military action. The international community is also eager to build on the successes of its ad hoc tribunals by having established, under the auspices of the United Nations, an independent International Criminal Court (ICC), a permanent international judicial body especially set up to try individuals for genocide, crimes against humanity and war crimes. This body became official in 2002, when the so-called Rome Statute received adequate ratification and was 'entered into force'.

Unfortunately, as of now, the United States has not been willing to ratify the treaty, fearing that US service men and women and officials could be brought before the court in politically motivated cases. This fear is unwarranted: the treaty stipulates that the International Criminal Court will take on only cases that national courts are demonstrably unable or unwilling to prosecute, and it includes numerous safeguards to protect against frivolous or unwarranted prosecutions.

The ICC will have a much wider jurisdiction than the earlier tribunals. This international court will complement existing national judicial systems, however, stepping in only if national courts are unwilling or unable to investigate or prosecute the crimes falling under the mandate of the ICC. The ICC will also help defend the rights of groups that have often had little recourse to justice, such as women and children. The establishment of such a court is more than just a symbolic move; it promises to end the impunity long enjoyed by gangster-like world leaders. It is a much-needed step in the direction of universal, global criminal justice.

The ICC will make international standards of conduct more specific, provide an important mechanism for implementation of these standards, and ensure that potential violators are brought to justice. In addition to determining the criminal responsibility of today's despots, it is expected to serve as a strong deterrent for possible future despots. Because it will be able to investigate and begin prosecutions at an early stage, it is also expected to shorten the span of violence and hasten expedient resolution of conflict. Furthermore it may have a positive impact on national laws around the world, because ratifying nations will want to ensure that crimes covered by the ICC can be tried within their own borders. It is the hope of the international community that the ICC will ensure that future Hitlers, Pinochets, Pol Pots, Mengistus, Amins, Savimbis and Mobutus will not escape justice. With the help of this new council, all despots will face a day of reckoning. Budding despots the world over had best beware.

That is the hope. Is it realistic? Would the existence of such a criminal court have affected the behavior of Shaka for example? Would it have made him less bloodthirsty – or at least less determined to act on his bloodthirst? Would he have found a more humanitarian way of building a nation? Or is it true, as many people believe, that personality is destiny? Given the kind of person Shaka was, would he have been compelled to continue his destructive ways even in the face of international opposition? We will never know.

REPRISE: THE RISE AND FALL OF NARCISSISM

We do know, however, that as Shaka's delusions of grandeur increased – and by the end they *were* delusions, despite his earlier stunning accomplishments – he lived more and more in a world of his own, and he forced that distorted reality on others. As noted, he had become the ultimate court of appeal, the sole source of law, the commander-in chief and the high priest, all in one. With that absolute sovereignty a process of mutual regression occurred, as it always does between a hubristic leader and dependent followers, giving rise to inappropriate behavior and detouring people from reality.

Narcissistic personalities typically deteriorate when they get older, and as we have seen, Shaka was no exception. As the combined effects of unbroken victories, unparalleled wealth, absolute and unchallenged power, extraordinary physical strain, and isolation began to take their toll, Shaka became increasingly domineering and grandiose. His temper, always quick, became more and more unpredictable: at the slightest provocation he erupted in an outburst of rage. His suspiciousness also heightened as time went on, making him ready to believe any rumor of perfidy, whatever its source. With not much needed to arouse his suspicion, it became increasingly dangerous to be part of his inner circle.

Although initially Shaka was one of the warriors, giving him the sense of belonging he had longed for as a child, he grew more isolated and lonely as his power increased. The obsequious behavior of his troops and his entourage reinforced his reactive sense of superiority and distanced him further from them. As the most powerful king in Africa – a land where even lesser kings were seen as godlike – only his mother had any influence on him by the end. None of the 'yea-sayers' who populated his retinue had the courage to stand up to him, and there were no systemic checks and balances to contain him. By the time his mother died, his sense of reality-testing had become totally defective. As I noted earlier, the bizarre edicts he forced on his increasingly bewildered population suggest that he suffered from a full-fledged psychotic episode.

With the disappearance of the last bastion of reality-testing – his mother – Shaka's delusions had free rein. No wonder his paranoid ideation intensified. No wonder his actions became increasingly bizarre. No wonder he became more and more violent with his own population. The man had become delusional. Ironically, as his unpredictability increased, his paranoia became more 'rational': the greater his restrictions and atrocities, the more likely an assassination attempt. As if in self-fulfilling prophecy, he was finally killed.

In his paranoia, Shaka both built up and tore down the Zulu people. He created a powerful nation, but he did so by legitimizing violence, weaving it throughout the entire social structure. As Alfred Bryant (1929) observed very accurately:

> The *magnus opus* of Shaka's genius was the creation, organization, training and application of an unconquerable army to the purpose of building up a supreme Zulu nation. Step by step, with intuitive wisdom and skill, the plan was conceived and carried out with amazing rapidity. ... But in accomplishing his 'glorious' work, he ruined himself – if, indeed, he was not ruined already; in gaining the world, he lost his own soul. For the brutal methods and vicious deeds necessarily and continuously practiced in pursuance of his plan naturally involved an abnormal development of the baser qualities, and a gradual deadening and final extinction of those more noble. Whatever he may have been in childhood and youth – and we have an idea that with him the child was but father of the man – certainly, in adult life, every virtue seemed lacking and every vice was rampant. He was man reverted, not to the savage, but to the brutish stage, in which all altruistic elements are absent, and the animal instincts reign supreme. (p. 648)

Shaka's inability to form attachments, his incapacity to connect with others, was transformed by hardship into a desire to destroy others. By institutionalizing that desire, Shaka destroyed the moral fiber of a formerly relatively benign society. By the end of his reign, not only his warriors, but also his subjects, were willing ruthlessly to kill others – even women and children, even close friends and family members – if the king so desired. The people participated in a veritable orgy of killing after Nandi's death. How could they do this? In the manner of subjects everywhere, throughout time: by subordinating their conscience to that of their leader. Thoroughly socialized to violence, they cognitively and emotionally restructured the moral value of killing, exempting it from their own conscience. Loyalty to the system as created by their leader took precedence over all other considerations, and loyalty protected them from moral liability for actions executed in the line of duty. But when morally abhorrent conduct is enacted by what seem to be decent people in the name of a leader or a secular or theocratic ideology, the absolution of conscience is generally only superficial and temporary; the emotional cost is itself often deadly.

Some historians have argued that Zulu society was more tolerant of violence than other societies. Others, as suggested earlier, have argued that Shaka could not have unified so many diverse clans without relying on violence. Had he taken a more democratic approach, they say, the result would have been fragmentation and murderous implosion. This theory has a contemporary ring: as we could see in Iraq after the fall of Saddam Hussein.

Whether or not the Zulus were more tolerant than others of violence, Shaka was clearly a 'culture innovator'. The early history of the Zulus and the neighboring clans reveals that his way of interacting with others was quite different from that of the kings or chiefs before him. Dingiswayo for example was much more forgiving of his enemies than Shaka. He once captured and then released the great enemy Zwide, though Shaka argued for Zwide's death. His innovations were so impressive, even to the cadre that overthrew him, that they retained the civic code he created – a code based on terror. In fact that code outlasted even Shaka's successor.

Though Shaka never had a formal day of reckoning, he was locked in a psychic prison of his own making. Though unrestrained physically – with no boundaries to constrain him, no countervailing powers to control him – he could not combat the psychological forces of narcissism and paranoia. Eventually those forces sent him across moral boundaries from which he could not return. His craving for admiration, affirmation and power prompted such extremes of cruelty that he eventually overreached himself, damaging his own power base. At the time of his assassination, the Zulu nation had become a military parasite terrorizing outlying clans.

Shaka's rise and fall – like that of most despots throughout history – was accompanied by incredible bloodshed. Although some people still lionize this warrior-king and excuse his excesses, it is estimated that more than 2 million people died either directly or indirectly by his hand – through internal purges, through warfare and through the upheaval left in his wake as his 'nomads of wrath' wandered aimlessly through southern Africa, attacking and terrorizing other tribes. When the white men arrived in Zululand Natal – Shaka's buffer zone against attack – the landscape was desolate, littered with skeletons.

Due to – and despite – Shaka's endeavors, southern Africa was left with a few powerful nations: the Matabele, the Basuto and the Swazi. But the most powerful of them all, for a good long time, were the Zulu. Notwithstanding all his shortcomings, Shaka had established a state system that was robust enough to last another 50 years, in spite of the rule of two incompetent successors. Shaka's Zulu kingdom became his monument, and it continued to be a source of pride for the Zulus after his death. It took Great Britain, the world's most sophisticated military nation during Shaka's heyday, to destroy the Zulus' military apparatus – and that only after a dramatic British defeat at Isandlwana. Still today the Zulus are proud of the fact that they were once the most powerful tribe in southern Africa, and remnants of the alertness and discipline of the old military system remain.

Shaka's great homestead at Dukuza is gone, the modern town of Stanger built up around it. There is little left of the other homesteads he built. A monument can be found on the site of his grave near Stanger, however, and nearby lies the boulder on which Shaka was sitting when attacked. Many people have made a pilgrimage to this monument, searching for answers about the enigmatic Shaka. But the mystery remains, as the Zulu poet Vilakazi asserts in his poem *Ushaka KaSenzangakhona* ('Shaka, Son of Senzangakhona'):

> The nations, Shaka, have condemned you,
> Yet still today, they speak of you,
> Still today their books discuss you,
> But we defy them to explain you. (Roberts, 1974, p. 163)

Bibliography

Adorno, T., E. Frenkel-Brunswik, D.J. Levinson and N. Sanford (1950), *The Authoritarian Personality*, New York: Harper.

American Psychiatric Association (1987), *Diagnostic and Statistical Manual of the Mental Disorders, DSM-III-R* (3rd rev. edn), Washington, DC: American Psychiatric Association.

American Psychiatric Association (1994), *Diagnostic and Statistical Manual for Mental Disorders, DSM-IV* (4th edn), Washington, DC: American Psychiatric Association.

Angas, G.F. (1849), *The Kafirs Illustrated*, London: J. Hogarth.

Arendt, H. (1969), *On Violence*, New York: Harcourt, Brace and World.

Arendt, H. (1973), *The Origins of Totalitarianism* (new edn), New York: Harcourt Brace Jovanovitch.

Athens, L.H. (1992), *The Creation of Dangerous Violent Criminals*, Urbana, IL: University of Illinois Press.

Bion, W.R. (1959), *Experiences in Groups*, London: Tavistock.

Bird, J. (ed.), (1888/1965), *The Annals of Natal: 1495–1945* (Vol. 1), Cape Town: Struik.

Boesche, R. (1996), *Theories of Tyranny: From Plato to Arendt*, University Park, PA: Pennsylvania State University Press.

Bowlby, J. (1969), *Attachment and Loss* (Vol. 1: *Attachment*), New York: Basic Books.

Breuer, J. and S. Freud (1893–95), 'Studies on Hysteria', in J. Strachey (ed.), *The Standard Edition of the Complete Psychological Works of Sigmund Freud* (Vol. 2), London: Hogarth Press and the Institute of Psychoanalysis.

Bryant, A.T. (1929), *Olden Times in Zululand and Natal*, London: Longmans.

Bryant, A.T. (1949), *The Zulu People*, Pietermaritzburg: Shuter & Shooter.

Cameron, N. (1963), *Personality Development and Psychopathology*, Boston: Houghton-Mifflin.

Campbell, J. (1949), *The Hero with a Thousand Faces*, Princeton, NJ: Princeton University Press.

Canetti, E. (1960), *Crowds and Power*, Harmondsworth: Penguin Books.

Castelnuovo-Tedesco, P. (1974), 'Stealing, Revenge and the Monte Cristo Complex', *International Journal of Psychoanalysis*, **55**, 169–77.

Chirot, D. (1994), *Modern Tyrants*, Princeton, NJ: Princeton University Press.

Cope, T. (1968), *Izibongo: Zulu Praise-Poems Collected by James Stuart* (D. Malcolm, trans.), Oxford: Oxford University Press.

Delegorgue, A. (1847), *Voyage dans l'Afrique Australe* (Vols 1, 2), Paris: A. René.

Derwent, S. (1998), *Zulu*, London: Struik New Holland Publishing.

Des Pres, T. (1976), *The Survivor: An Anatomy of Life in the Death Camps*, New York: Oxford University Press.

Deutsch, H. (1965), *Neurosis and Character Types: Clinical Psychoanalytic Studies*, New York: International Universities Press.

Devereux, G. (1978), *Ethnopsychoanalysis*, Berkeley and Los Angeles, CA: University of California Press.

Emde, R.N. (1981), 'Changing models of infancy and the nature of early development: remodelling the foundation', *Journal of the American Psychoanalytical Association*, **29**, 179–219.

Erikson, E.H. (1963), *Childhood and Society*, New York: W.W. Norton & Society.

Erikson, E.H. (1971), 'On the nature of psycho-historical evidence: in search of Gandhi', in B. Mazlish (ed.), *Psychoanalysis and History*, New York: Grosset & Dunlap.

Erikson, E.H. (1975), *Life History and Historical Moment*, New York: W.W. Norton.

Fenichel, O. (1945), *The Psychoanalytic Theory of Neurosis*, New York: W.W. Norton.

Ferguson, W.S. (1918), 'The Zulus and the Spartans: a comparison of their military systems', *Harvard African Studies*, **2**, 197–234.

Fernandez, J.W. (1967), 'The Shaka Complex', *Transition*, **29**, 11–14.

Freud, A. (1966), *The Ego and the Mechanisms of Defense* (rev. edn), Madison, CT: International Universities Press.

Freud, S. (1900), 'The interpretation of dreams', in J. Strachey (ed.), *The Standard Edition of the Complete Psychoanalytical Works of Sigmund Freud* (Vol. 5), London: Hogarth Press and the Institute of Psychoanalysis.

Freud, S. (1917), 'A childhood collection from Dichtung und Wahrheit', in J. Strachey (ed.), *The Standard Edition of the Complete Psychological Works of Sigmund Freud* (Vol. 17), London: Hogarth Press and the Institute of Psychoanalysis.

Freud, S. (1920), 'Beyond the Pleasure Principle', in J. Strachey (ed.), *The Standard Edition of the Complete Psychological Works of Sigmund Freud* (Vol. 18), London: Hogarth Press and the Institute of Psychoanalysis.

Freud, S. (1921), 'Group psychology and the analysis of the ego', in J. Strachey (ed.), *The Standard Edition of the Complete Psychological Works of Sigmund Freud* (Vol. 7), London: Hogarth Press and the Institute of Psychoanalysis.

Freud, S. (1933), 'New introductory lectures', in J. Strachey (ed.), *The Standard Edition of the Complete Psychological Works of Sigmund Freud* (Vol. 22), London: Hogarth Press and the Institute of Psychoanalysis.

Friedrich, C. (1954), *Totalitarianism*, Cambridge, MA: Harvard University Press.

Friedrich, C. and Z. Brezezinsky (1965), *Totalitarian Dictatorship and Autocracy*, Cambridge, MA: Harvard University Press.

Fromm, E. (1973), *The Anatomy of Human Destructiveness*, New York: Holt, Rinehart & Winston.

Fuze, M.M. (1921/1998), *The Black People and Whence They Came* (H. Lugg, trans.), Pietermaritzburg: University of Natal Press.

Fynn, H.F. (1833/1950), *The Diary of Henry Francis Fynn*, Pietermaritzburg: Shuter & Shooter.

Gadpaille, W.J. (1989), 'Homosexuality', in H.I. Kaplan and B.J. Sadock (eds), *Comprehensive Textbook of Psychiatry* (Vol. 1), Baltimore, MD: Williams & Wilkins.

George, A.L. (1969), 'The "Operational Code": a neglected approach to the study of political leadership and decision-making', *International Studies Quarterly*, **13**, 190–222.

Gibson, J.Y. (1911), *The Story of the Zulus*, London: Longmans, Green & Co.

Glass, J.M. (1995), *Psychosis and Power: Threats to Democracy in the Self and the Group*, Ithaca, NY: Cornell University Press.

Gluckman, M. (1960), 'The rise of a Zulu empire', *Scientific American*, **202** (4), 157–69.

Golan, D. (1990), 'The life history of King Shaka and gender tensions in the Zulu state', *History in Africa*, **17**, 95–111.

Grossman, D. (1996), *On Killing: The Psychological Cost of Learning to Kill in War and Society*, Boston, MA: Little, Brown.

Gump, J. (1988), 'Origins of the Zulu kingdom', *Historian*, **50**, 521–34.

Haggard, R.H. (1882), *Nada the Lily*, London: Longmans.

Hamilton, C. (1998), *Terrific Majesty: The Powers of Shaka Zulu and the Limits of Historical Invention*, Cambridge, MA: Harvard University Press.

Herschman, J. and J. Lieb (1994), *Brotherhood of Tyrants: Manic Depression and Absolute Power*, Amherst, NY: Prometheus Books.

Hodgsdon, R.C., D.J. Levinson and A. Zaleznik (1965), *The Executive Role Constellation*, Boston, MA: Harvard University, Graduate School of Business Administration.

Hofstede, G. (1991), *Culture's Consequences: Software of the Mind*, New York: McGraw-Hill.

Horney, K. (1945), *Our Inner Conflicts*, New York: Norton.

Horowitz, M.J., C. Marmor, J. Krupnick, N. Wilner, N. Kaltreider and R. Wallerstein (1984), *Personality Styles and Brief Psychotherapy*, New York: Basic Books.

Isaacs, N. (1836/1970), *Travels and Adventures in Eastern Africa*, Cape Town: C. Struik.

Janis, I.L. (1971), 'Groupthink', *Psychology Today*, Nov, 43–6.

Kernberg, O. (1975), *Borderline Conditions and Pathological Narcissism*, New York: Aronson.

Kernberg, O. (1980), *Internal World and External Reality*, New York: Jason Aronson.

Kernberg, O. (1992), *Aggression in Personality Disorders and Perversions*, New Haven, CJ: Yale University Press.

Kets de Vries, M.F.R. (1980), *Organizational Paradoxes: Clinical Approaches to Management*, New York: Routledge.

Kets de Vries, M.F.R. (1989), *Prisoners of Leadership*, New York: Wiley.

Kets de Vries, M.F.R. (1993), *Leaders, Fools, and Impostors*, San Francisco, CA: Jossey-Bass.

Kets de Vries, M.F.R. (1995), *Organizational Paradoxes* (2nd edn), London: Routledge.

Kets de Vries, M.F.R. (2000), 'The clinical paradigm: Manfred Kets de Vries's reflections on organizational theory: interview by Erik van de Loo', *Academy of Management Executive and European Management Journal*, **18** (1 February), 2–21.

Kets de Vries, M.F.R. (2001a), 'The anarchist within: clinical reflections on Russian character and leadership style', *Human Relations*, **54** (5), 585–627.

Kets de Vries, M.F.R. (2001b), *The Leadership Mystique*, London: Financial Times/Prentice Hall.

Kets de Vries, M.F.R. (2001c), *Struggling with the Demon: Essays in Individual and Organizational Irrationality*, Madison, CT: Psychosocial Press.

Kets de Vries, M.F.R. (2004), *Global Executive Leadership Inventory: Facilitator's Guide*, San Francisco: Pfeiffer.

Kets de Vries, M.F.R., and D. Miller (1984), *The Neurotic Organization*, San Francisco, CA: Jossey-Bass.

Klein, M. (1948), *Contributions to Psychoanalysis, 1921–1945*, London: Hogarth Press.

Klein, M. (1959), *The Psychoanalysis of Children*, London: Hogarth Press.

Knight, I. (1989), *The Zulus*, Oxford: Osprey Publishing.

Knight, I. (1994), *Warrior Chiefs of Southern Africa*, Poole: Firebird Books.

Knight, I. (1995), *The Anatomy of the Zulu Army from Shaka to Cetshwayo 1818–1879*, London: Greenhill Books.

Knight, I. (1999), *Great Zulu Commanders*, London: Arms and Armour.

Kohut, H. (1971), *The Analysis of the Self*, New York: International Universities Press.

Kohut, H. (1977), *The Restoration of the Self*, Madison, CT: International Universities Press.

Kohut, H. and E.S. Wolf (1978), 'The disorders of the self and their treatment: an outline', *International Journal of Psychoanalysis*, **59**, 413–26.

Krige, E.J. (1936), *The Social System of the Zulus*, Pietermaritzburg: Shuter & Shooter.

Kunene, M. (1979), *Emperor Shaka the Great*, London: Heinemann.

Laband, J. (1995), *Rope of Sand: The Rise and Fall of the Zulu Kingdom in the Nineteenth Century*, Johannesburg: Jonathan Ball Publishers.

Laband, J. (1997), *The Rise and Fall of the Zulu Nation*, London: Arms and Armour.

Lasswell, H. (1960), *Psychopathology and Politics*, New York: Viking Press.

Levine, R.A. (1980), *Culture, Behavior, and Personality*, New York: Aldine.

Levi-Strauss, C. (1955), 'The structural study of myth', *Journal of American Folklore*, **68**, 428–44.

Levi-Strauss, C. (1969), *The Raw and the Cooked*, New York: Harper & Row.

Lewis, D.O. (1992), 'From abuse to violence', *Journal of the American Academy of Child and Adolescent Psychiatry*, **31**, 383–91.

Lichtenberg, J.D. (1991), *Psychoanalysis and Infant Research*, New York: Lawrence Erlbaum.

Lifton, R.J. (1961), *Thought Reform and the Psychology of Totalism*, New York: W.W. Norton & Company.

Loewenberg, P. (1982), *Decoding the Past: The Psychohistorical Approach*, New York: Alfred A. Knopf.

Lyndon Dodds, G. (1998), *The Zulus and Matabele: Warrior Nations*, London: Arms and Armour.

Machiavelli, N. (1966), *The Prince* (D. Donno, trans.), New York: Bantam.

MacLean, C. (1992), *The Natal Papers of 'John Ross'*, Pietermaritzburg: University of Natal.

Malinovsky, B. (1926), *Myths in Primitive Psychology*, London: Kegan Paul.

McDougall, J. (1985), *Theaters of the Mind*, New York: Basic Books.

McDougall, J. (1989), *Theaters of the Body*, New York: W.W. Norton.

Meissner, W.W. (1978), *The Paranoid Process*, New York: Jason Aronson.

Milgram, S. (1975), *Obedience to Authority*, New York: Harper and Row.

Millon, T. (1986), 'A theoretical derivation of pathological personalities', in T. Millon and G.L. Klerman (eds), *Contemporary Directions in Psychopathology: Toward the DSM-IV*, New York: Guilford Press.

Millon, T. (1996), *Disorders of Personality: DSM IV and Beyond*, New York: John Wiley.

Mofolo, T. (1981), *Chaka* (D.P. Kunene, trans.), Johannesburg: Heinemann.

Morris, D.R. (1966), *The Washing of the Spears: The Rise and Fall of the Zulu Nation*, London: Da Capo Press.

Nabokov, V. (1975), *Tyrants Destroyed and Other Stories*, New York: McGraw-Hill.

Omer-Cooper, J.D. (1966), *The Zulu Aftermath: A Nineteenth-Century Revolution in Bantu Africa*, London: Longman.

Pinel, P. (1801), *Traite Medico-philosophique sur l'Alienation Mentale*, Paris: Richard, Cailleet Ravier.

Plato (1955), *The Republic* (H.D.P. Lee, trans.), Harmondsworth: Penguin.

Rank, O. (1932), *The Myth of the Birth of the Hero and other Writings*, New York: Vintage Books.

Reader, J. (1998), *Africa: A Biography of the Continent*, London: Penguin Books.

Redl, F. and D. Wineman (1951), *Children who Hate: The Disorganization and Breakdown of Behavior Controls*, Glencoe, IL: Free Press.

Reich, W. (ed.) (1990), *Origins of Terrorism: Psychologies, Ideologies, Theologies, States of Mind*, Washington, DC: Woodrow Wilson Center Press.

Rhodes, R. (2002), *Masters of Death*, New York: Alfred A. Knopf.

Ritter, E.A. (1978), *Shaka Zulu*, London: Penguin Books.

Roberts, B. (1974), *The Zulu Kings*, London: Hamish Hamilton.

Robins, R.S. and J.M. Post (1997), *Political Paranoia: The Psychopolitics of Hatred*, New Haven, CT: Yale University Press.

Rycroft, D. and A. Ngcobo (eds) (1988), *The Praises of Dingana*, Durban and Pietermaritzburg: Killie Campbell Africana Library and the University of Natal Press.

Shapiro, D. (1965), *Neurotic Styles*, New York: Basic Books.

Socarides, C.W. (1966), 'On vengeance: the desire to "get even"', *Journal of American Psychoanalytical Association*, **14**, 356–75.

Stuart, J. (1976), *The James Stuart Archive* (Vol. 1), Pietermaritzburg: University of Natal Press and Killie Campbell Africana Library.

Stuart, J. (1979), *The James Stuart Archive* (Vol. 2), Pietermaritzburg: University of Natal Press and Killie Campbell Library.

Stuart, J. (1982), *The James Stuart Archive* (Vol. 3), Pietermaritzburg: University of Natal Press and Killie Campbell Library.

Stuart, J. (1986), *The James Stuart Archive* (Vol. 4), Pietermaritzburg: University of Natal Press and Killie Campbell Library.

Stuart, J. (2001), *The James Stuart Archive* (Vol. 5), Pietermaritzburg: University of Natal Press and Killie Campbell Library.

Stuart, P.A. (1927), *An African Attila: Tales of Zulu Reign of Terror*, London: T. Fischer Unwin.

Thompson, G. (1967), *Travels and Adventures in Southern Africa*, Cape Town: Van Riebeeck Society.

Van der Kolk, B.A. and R.E. Fisler (1994), 'Childhood abuse and neglect and loss of self-regulation', *Bulletin of the Menninger Clinic*, **58** (2), 145–68.

Volkan, V. (1988), *The Need to have Enemies and Allies*, Northvale, NJ: Jason Aronson.

Von Lang, J. and C. Sibyll (eds) (1983), *Eichman Interrogated*, New York: Farrar, Straus & Giroux.

Walter, E.V. (1969), *Terror and Resistance: A Study of Political Violence*, New York: Oxford University Press.

Webb, C. d. B. and J.B. Wright (eds) (1978), *A Zulu King Speaks: Statements made by Cetshwayo kaMpande on the History and Customs of his People*, Pietermaritzburg and Durban: University of Natal Press and Killie Cambell Africana Library.

Weber, M. (1924/1947), *The Theory of Social and Economic Organization*, New York: Oxford University Press.

White, R. (1966), *Lives in Progress*, New York: Holt, Rinehart & Winston.

Winnicott, D.W. (1965), *The Maturational Process and the Facilitating Environment*, London: Hogarth Press.

Winnicott, D.W. (1975), *Through Paediatrics to Psycho-Analysis*, New York: Basic Books.

Worger, W. (1979), 'Clothing dry bones: the myth of Shaka', *Journal of African Studies*, **6** (3), 144–58.

Wylie, D. (1992), 'Textual incest: Nathaniel Isaacs and the development of the Shaka myth', *History in Africa*, **19**, 411–33.

Wylie, D. (1993), 'A dangerous admiration: E.A. Ritter's *Shaka Zulu*', *South African Historical Journal*, **28**, 98–118.

Zaleznik, A. and M.F.R. Kets de Vries (1975), *Power and the Corporate Mind*, Boston, MA: Houghton Mifflin.

Index

accountability 151–3
adultery 87
adversity, reaction to 77
age-grades 25, 29
ageing, fear of 67–8, 88
aggressor, identification with 135–6
alienation, and despotism 165
amabutho (regiments) 25–6, 29, 42, 44–5, 146
  competition between 35–6, 43, 151–2
  training 154–5
  and violence 130–31, 154
Angas, G.F. vii, 85
antisocial personality 104–8
Arendt, H. 129–30, 167
armed forces, control over, and despotism 169
army 141
  accountability 151–3
  discipline 33–4, 44, 111–12, 145, 154–5
  resources required 41, 42–3
  rewards to warriors 41, 153–4
  speed of travel 145
  strains on 51, 52
  tactics 34, 142–3, 155
  training 32–6, 154–5
  war, eagerness for 43, 128–9, 148
  see also amabutho (regiments)
assassination attempts/plots 49, 52–3
assegai (stabbing spear) 32–3, 142
authoritarianism, definition of 4

blacksmiths 33
body image, preoccupation with 67–8
boys
  development of 25–6, 29
  role of 25, 34
brutality (of Shaka) 39–41, 47–52, 78–80, 85, 109–10, 111–12, 124–7, 152–3

Bryant, A.T. 44, 51, 79, 107, 111–12, 130, 183
'bull's horns' 34, 142

Canetti, E. 95
cattle
  importance to Zulus 20–21, 27
  as rewards 41, 153
Ceausescu, N. 177–8
change, discontinuous 155
character
  concept of 93–4
  disorders 94
child development 162–3
  and 'family romance' 58
  and maternal distress 75–6
  and narcissism 63–5
  and Oedipal myth/victory 58, 80
  and paranoia 96–8
children
  indoctrination of 173
  killing of 40
  role of 25, 26, 34
Chile 179
circumcision 25, 29
clinical historians 11–12
collectivism, Zulus 20, 23
corruption 177
'countertransference' 11
cowardice, punishment for 111–12, 152–3
'Coward's Bush' 40–41, 112, 152–3
'crushing' 41–2

Damocles vii–viii
dehumanization, process of 134–5, 157
delegation 145–7, 150
delusions 98
democracy 166, 176
  transition to 165
dependency assumption 99–100

depression, as response to terror 137
despotism 2–7, 117–24, 175–7
    action against 178–82
    advantages of 165
    collusion with 127–31
    conditions for 164–5, 168
    costs of 173–4
    and democracy, transition to 165
    effects of 5–6, 166–7
    examples of 1–2, 177–8
    followers, coping mechanisms 131–8
    human tendency towards 2
    and ideology 3, 167–70, 173
    isolation of subjects 170
    and nation-building 163–4
    overthrow of 177–8
    perpetuation, methods of 6, 167–73
    and random terror 124–7
    and scapegoats 122–3, 171–2
    state apparatus, subversion of 172–3
    subjugation of population 172–3
    tendency to intensify 165–6
    totalitarianism, definition of 3–4
    and trust 157–8
    violence, ease of engaging in 177
Dingane (half-brother of Shaka) 52,
    53–4, 89
Dingiswayo, King 19, 20, 25–6, 27–30,
    36, 141, 184
    and Shaka 29–30, 36, 81, 90–92, 156
Dionysius vii–viii
dissociative thinking 136–7
divide-and-conquer 101, 123–4, 146
double identification 79–80
drought 27
Dumas, A. 78

empowerment of subordinates 145–7
entrepreneurship 147
Erikson, E.H. 11–12
errors, intolerance of 147
exhibitionism 66–7

family, role of 121
'family romance' 58
fight–flight assumption 99–100
flight behavior, as response to terror
    137
followers 69, 117–19, 122
    collusion with despotism 127–31

coping mechanisms/responses to
    despotism 131–8
fear of 132, 133
idealization of leader 69–71
identification with aggressor 135–6
identification with leader 134–5
isolation of 164–5, 170
and megalomania of leader 71–4
and paranoia of leader 98–100
and random terror 124–7
reward, as motivation 132–3, 135
and scapegoats 171–2
'true believers' 132, 133, 168
freedom, importance of 173–4
freedom-fighters 137–8
Freud, S. 61, 65, 118, 135
Fromm, E. 63, 111
frustration 63–4
Fuze, M.M. xvii, 60, 140, 175
Fynn, H.F. xvi, 49–50, 51–2, 60–61, 62,
    67, 68, 79, 84, 111, 151, 152

Gala 50–51
gender-orientation 90
girls, role of 25, 26
government of Zulu empire 43–7
Gqokli Hill, battle of 37, 143, 144
groups 118
    and conformity 133–4
    and paranoia 99–102
guilt, transference of 133–4
guns 143, 155

Haggard, R.H. 54
historians, clinical 11–12
Hodgsdon, R.C. 150
homesteads, royal 45–6
homosexuality 90
hubris 72–4, 156–7

identification
    with aggressor 135–6
    double 79–80
    with leader 134–5
ideology, and despotism 3, 167–70,
    173
illegitimacy 16–17
impondo zenkomo ('bull's horns') 34,
    142
incest 23

information
  gathering 124, 144, 146
  management 123–4, 142, 145–6
  propaganda 169, 170–71
inkatha (sacred coil) 35, 42, 149
innovation, strategic, importance in
  leadership 141–3
International Criminal Court (ICC)
  181–2
International Criminal Tribunals 179
International Military Tribunals 178–9
Isaacs, N. xvi, 61, 68, 84, 87, 89, 90, 95,
  117, 125–6, 136, 144
isicoco (head ring) 26, 43
isolation of subjects, and despotism
  164–5, 170
ivory 27, 28
izangoma (diviners) 22, 24–5, 47, 101,
  146
izinduna (king's representatives) 46–7,
  150
izinyanga (war doctors) 35

Jobe (father of King Dingiswayo) 19, 28

Kernberg, O. 104
kings
  care of 24
  power of 23–5
Knight, I. 152

Laband, J. 53
leaders
  abuse of power 2–7, 175–7
  functions of 69
  idealization of 69–71
  identification with 134–5
  megalomania 71–4, 156–7
  paranoia 95–6, 97–8, 99–100, 176,
    177
  sadism 110–11, 112–13
  see also followers
leadership, lessons from Shaka 140–58
  accountability 151–3
  action, importance of quick and
    decisive 144–5
  competition, knowing 143–4
  discontinuous change 155
  empowerment of subordinates 145–7
  entrepreneurship, promotion of 147

  example setting 150–51
  fair rewards 153–4
  hubris, guarding against 156–7
  selection and promotion 149–50
  strategic innovation 141–3
  symbol manipulation 147–9
  training and development 154–5
  trust, culture of 157–8
  vision, development of clear 140–41
Lifton, R.J. 167

Machiavelli, N. 5, 93, 163–4, 165
malevolent antisocial character disorder
  104–8
'malignant' aggression 109
marriage 17, 26, 45, 89
meals 45
media, role of 180
megalomania 71–4, 94, 156–7
men
  loyalty of 44–5
  old 47, 67, 79, 123
  role of 20, 26
mfecane ('crushing') 41–2
Mhlangana (half-brother of Shaka) 52
Milgram experiment 133–4
military intelligence 144
Mnkabayi kaJama (aunt of Shaka) 30, 52
Mofolo, T. 1, 71–72
Monte Cristo complex 76–80
Morris, D.R. 106
myths and legends 8–9, 12

Nabokov, V. 57, 131–32
Nandi (mother of Shaka) 16–20
  death of 49–51, 84–5, 119
  influence on Shaka 65, 76, 80, 81–2,
    84
  later pregnancies 86–7
narcissism 61, 62–3, 182–3
  and body image/exhibitionism 66–8
  constructive versus reactive 63–6
  and leadership 70–74
  and malevolent antisocials 107–8
  and rage 76–7
9/11 attacks 180
Nthombazi, Queen 36, 37

obedience, culture of 130, 147, 157
Oedipal myth/victory 58, 80

paranoia 94–6, 118, 176, 177
    origins of 96–8
    regression in groups 99–102
    of Shaka 98–9, 100–102
    and trust 96–9
past, importance to Zulus 20
patriarchal society 23–5
Plato 1, 5, 15, 39, 161
police, control over 169
power, abuse of 2–7, 175–7
pregnancy 86–8
propaganda 169, 170–71
'protective reaction' 177

Rank, O. 8–9
rape 35, 128–9
religion 21–3, 24, 42, 172; *see also*
    spirituality; witchcraft
representatives of king 46–7, 150
revenge 76–80, 81
rewards, after battle 41, 153–4
Ritter, E.A. xvii, 1, 53, 81–2, 126
Roberts, B. 53
Romania 177–8
Rwanda 179

sadistic personality/character disorder
    104, 108–13
sandals 33
scapegoats 112, 122–3, 171–2
secret service 47, 124, 144
self-control, and sexuality 85–6
semen 87–8
Senzangakhona kaJama (father of Shaka)
    16–18, 30, 80–81
sex 26
    and battle 35, 88, 89, 128–9
    exogamy rules 17, 23
    pre-marital 16, 26
    ukusoma (thigh sex) 16, 86
sexuality issues 85
    gender-orientation 90
    marriage 89
    pregnancy 86–8
    self-control 85–6
    succession 88–9
Shaka Zulu (Shaka kaSenzangakhona)
    army training 32–6, 154–5
    birth/conception 16–17
    brutality 39–41, 47–52, 78–80, 85,

        109–10, 111–12, 124–7, 152–3
    bullying of 18–19, 65, 67, 77, 112
    consolidation of power 42, 47–8,
        145–6, 150, 156, 163
    death 53–4
    decline 48–54, 163, 184
    as despot 119–24, 163–4
    early life 15–20
    example setting 150–51
    fighting ability 19, 29–30, 79–80
    followers, collusion of 127–31
    government of Zulu nation 43–7
    hubris 156–7
    innovation by 142–3, 155, 184
    isolation 108
    and King Dingiswayo 29–30, 36, 81,
        90–92, 156
    knowledge, thirst for 143
    lessons from leadership 140–58
    life story, significance of 7–8, 12,
        57–9
    as malevolent antisocial 106, 107, 108
    military conquests 36–7, 40, 41,
        142–3
    narcissism 61, 64, 65, 66–8, 71–2,
        73–4, 182–3
    paranoia 98–9, 100–102
    parents, influence of 65, 76, 80–82, 84
    personality 62, 161–2
    physical characteristics/appearance 18,
        19, 60–61, 67–8
    portrayals of/sources of information
        on xvi–xvii, 8, 9–11
    punishment, unconscious need for 108
    random terror 124–7
    relationships, ability to form 83–4
    revenge, as motive 76–80, 81
    rise to leadership 29–30, 91–2, 119
    as sadist 109–10, 111–13
    sexuality, issues of 85–90
    symbol manipulation 148–9
    verdicts on 9–11, 139–40, 182–5
    and Zulu nation, building of 7, 37–8,
        40, 41–3, 54, 113, 141, 162, 183,
        184–5
shields 33, 45
Sigujana (half-brother of Shaka) 30
slave trade 27, 28
Sparta, comparisons with 42–3
spies 47, 124, 144

spirituality 21–3, 24, 35, 99
use by Shaka 42, 101–2, 121, 125, 148
see also witchcraft
Stuart, J. xvii, 21, 35, 37, 38, 49, 53, 110, 126, 130, 152
subjects, *see* followers
subordinates, empowerment of 145–7
succession issues 88–9
Sword of Damocles vii–viii
symbol manipulation 148–9

terrorism 180
thought-control 3, 121–3, 131–2
total war 79
totalitarianism, *see* despotism
treason 23–4
trust 96–9, 157–8
tyranny, *see* despotism

ukusoma (thigh sex) 16, 86
umkhosi wokweshwama festival 24
umndlunkulu ('Great-hut Troupe') 46
uMvelinqangi ('Ancient One') 21, 22
United Nations 179–80, 181

victims
and double identification 80
identification with aggressor 135–6
of malevolent antisocials 105, 106
of sadists 110, 111

violence, indoctrination into 130–31, 154, 162, 172, 183–4

war
and despotism 177
eagerness of army for 43, 128–9, 148
pre-Shaka 27, 28, 29, 31–2
total 79
war crimes trials 178–9, 181–2
Weber, M. 69
white settlers/traders 27, 28–9, 155
Winnicott, D.W. 63
witchcraft 22, 35, 36, 47, 68, 81, 87
assegai of Shaka 33
and paranoia 99, 101–2
punishment for 22–3, 40–41, 51–2
women
attached to an *ibutho* 45
attached to Shaka 46, 85–6, 87
role of 20, 23
wounded, fate of 39

yea-sayers 48, 70, 73, 98–9, 123–4, 156
Yugoslavia 179

Zulus
building of nation 7, 37–8, 40, 41–3, 54, 113, 141, 162, 183, 184–5
descent/early history 16
way of life 20–26
Zwide, King 36, 37, 119, 142–3